The **Last**
Virtual Volunteering
Guidebook

The **Last**
Virtual Volunteering
Guidebook

Fully Integrating Online Service into Volunteer Involvement

Jayne Cravens and Susan J. Ellis

Energize, Inc.
Philadelphia

Energize, Inc.
5450 Wissahickon Avenue
Philadelphia, PA 19144 USA

www.energizeinc.com

ISBN-13: 978-0-940576-65-0 (paperback)
ISBN-13: 978-0-940576-66-7 (e-book)
ISBN-13: 978-0-940576-67-4 (PDF)

This book is a complete revision of *The Virtual Volunteering Guidebook: Applying the Principles of Real-World Volunteer Management to Online Service* by Susan J. Ellis and Jayne Cravens, published electronically by Impact Online in 2000.

Library of Congress Cataloging-in-Publication Data

Cravens, Jayne, 1966–
    The last virtual volunteering guidebook : fully integrating online service into volunteer
        involvement / Jayne Cravens and Susan J. Ellis.
        pages cm
    Includes bibliographical references and index.
    ISBN 978-0-940576-65-0 (pbk.) – ISBN (978-0-940576-66-7 (e-book)
1. Voluntarism. 2. Volunteers. I. Ellis, Susan J. II. Title.
    HN90.V64C73 2014
    361.3'7—dc23   2013034420

Printed in the United States of America

Table of Contents

5 Orienting and Training Online Volunteers   **55**

6 Basic Techniques for Working Online with Volunteers: What Everyone Should Know   **69**

12 For Online Volunteers

Preface

It has been 14 years since we published the first *Virtual Volunteering Guidebook*, and since then so much about volunteering and the Internet has changed.

When Impact Online launched the Virtual Volunteering Project in 1996, the idea of online volunteer service was revolutionary for most people and organizations—even though the practice was already well under way in at least a few hundred organizations and already growing rapidly.[1] Yet in the years that immediately followed, we faced skeptical, fearful, and at times hostile audiences among nonprofit organizations, public-sector organizations, and other groups that involved community members in philanthropic activities. This initial skepticism and fear has given way to acceptance at most organizations, as it becomes commonplace to hear about successfully engaging online volunteers in a variety of organizations and initiatives, from political campaigns, to service to vulnerable clients, to high-responsibility leadership roles.

One of the primary areas of change since the first publication? Language. Instead of talking about the information superhighway or cyberspace, the hot term at the time of this revision is *the cloud*. Instead of talking about *byte-sized volunteering* activities that take just a few hours to complete, the new buzzword is *micro-volunteering*. We struggled with this ever-changing language—and today's challenge of writing about anything tech related with relevant, appropriate terminology—as we worked to determine a relatively timeless title for this second edition. With tongue in cheek, Jayne at one point proposed:

Virtual Volunteering: Coalition-Based Social Capital Refocusing Cross-Sector, Cloud-Based Collaborations and Cultivating Robust, Best-in-Breed, Synergistic Strategies for Results-Based Actions through Emerging Pipelines

The title we eventually chose—*The **Last** Virtual Volunteering Guidebook*—became the title after Susan repeatedly listened to Jayne say, "I never want to write another edition of this book—virtual volunteering should be a part of all volunteering!" Jayne's statement actually highlights the biggest and best change in the last decade: the notion of volunteering online is no longer new and has, in fact, been adopted in one way or another by a majority of organizations. As we explain in more detail in chapter 1, it is time—even long overdue—to consider virtual service as fully integrated with all sorts of real-world volunteering, not off on its own in an isolated silo. And the integration is two-way: increasingly traditional onsite volunteering has an online component as well. So our hope is that, from now on, the issues discussed in the book—while possibly specific to working with volunteers online—will be included naturally and without fanfare in any basic volunteer management text.

NOTE

1. Jayne Cravens, "A Brief Review of the Early History of Nonprofits and the Internet (before 1996)," 2009 <http://www.coyotecommunications.com/tech/npo_and_net_history.shtml>.

Introduction

Evolving Technology

Since the first edition, there has been enormous growth in the ease and popularity of communicating online with photos and video. The original book focused almost exclusively on text-based communications, which hide our weight, ethnicity, hair color, age, and other physical traits from each other online. That created a lot of freedom for online volunteers; they could be judged by the quality of their work, not their physical appearance or regional accent. Today's preference to actually see and hear each other online is a double-edged sword: it can make electronic communication more personal and personable, but it can also inject offline prejudices evoked by how someone looks. Will online volunteering candidates be turned away because of possible but unacknowledged biases?

Another change that has greatly altered this new edition is the explosion of multiple contact points for people online. People do not communicate primarily via e-mail anymore. Now they talk together via online social networks and in the comments section of blogs, photo-sharing sites, and video-sharing sites. Upon meeting someone, our question to each other has gone from "What's your e-mail address?" to "Will you 'friend' me on Facebook?" or "What's your Twitter hashtag?"

It is also much easier today to be online anywhere, through free wireless access in various public spaces and fee-based access elsewhere on the ground and in the sky (even at almost any hotel in Kabul, Afghanistan, to which Jayne can attest firsthand!). And then there is the explosion of networked handheld technologies. Cell phones and personal digital assistants (PDAs) were already in use by some nonprofits and by volunteers at the time of our *Guidebook*'s original publication, but these technologies have now merged into smartphones and tablets such as the iPad. Today's online volunteers are not limited to laptop or desktop computers at home or work; they can and do engage in service just about anywhere.

In this new edition, we have tried to capture these and other changes in the technology landscape. And that has been relatively easy for two reasons:

- *We have stayed involved and connected to online volunteering efforts.* Despite the Virtual Volunteering Project going into hiatus and both authors moving on to many other activities, we have stayed on top of what is happening regarding the engagement of volunteers online. We both have continued to research, write about, and present on the subject. We have also become involved first-hand in various virtual volunteering activities over the years.

- *So much has also stayed the same about what is fundamental to successfully engaging volunteers online.* While the language and tools have evolved, the elements for success in virtual volunteering are still largely the same. It has been gratifying—and, at times, downright surprising—to see so many of our recommendations from that first *Guidebook* stand the test of time.

What we still struggle with ourselves, as well as in our recommendations to readers and those who attend our trainings, is time management. Being available anytime, anywhere, to anyone has increased our number of distractions, making it harder to get messages to their intended audiences amid all of the other diversions and disruptions going on. It can be hard to maintain or even identify boundaries between work and rest, between official and social activities, when electronic communications permeate our lives. This most definitely influences how virtual volunteering happens—or does not—at a variety of organizations.

When all is said and done, we believe that if a task at an organization can be done by a human, it can be done by a qualified volunteer and, based on our experience and observations over the years, we believe the possibilities for what can be done through online volunteer involvement are endless. We hope this second, *Last* edition of this *Guidebook* captures that and empowers a variety of organizations and institutions to benefit from virtual volunteering in more and more ways.

What This *Guidebook* Is Not

This is not a computer technology manual. A lot of computer and Internet tools will be mentioned here, but no primers will be offered on how to use them in general—only on how to use them to work with volunteers. If you come upon a technology tool you do not understand, or if you need more background on how to use that tool in general, we recommend looking up the tool name on either or both of these Web sites:

- Wikipedia, http://www.wikipedia.org, the extensive, ever-growing online encyclopedia (that, please note, was developed and is maintained entirely by online volunteers)

- TechSoup Global, http://www.techsoup.org, a nonprofit initiative focused on helping nonprofit organizations with computer and Internet technology issues

This *Guidebook* is also not a list or review of every organization engaged in virtual volunteering. That kind of review would be impossible, just as it would be impossible to list every organization engaged in traditional volunteering, because of the sheer numbers of such organizations and the unmanageable task of tracking those data. For the same reason, we also have not listed every resource related to virtual volunteering.

Technology, and how we use it, is ever-changing and happens so quickly that any book is out of date before it is published! So, to ensure that we all stay on top of the most-used tools and practices

regarding virtual volunteering, we have created the "Virtual Volunteering Wiki"[1] (you'll learn more about wikis throughout this book). That is where we *can* list the many resources that have contributed to our learning, continue to add new resources over time, and *you* can submit resources as well. We hope you will help us build a dynamic site—our effort to crowdsource the concept of virtual volunteering (you'll learn more about crowdsourcing later, too).

This *Guidebook* is also not a volunteer management textbook. We believe *that understanding and practicing the fundamentals of volunteer management are essential to the success of virtual volunteering.* Understanding these elements is more important in working with volunteers virtually than the Internet skills a reader may or may not have. However, we cannot teach the fundamentals of effective volunteer engagement here; instead, we detail how to *apply* these fundamentals to online service.

In appendix B, there is a starting list of recommended books and Web sites that can help you further understand the elements of traditional volunteer engagement and support. The Virtual Volunteering Wiki also provides additional Web sites, publications, research, and more related to volunteer management.

Virtual Volunteering Is Part of All Volunteering

While we frequently use the term *virtual volunteering*, we never use the term *virtual volunteers*. All volunteers are *real*. Instead, we talk about *online volunteers* to emphasize that these are real volunteers contributing real time and skills, but through the Internet.

Which brings us to an explanation of the title of this second and *Last Virtual Volunteering Guidebook.*

We challenge you to abandon any notion that there is a distinct, hard line that separates online volunteers from all other volunteers. When we refer to online volunteers, we are referring to *all* volunteers who provide some or all of their interaction with the organization via the Internet. And that means people who may never think of themselves as *online volunteers* but, rather, simply as *volunteers*.

Ten years ago the very concept of online service was revolutionary to many and often met with skepticism. We realize that many are still learning about virtual volunteering today, but we are also happy to note that it has been adopted by many thousands of organizations of all kinds and in all places. This means that any effective volunteer involvement strategy should be integrating online interaction with and by all volunteers as a natural and expected part of operations. Some people will volunteer solely online; others will incorporate a virtual component into an onsite placement, and others may do their service totally hands on. But even for this last group, increasingly we can expect some Internet contact, whether in recruitment, training, recordkeeping or simply to communicate information. The Internet is a tool to support *all* volunteers, regardless of their role in an organization or where they physically perform their service.

Yes, in this book we focus on virtual volunteering, but it is our goal to get to the point where there is no longer any need for a special guidebook just for this subject. In the future, *we hope all volunteer management books and training sessions will include online service as a matter of course, just as they already examine onsite and remote volunteering.*

Who Should Read This Book?

The Last *Virtual Volunteering Guidebook* is written for those working with or for:

- Volunteer-involving nonprofit organizations or non-governmental organizations (NGOs), regardless of mission or services provided

- Community-focused public-sector agencies such as schools, courts, parks, and other government programs that engage volunteers

- Grassroots groups or all-volunteer membership associations

- For-profit corporations supporting any of the above with employee volunteers

Readers may be employees or volunteers, managers or frontline workers, or even funders, who want to see the introduction or expansion of virtual volunteering in an organization or in one department or program. Because of the global nature of the Internet, almost everything covered here applies to any country, with the understanding that the authors are from the U.S. and the text is in English. The ideas and principles put forward here

for working with volunteers could also help anyone working with *employees* remotely through the use of Internet and networking technologies and anyone (paid or not) looking for ways to keep a dispersed team energized.

This *Guidebook* frequently refers to *volunteer resources managers* (VRMs), meaning the people who are in charge of an organization's volunteer involvement. These people may fill the role of a VRM but have a different title, such as volunteer coordinator, director of volunteer services, or any other of a dozen or so names used for this role. However, this book is for *all* staff, paid or volunteers themselves, no matter what their title is, who work with volunteers in any leadership/supervisory/support capacity.

If you are the designated VRM, this *Guidebook* is written so that you will become the virtual volunteering expert within your organization. After reading the entire book, you will be well versed in virtual volunteering, ready to allay the most-commonly expressed fears and to address the most common challenges in engaging and supporting volunteers online.

While you may engage with volunteers in your daily work, perhaps you are *not* the central VRM for your organization, and might even have to convince that person to welcome virtual volunteering. We have customized advice specifically for you throughout the book to help you introduce virtual volunteering in a non-threatening manner, so as to quickly win over the VRM and any other potential naysayers.

We acknowledge that not all of the information in this book may be applicable to every organization or to every volunteering effort. We offer the essentials for virtual volunteering success, based on: our own experience as volunteers and managers of volunteers; extensive feedback from and observation of hundreds of organizations in many different countries engaged in virtual volunteering; and feedback from thousands of individuals, also from many different countries, who volunteer online. However, just as there is no one absolute blueprint for the involvement of onsite volunteers, there is no absolute blueprint for involving online volunteers. The nature of an organization's work, its organizational culture, the attitudes of those involved with the organization, and the changing times regarding technology will all influence how an organization does, or does not, embrace virtual volunteering. As is said on many online communities and text messages regarding advice, YMMV (Your Mileage May Vary).

Also, please note that *you may not need to read this entire book*. Your organization may already be using Internet tools, even smartphone applications, to engage and support volunteers successfully. We have divided the book into chapters that will allow those who are not starting from scratch to easily jump to the sections they need most to expand or improve their online volunteer engagement. The index at the end of this book and chapter references throughout the book will help you easily troubleshoot issues you face in working with online volunteers.

Whether you are new to virtual volunteering or already experienced in working with volunteers online, we hope this book will make you feel confident and supported in joining the parade.

Welcome!

NOTE

1. Virtual Volunteering Wiki <http://virtualvolunteering.wikispaces.com>.

A Word about Web Addresses (URLs), Products, Tools, and Sites Named in This Book

This book obviously references many Web sites. If we mention a site or an organization and its URL is based on its name or is commonly known (such as Google or Yahoo!), we will not provide the URL each time. However, if we refer to specific information appearing within a site, that Web address will be given in a footnote (at first reference) at the end of the chapter. In the Virtual Volunteering Wiki, we give an alphabetical list of all organizations and sites mentioned in the book, with their URLs, and will keep that list updated as much as possible.

Be aware that Web site addresses change frequently. At least some will be outdated the moment this book is published. If you cannot find the new address of an expired Web site mentioned here, type the old URL into the Internet Archive's Wayback Machine, http://www.archive.org. The Internet Archive is a U.S.-based nonprofit that archives Web sites (type in your own organization's URL to see its earlier versions), as well as providing archives of various public domain texts, audio files, moving images, and software. And, yes, the site involves online volunteers!

A lot of different online products and services produced by various companies are named in this book. We each have our personal preferences when it comes to software and Internet tools, and no doubt our preferences show up in this *Guidebook*. Please do not see one or more mentions of a particular company or tool as an endorsement of a product, nor the exclusion of a tool as a negative assessment. For example, it is impossible to name every photo-sharing site out there, so you are going to see the names of only those services with which the authors are very familiar and either use regularly or have seen used regularly.

To research the variety of products available for a particular online function, be it smartphones, project management, shared work spaces, online conferences, or anything else, type the name of that function or service into Wikipedia, the most likely place to find a comprehensive list of products and services for a specific online function or technology. In addition, please see the Virtual Volunteering Wiki we created in conjunction with this book for more suggestions of specific products and tools (your contributions to that Wiki are welcomed!).

Chapter 1
Understanding Virtual Volunteering

What Is "Virtual Volunteering"?

Virtual volunteering refers to volunteering activities completed, in whole or in part, using the Internet and a home, school, telecenter, or work computer or other Internet-connected device, such as a smartphone (a cell phone with Internet functions) or personal digital assistant (PDA).

Virtual volunteering goes by many names. It has been called online volunteering, cyber service, Internet-mediated service, telementoring, e-mentoring, teletutoring, micro-volunteering, crowdsourcing, and various other names. You may also hear it described as crowdcasting, distributed development, distributed thinking, micro-tasking, smart mob,

virtual teams, virtual workforce, the wisdom of the crowd, or various other terms used when talking about online contributors to a project who are not employees of the company or organization soliciting advice or service online.

Virtual volunteering can be described as the same as telecommuting, but it involves unpaid volunteers instead of paid employees. Just as telecommuting employees work part-time or full-time remotely from a company, online volunteers work remotely from the organization they support, part-time or full-time. When volunteers are working on tiny tasks that take just a few minutes, the telecommuting analogy might not work, but the terms we used earlier—crowdsourcing, micro-tasking, and so on—certainly do.

tagxedo.com

1

Contested Terms: Can't
We All Get Along?

Not everyone agrees on who is and is not a volunteer (some define it by the person's motivation; others define it by whether or not the person is paid). The definitions of virtual volunteering, and all the terms related to online service used in this book, are contested as well. We include *crowdsourcing* as a form of virtual volunteering, for instance; others would say no, because contributors might never be called "volunteers" by the organization soliciting service, even though they are unpaid by that organization. We've heard people say that "the cloud" is different from "the Internet." Jayne and Susan themselves don't agree on what is and isn't micro-volunteering.

As you read through all these terms and definitions, you may come across a definition or label you don't agree with. That's fine. What we ask you, the reader, to do is what we, the authors, try to do: don't get caught up in absolute labels. Instead, try to look at the concepts and practices being discussed and always have one thing in mind: what does this mean for volunteers—any volunteers—and the organizations that involve volunteers in *any* way?

And keep in mind the title of this *Guidebook*. We chose the word "*Last*" because we want to discourage the compartmentalization of volunteers and volunteering. We want all kinds of virtual volunteering to be talked about and fully integrated into all future volunteering resources so that we no longer distinguish between online and traditional volunteers and instead talk about volunteers and volunteerism, encompassing all contributed services.

The beneficiary of online volunteer service is usually a nonprofit organization, a non-governmental organization (NGO), a grassroots group, or a community-focused government agency, such as a public school or state park. However, there are also volunteers who donate their service to for-profit businesses, such as people who answer questions on Yahoo! Answers, online volunteers who have helped Ancestry.com with its record indexing, or Apple users who help other users via Apple's user forum.[1] Many Open Source software initiatives, both commercial and not-for-profit, involve online volunteers—people not paid by the initiative—to design or code the software, test it, and identify and solve bugs in the programming. Some of the best known of these are OpenOffice, Gentoo, and Drupal.

What do online volunteers do to help the causes they support? Many things! They:

- Translate documents
- Research topics and gather data
- Develop Web sites or databases
- Design or code software
- Edit, critique, or prepare proposals, press releases, newsletter articles, speeches, and blogs
- Develop curricula
- Provide expert advice, such as legal, medical, marketing, human resources management, or business expertise
- Transcribe a video or podcast (audio recording)
- Critique an online resource from a user's perspective (beta testing)
- Design graphics
- Tutor students
- Mentor young people, new employees, or someone starting a new business
- Visit virtually with someone who is home-bound, in a hospital, or in an assisted living facility
- Moderate or facilitate online discussion groups
- Review contributions from other online volunteers
- Manage other online volunteers
- Blog or tweet live from an event, providing frequent updates about what they are seeing and hearing
- Prepare and tag photos for online sharing
- Compose songs and write plays with others

- Create and edit videos and podcasts
- Caption online videos (so that they can be understood by people with hearing impairments or people who are not native English speakers)
- Monitor the news
- Serve on an advisory committee
- And much more. . . .

In *Successful Management in the Virtual Office*—a seminal work in relation to the Virtual Volunteering Project,[2] which first researched virtual volunteering—Bernie Kelly and Bruce McGraw identified the following categories of tasks as appropriate for telecommuting jobs.[3] They are also appropriate for online volunteers:

- Administrative
- Analysis
- Calculating
- Data analysis
- Data entry
- Data manipulation
- Data processing
- Data programming
- Maintaining databases
- Meeting with clients
- Planning
- Project-oriented work/management
- Reading
- Recordkeeping
- Research
- Sending/receiving electronic mail
- Spreadsheet analysis
- Support activities
- Thinking
- Typing
- Using a computer
- Word processing
- Writing

Note that the majority of virtual volunteering tasks listed, as well as the majority of telecommuting jobs identified, are *not* specifically computer or Internet technology related; they are, rather, expertise that can easily be shared remotely and electronically. For instance, moderating an online discussion group has much more to do with communicating clearly via written communications, having excellent facilitation skills, and having an understanding of group dynamics than it has to do with technical computer skills. A survey of online volunteering assignments posted to the United Nations Volunteers Online Volunteering service (formerly NetAid) shows that more than 50 percent of assignments are not technology specific.

It is increasingly hard to say that someone is *only* an online volunteer and someone else is *only* an onsite volunteer because the Internet can be integrated in many ways. How would you classify someone who:

- Mentors a student both in the school cafeteria and via the Internet?
- Volunteers as a firefighter but also maintains the fire department's Web site from home?
- Serves onsite but at a remote location, such as at a satellite office or in a client's home, and mainly interacts with headquarters via the Internet?
- Staffs an information booth for your organization once a week but also spends spare time from anywhere tagging photos your organization posts to a photo-sharing site so they will be easier to find by people searching for specific topics?
- Leads a youth group but also serves on a committee that collaborates primarily via e-mail?

Does it really matter what label you apply to these perfectly natural mergers of real-world and electronic service? Again, when we refer to online volunteers, we are referring to *all* volunteers who provide some or all of their service via the Internet, whether or not they think of themselves as *online* volunteers.

History of Virtual Volunteering

Virtual volunteering is *not* a new concept, and the practice has been widespread for many years. To fully understand virtual volunteering, it is helpful to understand its history.

Virtual volunteering has been going on probably as long as there has been an Internet (which itself is more than 30 years old). The first instance of organized virtual volunteering was probably Project Gutenberg, a volunteer effort that began in 1971 to digitize, archive, and distribute written cultural works. Most of the items in its collection are the full texts of public-domain books, such as works by Jane Austen, Charles Dickens, Sir Arthur Conan Doyle, and Mark Twain. These works continue to be typed in and proofread by online volunteers.[4]

Tim Berners-Lee, who is credited as the inventor of the World Wide Web, made an online appearance at the United Nations Open Day in Geneva in 2001 and noted the role online volunteers had played in his development of the Web a decade earlier.[5]

What's in a Name?

In 1995, the Support Center for Nonprofit Management in San Francisco, now Compass Point Nonprofit Services, asked Jayne Cravens to do a workshop for their membership on how volunteer resources managers could use the Internet as a part of their work; the members had already seen Jayne promote the idea on soc.org.nonprofit, an online community and USENET newsgroup for nonprofit managers. A few months later, a representative of Impact Online contacted Jayne and asked her if she might be interested in learning more about what Impact Online was doing to promote virtual volunteering. "What's virtual volunteering?" Jayne asked. The representative replied, "It's what you keep talking about online and you did that workshop in San Francisco on!" It was the first Jayne had heard that the practice had a name. Jayne later went on to lead the Virtual Volunteering Project.

In 1995, a then-new nonprofit organization called Impact Online, based in Palo Alto, California, began promoting the idea of *virtual volunteering*,[6] a phrase that was probably first used by one of Impact Online's co-founders, Steve Glikbarg. In 1996, Impact Online received a grant from the James Irvine Foundation to launch an initiative to research the practice of virtual volunteering and to promote the practice to nonprofit organizations in the United States. This new initiative was dubbed the Virtual Volunteering Project, and its Web site was launched in early 1997.[7] After one year, the Virtual Volunteering Project moved to the Charles A. Dana Center at The University of Texas at Austin, and Impact Online became VolunteerMatch.

The first two years of the Virtual Volunteer Project were spent reviewing and adapting telecommuting manuals and existing volunteer management recommendations with regard to virtual volunteering, as well as identifying organizations that were involving online volunteers. By April 1999, the Project had identified almost 100 organizations as involving online volunteers and listed them on the Project's Web site. By the end of 1999, as the numbers grew exponentially, the Project stopped listing every organization involving online volunteers and instead identified only those organizations with large or unique online volunteering programs. The Project used its research about these organizations to continually create and refine guidelines for engaging and supporting online volunteers.

Until January 2001, the Virtual Volunteering Project compiled a list of all telementoring, e-mentoring, and teletutoring programs in the U.S. (in which online volunteers mentored or tutored others through a nonprofit organization or school). At that time, 40 programs were identified.[8] This was the first and only effort to list *all* such programs and to track what made them successful.

In the last few years, there has been more and more recognition of *micro-volunteering*—online volunteers undertaking very quick, small tasks that usually require little specialized expertise, such as tagging photos or trying out a new online resource for even just a few minutes and providing feedback. While the practice of micro-volunteering has always been a part of virtual volunteering and, therefore, is as old as the Internet, the name for the practice is relatively new (back in the 1990s, we called it *byte-sized* volunteering). This type of service has grown into a significant and distinct part of virtual volunteering, so much so that there are Web sites and research papers devoted only to this aspect.

There is no longer any current research that measures how widespread virtual volunteering is, and so we offer no statistics on that. While the lack of data is unfortunate in some ways, it also furthers our contention that online service should be treated less and less as something unique from other volunteering. In this edition, we therefore focus on what practitioners and academics have identified as essential for the successful involvement of online volunteers. Readers can find links to research articles and projects relating to virtual volunteering, including lists of organizations involving volunteers, online in the Virtual Volunteering Wiki.

Who Volunteers Online and Why

Who are online volunteers? They are:

- Professionals: lawyers, doctors, accountants, teachers, Web designers, nurses
- Students
- Stay-at-home parents
- People with disabilities
- Seniors/elders
- Teenagers
- Women
- Men
- Vivacious people
- Shy people
- Techies
- Non-techies
- People in developing countries
- People in developed countries
- People in big cities
- People in rural areas
- People across the street
- People across the world

In short—*anyone.*

This diversity of people who volunteer online should immediately dispel any myths regarding virtual volunteering appealing only to twenty-something computer professionals in Silicon Valley. Online volunteers come from all age groups of people who can use the Internet independently and have a particular skill to offer. They come from various educational and work backgrounds and from various geographies and ethnicities. The breakdown of online volunteers for the UN's Online Volunteering service in 2004 is telling: almost 40 percent were based in developing countries in Africa, Asia, South America, and Eastern Europe.[9] Of course, each organization that involves online volunteers will have different online volunteering demographics, but the point is that one cannot make sweeping generalizations about who online volunteers are.

More Myths to Dispel

Another virtual volunteering myth to dispel quickly is that online volunteers are geographically remote from the organizations they assist. While there are certainly thousands of volunteers located at a distance from the organizations receiving their services, research shows that the overwhelming majority of online volunteers *also* volunteer in face-to-face settings, often for an organization in their same city or region, and often onsite in a traditional role for the same organization they are helping virtually as well. More information about this research can be found on the Virtual Volunteering Wiki.

Another myth: Online volunteers are substitutes for onsite volunteer service. We have yet to find an organization that has involved online volunteers in order to do away with onsite volunteers; there may be organizations who involve *only* online volunteers, but none have done so to replace traditional, onsite service. Many organizations offer virtual assignments to give current onsite volunteers new roles and to involve new volunteers in different ways. While volunteering exclusively online may be the preferred avenue of volunteering for some people, the vast majority of people volunteer online as an *additional* way of contributing time and talent.

For individuals, the appeal of virtual volunteering is that it:

- Gives additional support to help an organization they are already volunteering with onsite

- Uses the time they have to volunteer but without leaving their home, school, or workplace to do so (whether by circumstance or preference)

- Allows them to serve despite disabilities that limit their mobility, or with no way of traveling to volunteer

- Contributes to a cause or issue of great importance to them but for which there are no conveniently-located onsite opportunities

- Helps an organization in a geographic area that they cannot travel to

- Applies their love of computers or smartphones to the idea of using technology for doing good

A complete list of "Virtual Volunteering Myths" can be found in appendix A.

Why Involve Online Volunteers?

There are many reasons why organizations or initiatives involve online volunteers, and they are pretty much the same reasons organizations involve onsite volunteers. Here are but 10 reasons for an organization to engage in virtual volunteering:

1. *Online volunteers, just as those volunteers who work onsite, extend the resources of an organization.* The additional help augments core staff efforts and allows an organization to do even more. They and other volunteers are not, however, replacements for employees.

2. *An organization that embraces virtual volunteering gives volunteers new ways of supporting causes they feel passionate about.* This can lead both to expanding the involvement of onsite volunteers and to involving new volunteers altogether.

3. *Virtual volunteering can remove some time and physical barriers for both current and new volunteers.* While the time required for volunteering online is real, not virtual, volunteers can provide a service, ask questions, or provide feedback at whatever time is convenient for them, outside of a few required live meetings with staff or other volunteers.

4. *An organization that uses the Internet to support and involve volunteers is sending a message to its supporters that it is modern and efficient, that it wants to provide convenience to its volunteers, and that it understands the realities of the 21st-century workplace.* As the competition for press coverage and funding becomes more intense, it has never been more important for nonprofits, NGOs, government agencies, and others to exude such an image.

5. *Virtual volunteering allows for the participation of people who might find onsite volunteering difficult or impossible because of a disability, mobility issue, home obligation, or work schedule.* This, in turn, allows agencies to benefit from the additional talent and resources of more volunteers and allows the organization to demonstrate its commitment to being an accessible organization.

6. *Potential volunteers not reached by traditional means may be reached online.* The Internet makes it easy to reach particular audiences quickly, such as people with a specific skill or representing a specific demographic. This does not mean the Internet will totally replace other forms of volunteer recruitment, such as a booth at a community event or registering with your local volunteer center (which these days is likely to put local information online as well). It simply means you have an additional avenue to use to recruit volunteers. Recruiting online volunteers is discussed in depth in chapter 11.

7. *The Internet offers a proven tool for recruiting younger volunteers, a difficulty many organizations face.* We have noted earlier that online volunteers may represent a variety of populations. While it is certainly true that people

under the age of 30 are more prone to use online technologies than any other age group, even people in their 40s have used the Web for most of their professional lives.

8. *Some or most of your organization's mission may be best served by online volunteers, especially if your organization's membership is dispersed across a region or a country, or even around the world.* Three examples of entirely virtual organizations are: Project Gutenberg, mentioned earlier in this chapter; LibriVox, a nonprofit that coordinates volunteers making freely-available online recordings of public-domain books; and the Aid Workers Network, an online resource for people working in aid, relief, and development. These entirely virtual organizations could not exist if they only or primarily involved onsite volunteers.

9. *Online volunteers can be environmentally friendly.* Online volunteers create no car exhaust, do not require a parking space, and do not need the organization to provide them with a desk or chair. And people are not buying new, additional technology just to volunteer online; they are using technology for a variety of other tasks. Even so, you may want to encourage your online volunteers to dispose of electronic waste in an ecologically-friendly manner.[10]

    Moreover, volunteer resources managers (VRMs) who work online have no restrictive limits on giving and sharing information with volunteers. For instance, instead of printed volunteer policies, which must be copied for onsite distribution and quickly go out of date, managers can share the most current policies online, in a public or private area, for any volunteer to access at any time. Instead of giving a volunteer mounds of printed material that are not environmentally friendly, the manager can point to online resources for the volunteer to read from home. And the volunteer can read as much as he or she needs to for an assignment (and, beyond that, what he or she wants to).

10. *Managing volunteers virtually can create automatic, extensive records of both volunteer activities and interactions with volunteers— records that can be used to generate statistics, provide quotes for an upcoming grant proposal, or evaluate the overall volunteering initiative.* An organization that manages virtually gains an archive of e-mails, instant messages, chats, online forum messages, photos, and audio and video recordings relating to volunteer discussions and activities.

Is Your Organization Ready for Virtual Volunteering?

As we will emphasize again and again, understanding and practicing the fundamentals of volunteer management are essential to the success of virtual volunteering options. Good volunteer management practice dictates that an organization be able to say why it wants to involve volunteers; identify what tasks and roles would be best done by volunteers; recruit the right people to fill those roles; and support the volunteers in whatever ways are necessary.

In line with this approach, we do not recommend deciding to launch a virtual volunteering project simply to explore what it's all about. The best approach is to look at all the things you have identified as needs and consider whether you might actually address them more effectively online rather than onsite (or in addition to onsite) or whether you will be likely to recruit more qualified/appropriate candidates by offering an online option. This makes online service an intentional approach to meaningful service delivery. Once you have identified virtual roles, you should approach your first attempt as a pilot project to learn what might be special about working with this sort of service.

Before your organization decides to involve volunteers virtually—or expand existing involvement— do some self-evaluation of both yourself and your organization regarding basic volunteer management practice at your organization. Consider these factors:

- If your organization is already successfully involving volunteers in traditional settings, you should have an established system in place for volunteer recruitment, screening, matching to assignments, supervision, feedback, and evaluation (measures of success for both volunteer assignments and your volunteer program in general). This goes for all kinds of volunteers, from people providing episodic volunteering (showing up just one day to clean a beach) to people serving on a committee or leading a project for a year or more. Alternatively, your organization could have staff with such experience from previous workplaces, who know how to establish a reliable volunteer management system (whether that system is software or a human system of procedures).

- All employees and all board members, as well as all volunteers, should understand how and why the organization involves any volunteers and be committed to the success of current volunteer involvement.

- All of the organization's employees or core volunteer staff should have training and/or experience in basic volunteer supervision and management. They do not all have to be experts, but they should understand the basics of things like interviewing, supporting volunteers working on an assignment, and tracking volunteer progress.

- All staff should know how to route calls and e-mails from current volunteers and inquiries from potential volunteers and be committed to reading and responding to e-mails regarding volunteering within 72 hours of receipt.

- There should be an established system for employees or core volunteer staff to define possible tasks or roles for volunteers to support their own areas/departments (e.g., the development office needs volunteers for a special event or to write grants; the marketing manager needs volunteers to prepare a mailing; the human resources officer needs an expert advisor). There should also be an established system to communicate these roles to the VRM.

- There should be one person who is ultimately responsible for volunteer management at the organization, even if multiple people at the organization work with volunteers. This person should oversee the organization's volunteer engagement process, including recruiting and evaluation; understand the basic legal requirements associated with volunteer involvement (or at least know where to get such questions answered); and know which staff members are working with volunteers and what volunteers are doing at the organization or initiative. In addition, this person should have regular access to e-mail and the Internet during the work day. As already noted, this person may have the title of *volunteer resources manager* or may have this duty in addition to other responsibilities (and therefore be called something else).

- The same person who is in charge of coordinating the current volunteer involvement effort should also coordinate virtual volunteering. Virtual volunteering should be seen as an integrated part of traditional volunteer management—which always needs to adapt to new trends and tools.

- All who work with online volunteers should be able to freely access online resources for advice and information on involving volunteers virtually. Suggested resources are in appendix B and in the Virtual Volunteering Wiki.

Well-organized, responsive volunteer engagement does not come from funding or a software program. It comes from thoughtful application of existing resources and commitment to developing the best management system—and by *system*, we mean a human system of procedures, not just software. Having the above criteria in place before engaging online volunteers will prevent a significant increase in administrative burdens and ensure quality and success all around.

If you feel you meet all of the above criteria, you are ready to start engaging online volunteers.

The Challenges of Cyberspace

In a virtual environment, some adjustments in style and approaches to volunteer engagement and support must be made to ensure success. For instance, volunteers working via home or work computers

12 Elements of Successful Volunteer Management

In this book, we repeatedly write that "understanding andpracticing the fundamentals of volunteer management are essential to the success of a virtual volunteering program." To clarify, the best volunteer programs pay attention to 12 major elements of successful volunteer management, and these elements are the same for virtual volunteering:

- Planning and Resource Allocation
- Volunteer Work/Task Design
- Recruitment/Outreach/Public Relations
- Interviewing, Screening and Matching/Assigning
- Orientation and Training
- Volunteer/Employee Relations
- Coordination and Support
- Supervision
- Evaluation
- Recognition
- Recordkeeping and Reporting
- Volunteer Input

None of these elements happen in a vacuum; it is impossible to address these elements strictly one at a time. Again, there are resources identified in the appendices to provide details about each of these elements. Throughout this book, we will address each in relation to virtual volunteering. More resources on volunteer management are given in appendix B and in the Virtual Volunteering Wiki.

can feel isolated from the organization, or undervalued in comparison to onsite volunteers, and gradually lose their inspiration for volunteering online. This is no different from the needs of any volunteer working offsite or in the field. Those working with such volunteers must employ various means to keep these volunteers feeling engaged and as valued

parts of the organization. There are tips throughout each chapter in this *Guidebook* on ways to do this.

Involving volunteers via the Internet comes naturally to some people. For others, there is a significant learning curve and need for a lot of guidance. Recognize now, if you do not already, that introducing or expanding virtual volunteering in an organization requires *managing change*—something that is rarely easy. This *Guidebook* will help you to introduce virtual volunteering in a way that helps staff see it as a benefit and a tool they want to embrace, not a burden and something to be afraid of.

As you begin the initial steps into virtual volunteering, you will face challenges inherent in the cyberspace[11] environment. Be patient with yourself and with everyone else; we are all learning together. Some of the following challenges have remained the same since the first edition of this *Guidebook*, while others have recently emerged:

- Everyone is suffering from information overload. There was a time when e-mail offered almost instantaneous communications; now, it is oh-so-easy to ignore or be forgotten in the sea of ways people communicate online. People accidentally delete or can't find an e-mail. Not all of your messages to volunteers via e-mail or a Web-based forum will be read by everyone.

- Working online takes *real* time; there is nothing virtual about it! Online communication will not replace all other communication (telephone calls, onsite meetings, etc.), and, if not well managed, can feel like yet another thing to deal with in an already-overwhelming work day.

- Online communication was primarily asynchronous when the first edition of this book was published; everyone did not have to be online at the same time to write and read messages. That meant that time zones were no longer important, and everyone could participate online at his or her convenience. However, this is no longer the case. Synchronous communication tools—instant messaging, text messaging, and live audio and video—mean time zones are important again, and sending and reading messages whenever convenient is not always an option.

- In addition, most online tools were once text based—nationalities, ethnicities, physical appearance, and dialects could be hidden or ignored. A person's age, appearance, or accent was not apparent, and online volunteers were judged primarily on the quality of their service and their written communication. In short, it was harder for prejudices, even those we may not be aware of, to creep into our choice or evaluation of volunteers. However, with the increasing use of live online audio and video, synchronous tools are bringing back face-to-face communication—and, possibly, managers will need to work just as diligently to avoid discrimination online as they do onsite.

- In the first edition, we touted online tools as less intrusive than, say, a telephone call. That is still true of asynchronous tools, but with the increasing use of synchronous tools, the intrusiveness is back; it is easier to be interrupted by an instant message than a text message.

- Not only can lack of *tech* literacy be a barrier to tech use, but illiteracy—not being able to read and write—can be a barrier to successful online activities. Even with the growing use of online audio and video, text-based tools, particularly e-mail, are the most-used tools on the Internet.

- Not everyone likes audio- and video-based communication. While it adds a more personal interaction that some people find lacking in text-based communication such as e-mail, it also benefits from a clear, confident speaking voice and an appropriate or appealing appearance (possibly negating the perk of sitting at the computer in pajamas or underwear!). Many people do not like speaking in front of an audience for these reasons, even a virtual one.

- Networking technology changes constantly and is often confusing. The constant barrage of upgrades and new tools, as well as new computer viruses, can make working online seem overwhelming.

- Technology fails. Hard drives crash, Internet connections go offline, popular platforms can have service outages, cloud-based applications become unavailable for hours at a time, and critical data can be temporarily or permanently out of reach. Also, not everyone has the latest and fastest software and Internet connection, meaning that accessing information on the Web can, for many people, be the world wide *wait*. As more and more data and software are stored on or operated from the Internet (or the cloud) rather than on or from a hard drive sitting right in your office, you become more vulnerable to these online problems—in other words, an online service outage could make critical data about volunteers inaccessible to you.

Undoubtedly the next generation of technology tools will bring still more issues. But with all that said, we still feel very strongly that pursuing virtual volunteering is extremely worthwhile and that the initial steps for integrating the Internet into volunteer support and engagement are essential for all VRMs. The point is simply to be aware of the realities of working in cyberspace.

Notes

1. Apple User Forum <http://discussions.apple.com/>.
2. The version of the Virtual Volunteering Project Web site used as a reference for this *Guidebook* is at http://www.coyotecommunications.com/vv/.
3. Bernie Kelly and Bruce McGraw, *Successful Management in the Virtual Office,* Object Services and Consulting, Inc., 1997 < http://www.objs.com/survey/vo.htm>. This document was a seminal work in relation to the Virtual Volunteering Project.
4. Most online volunteers supporting Project Gutenberg now do so under the auspices of Distributed Proofreaders <http://www.pgdp.net/>.
5. United Nations Technology Service (UNITeS), "Results So Far," 2007 <http://www.unites.org/results.htm>.
6. Marc Green, "Fundraising in Cyberspace: Direct Email Campaigns, Virtual Volunteers, Annual Fund Drives

Online. Does the Information Superhighway Lead to New Horizons or a Dead End?" *The Grantsmanship Center Magazine*, Fall 1995.

7. Jayne Cravens, "Who Funds the Virtual Volunteering Project?" The Virtual Volunteering Project, University of Texas at Austin, February 2001.

8. The archived version of the 2001 list of telementoring programs can be found at http://www.coyotecommunications .com/vv/direct/telem.shtml.

9. UN Online Volunteering Service, "Who Is Using the OV Service?" Report, April 8, 2004.

10. Jayne Cravens, "Electronic Waste Is EVERYONE'S Responsibility," 2009 <http://www.coyotecommunications.com/ tech/recycle.html>.

11. The authors acknowledge that, like the term *information superhighway*, the term *cyberspace* has fallen out of favor with many. However, the authors are rebels and are going to continue to use the term.

Sarah Parshall, volunteer recorder of books for LibriVox, which engages volunteers in making freely-available online recordings of public domain books.

Chapter 2
Getting Ready for Virtual Volunteering

Although the basic principles of volunteer management apply to onsite and online volunteers, the introduction of the Internet, technology tools, and intangible interaction add some unique considerations to virtual volunteering. The good news is that today everyone in a professional environment is already using e-mail and the Internet in some way and the comfort level keeps growing. Except perhaps for some who retired from the workforce before the Web, this is as true for volunteers as for paid staff.

If virtual volunteering is still hard for you to accept comfortably, consider that it is rare to find an organization where onsite volunteers are *constantly* under observation; most volunteers provide service out of sight of their manager, whether in a different cubicle, a different room, a different area of the facility, or away from the organization's headquarters altogether. Volunteers who are youth group leaders, home visitors, coaches, mentors, and tutors generally provide their service out in the field (for some, literally out in *a* field). Obviously, organizations have long ago resolved their concerns about allowing certain volunteers the freedom to do their work, make judgment calls, and act responsibly without constant staff surveillance, even when those volunteers are working with children.

As discussed in the first chapter, it is hard to imagine any volunteering effort where at least some integration of the Internet would not be appropriate or to imagine any volunteering effort in which some Internet use with volunteers is not *already* happening. In addition, organizations that are not Internet savvy are increasingly falling behind in their ability to engage volunteers. On the basis of these three factors, you can map how to introduce or expand virtual volunteering at your organization.

What Is Already Happening in Your Organization?

Is virtual volunteering already happening at your organization? There is a very good possibility that it is and you need to identify it. See what you can discover by asking some key questions:

- If your organization asks volunteers to visit clients in their homes, or to mentor or tutor people one-on-one at an offsite location or via the phone, or to do any sort of outreach into the community on your behalf, ask: *Do volunteers ever interact with these clients/community members online as well? How?*

- If there are volunteers helping with your organization's Web site or with any computer or Internet tech-related issue, *is all service being performed onsite, or are some activities being done via a volunteer's home, work, or school computer?* Ask this of both the employees who work with these volunteers and *the volunteers themselves.*

- Are there any pro bono consultants at your organization? If so, *are they interacting with employees online sometimes, in addition to onsite meetings, or doing their work (such as producing a report) offsite from your organization and submitting it via e-mail?* Again, ask both the paid staff and the volunteers.

- *Does the board of directors ever "discuss" issues via e-mail exchanges or live chat before a formal face-to-face meeting? What about various committees and advisory groups?*

The best way to gather this information is conversationally, one-on-one with employees and volunteers, through a friendly notice in a newsletter, at an onsite meeting, or by e-mail. This will elicit better response than by, say, announcing at a staff meeting: "I want to know who is engaged in virtual volunteering here." Your informal survey is fact finding and should not imply approval or disapproval of virtual service.

The person who wants to champion the work of online volunteers first needs to know if virtual volunteering is already happening at the organization. This person needs to identify existing activities on which to build; identify who can help expand the practice; and identify staff who seem most comfortable doing their own work online or who have a proven track record in partnering with volunteers in general.

Are Volunteers Visible on Your Web Site Today?

There is another tremendously important question to answer before doing anything related to virtual volunteering: *Are volunteers visible on your organization's Web site right now?* In other words, if we visited the current Web site that presents all the things your organization does, how much information would we find online about volunteer involvement? Unfortunately, there are still organizations that would answer "nothing." This is unacceptable no matter what; it sends the message that volunteers are not valued, and it is particularly bad if the site openly solicits money donors and not time donors. If you want to engage online volunteers, it should be obvious that your Web site has to support that outreach.

Hopefully you have been given a page or special section of the site to explain all about volunteering at your organization, whether onsite or online. Is that linked from the home page and easily found? What would we learn about what volunteers do and what positions are currently available? Could we express interest or complete an application online?

Assess the readiness of the Web site to attract a new group of volunteers who want to work virtually. Then develop a list of what needs to be added and prepare to talk to your IT staff or webmaster. We explain more throughout this book about using your

Web site effectively for active and prospective online volunteers.

Overcoming Resistance

If you want to involve online volunteers in significant ways at your organization, you cannot be subtle forever. You are eventually going to have to present clear goals for formal virtual volunteering activities.

Your fact-finding survey will discover who is already on board with the idea and who has the potential to welcome it. But anyone who wishes to initiate some type of virtual volunteering activity should anticipate at least some negative reactions from employees and volunteers because the idea sounds so different from traditional ways to give time. Those under age 30 could be called "cyber natives" or "digital natives" because they cannot remember a time without access to the Internet; that means everyone else is a "cyber immigrant" (and some will remain "cyber dinosaurs"!). So expect initial resistance even if you start slowly, as we are recommending. You may still need to prove the value of online service one successful assignment at a time.

One rationale for learning to involve volunteers online may resonate with reluctant adopters: It increases everyone's skill sets. Both employees and volunteers expand their knowledge and comfort online, which makes them more competitive in the job market. In other words, learning to engage in or manage virtual volunteering is professional development that looks great on a résumé.

Staff members may initially respond that volunteer involvement and management is already too time-consuming and that adding a virtual component will make it more so. Remind staff that online service options will be developed for work that can be done most successfully in a virtual fashion and will be fully integrated into what your organization does with and for volunteers. While there may be some new tasks to learn, they should not put an extra burden on anyone. The idea is to help staff do what needs to be done, not to add more to their work. You are not introducing new activities so much as a new way of working, and you are not trying to replace any onsite volunteering with online service. Be prepared to address other assumptions and misunderstandings about virtual volunteering; to help

---

Change Happens!

Introducing anything new to any organization requires that staff feel fully prepared and supported regarding the change, that they have trust in those driving the change, and that they see immediate benefits that make it worth the time to learn how to implement the change. Without such support, trust, and buy-in, there is frustration, friction, and hostility that is difficult to overcome. The same is true for introducing virtual volunteering to an organization:

■ Go slowly and deliberately.

■ Do not ask staff to do anything you are not doing yourself.

■ Have facts ready to illustrate potential benefits, address concerns, and head off misunderstandings.

■ Let what your organization already does regarding volunteer involvement and support be your guide for introducing virtual volunteering.

---

you, we have listed the most common myths about online volunteering and how to reply to them in appendix A.

Resistance from the Volunteer Resources Manager

If you are not your organization's volunteer resources manager (VRM), you may find that the VRM is delighted to work with you if you want to champion virtual volunteering. However, the VRM may not be comfortable with online interactions with volunteers and may react with:

• *fear* of the concept of virtual volunteering itself or of losing control of volunteering activities;

• *anger* that you are stepping into his or her territory; or

• *being overwhelmed* at the thought of something technology related, something new, or something that could create more work.

In our experience, VRMs are usually the first advocates for virtual volunteering, though we are also aware of instances in which the VRM initially resisted it. Find ways to gain a VRM's support. For example, approach the VRM with a need or opportunity to help and suggest that it might be done by a volunteer offsite, with e-mail interaction.

Resistance from IT Staff

Those in charge of computer and Internet technology at your organization may claim that your organization does not have the computer capacity to involve online volunteers. If so, you need to stand your ground and reiterate that, since your organization has access to the Internet, you *do* have the capacity to involve volunteers virtually—period. Indeed, your organization may not have the hardware and Internet speed to use live online and video tools, but e-mail can be used with even very old computers and slow Internet connections. You may need to recruit professional tech experts from among your volunteers to provide information for your argument.

What Will Virtual Volunteering Cost?

Invariably, someone will challenge any new idea with concern about the financial costs to launch and maintain it. The same is true for virtual volunteering: expect and be prepared to answer questions about how much engaging online volunteers costs.

To do simple assignments like proofreading a document or tagging photos on a photo-sharing site, there should be no more expenses for involving new online volunteers than there are for bringing aboard a few additional onsite volunteers. Online volunteers who undertake simple assignments to support staff and other volunteers will fit into the budget of the existing volunteer program that already includes the time of the VRM, the cost of forms, training materials and handbooks, background checks, insurance coverage, and so on. They won't bring any costs regarding office space or parking, as new onsite volunteers would. Involvement of online volunteers in most circumstances can be done with available e-mail software, computers, and Internet access. The existing volunteer engagement budget might have to grow some if *many* new volunteers are recruited for online work, just as costs would go up with a substantial increase in new *onsite* volunteers.

Here are some possible additional expenses and purchases that VRMs and other supervisory staff *might* need in working with online volunteers:

- A headset and a webcam if they want to talk to online volunteers via audio or video on their computers. In the U.S., all of this equipment can be purchased for around $50 (and most new computers come with these tools already).

- A new computer if current machines are not compatible with online audio and video and your organization feels these functions are essential for working with volunteers. In the U.S., basic laptops with this functionality can be purchased for just a few hundred dollars.

- Advanced software that allows for multi-voice-based conversations over the Internet, like Skype or iVisit; these are free for one-on-one conversations but might need upgrades that allow several people to see and hear each other at once.

- A private online work space to collaborate with volunteers that is more advanced than what a free online collaboration tool like Google Docs (now Google Drive) can provide. There are packages that can be accessed for a monthly subscription that won't be as much as your monthly cable or satellite TV fee.

- An online meeting tool that will allow a VRM to present in real time to several people via their laptops, each in a different location. There are services that offer subscriptions for such tools for less than $50 a month.

Note that all of these expenses are optional; none are absolute requirements to work with online volunteers in most circumstances. And not being able to afford any one of these tools should not be a barrier to involving online volunteers at the most basic level.

If you are initiating an entirely new project through online volunteers, there may be more substantial additional expenses. For instance, you may need to develop a specific online orientation or training video or need to write a volunteer handbook for certain online volunteering roles, such as an online mentoring program. Just as there are costs associated with a new initiative involving volunteers working entirely onsite—hiring someone part-time or full-time to manage such a project and providing a desk, a computer, and a phone to that manager or assistant and so on—the same is true for a new, large online initiative.

It is highly unlikely that your organization will need additional server space, faster Internet access, or specialized software in order to involve online volunteers, unless you are undertaking an online initiative that will create large amounts of digital materials, such as an online mentoring program focused on video interactions between a few hundred adults and children or a historic audio archive program where volunteers interview seniors about specific events or eras and share these recordings online.

Allocation of Staff Time

The real issue when it comes to costs for involving online volunteers is *staff time* to create online volunteering assignments and to support to online volunteers.

Just as with onsite volunteers, a staff person has to be designated as ultimately in charge of a virtual volunteering assignment and to develop an effective working relationship with the online volunteers involved. Their interactions may be mostly asynchronous or mostly connecting in real time, depending on the assignment and on the preferences of everyone involved. Is your organization willing and able to make regular, timely support to online volunteers a required part of a staff person's job? (We discuss ongoing working relationships in more depth in chapter 6.)

Tech-Related Issues

Naturally, virtual volunteering implies the availability of computers and Internet access, which means that your organization's level of technical ability must be considered in planning. Here are some issues to put on the agenda of the appropriate staff and managers so that collectively you can prepare for online service by volunteers.

- Do you, the person who will work with online volunteers or support other staff in doing so, have access to update the volunteer-related pages of your Web site, whenever you need to, or do you have to wait for an IT staff person to budget time to do so? If that IT person cannot make changes to the Web site when they are needed immediately by those working with volunteers, would the IT staff grant access to a fully-vetted, IT-savvy volunteer to make these changes in a more timely manner?

- If your organization's volunteer application isn't already on your Web site, will the designated IT person do this for you in a timely manner, or will you need a volunteer to prepare everything for the webmaster to upload?

- If you start an online discussion group for volunteers (as we recommend in a moment), is there someone in IT who will help you do this on a free platform like Yahoo! Groups or Google Groups, or do you need to recruit a volunteer to help you do this if you don't feel capable of doing it on your own?

- If there are any Internet access limitations now in place, especially if staff are now barred from using social media such as Facebook, Google+ ("Google Plus") or Twitter while at work, can you be given special dispensation to use those sites, as they will be vital to your online outreach strategy? Will IT staff modify your firewall to permit this?

- If you want to use other online tools, such as creating a digital photo archive on Flickr, do you already know enough to do so independently, or will your IT staff help you with any questions you have about using the site, or do you need to recruit a volunteer to help you do this?

- If you have the budget to buy the equipment necessary to have webinars or audio and video conferences on your computer, will whoever is in charge of IT issues at your organization help you with installing these and troubleshooting tech problems?

Those working with volunteers should not have to beg for a spot on the IT staff's to-do list or argue for basic functions they feel are necessary. If you encounter resistance, go higher and make your case to a manager above both functions. Detail in writing your technical needs to work with volunteers and explain why you are asking for certain postings or functionality. Just as the author of a book has more say over its contents than the printer, the *content* and *priorities* of a Web site or other Internet outreach should be determined not by IT staff but by those directly involved in what needs to be accomplished. While it is fair to mutually determine deadlines with IT staff, your tech-related requests should not be answered with "when we have the time." Settle for nothing less than real dates for completion of work, getting upper management to back you up.

If you initiate a particularly ambitious online volunteering project, the technical needs will have to be fully detailed and endorsed beforehand by the organization's executive leadership, who may have to hire additional tech staff either temporarily or permanently to make such an initiative a reality.

Policies and Procedures

If you have an established, effective volunteering strategy in place, then you should already have written policies and procedures for and about volunteers (covering expected code of conduct, confidentiality, sexual harassment, grounds for dismissal, and so on). Further, your organization may already have developed Internet and social networking policies for staff. You may need to make some adjustments and additions to these written policies to accommodate virtual volunteering, but all policies really should be parallel for paid staff and volunteers, or appropriate differences should be explained. In addition, policies and procedures should apply to all volunteers; do not create a unique set for online service.

New to Volunteer Policies?

If you are still creating all policies and procedures for new volunteer involvement in your organization, we strongly suggest you base these on established best practices in the volunteer management field (see appendix B for recommended volunteer management resources). You can start with the free online Volunteer Management Library offered on the Energize, Inc. Web site. You might also consider conducting a "Volunteer Management Audit," a tool also listed in appendix B.

Here are some specific policies, procedures, guidelines, and recommendations that you need to consider and have in place to work with online volunteers:

- Signatures on documents relating to volunteering, such as volunteer applications, liability releases, permission slips, and so on. Can these be scanned and sent as an attachment via e-mail, or are only original documents with real signatures acceptable? Have a justification for which you chose to do.

- Ownership and use of materials produced by volunteers in the course of their service. Who owns what a volunteer designs, such as a logo? What about photos a volunteer takes at an event? When do you need to credit the volunteer as author or designer publicly?

- How (and when) volunteers should represent the organization online, such as identifying their affiliation with you when sending an e-mail or posting a message to an online bulletin board.

- Use of official e-mail addresses or online accounts; some organizations prohibit these being used for personal communication.

- How virtual volunteering work will be backed up and how often. Will you designate organization server space, or should a volunteer back up information on a personal computer or smartphone if that computer or phone is used as a part of his or her service?

- Protecting the confidentiality of information regarding the organization and its clients (see chapter 5 for more information on confidentiality issues).

- Protocol for forwarding, copying, or blind copying e-mail from other volunteers, employees, or clients, focusing in particular on when *not* to do it.

- Reporting to the organization while engaged in virtual service.

- Reasons and procedures for terminating volunteering service.

- How to direct or report online press inquiries.

- Dealing with problems that may arise with staff or others in the course of the volunteer's service.

- Requirements regarding volunteers' anti-virus, anti-spyware and anti-malware systems[1] on their home or work computers used as part of volunteering service.

- Archiving correspondence. For instance, are staff, including volunteers, required to save all correspondence with clients?

- Protocol for sharing photos and names of volunteers in print publications and online. Do volunteers give permission—possibly on their application forms—that any photos taken of them at the organization or an event can be posted online or in a newsletter? Do these volunteers want their first and last names used in your print publications or on the Web site?

- Advice to volunteers who might want to blog about their experience on their own Web sites or online social networking profiles, such as Twitter, MySpace, Google+, or Facebook.

- How online volunteers and their work are evaluated and suggestions for those volunteers to provide feedback to the organization.

- Protocol for changing passwords to systems that departing volunteers have accessed.

- Consequences for the violation of Internet-related policies and procedures.

A keyword search on your favorite Internet search engine will turn up several free samples of volunteer policies at various organizations that you can adapt for your own use. You can also look at Workforce.com, a Web site focused on human resources management and featuring several sample employee policies that are easily adapted to volunteer settings. You might also ask your board members or other volunteers who work for large organizations or government offices if they would be willing to share their organization's employee Internet-related policies with you.

Communicating Your Policies

Equal to keeping policies current is effectively communicating these policies to volunteers (and paid staff). Key in doing this are constant reminders. Note policies, such as those relating to confidentiality, in volunteer task descriptions, review policies in volunteer orientation sessions (see chapter 5), and refer to them regularly on your online volunteer community and in your newsletter for volunteers. Be sure to ask volunteers for their opinions on any policies that are about to be updated.

Recordkeeping Systems

Your system for tracking, managing, and reporting on volunteer data may be as basic as sign-in sheets and spreadsheets or as sophisticated as a customized software platform. Hopefully no one reading this book is still using index cards! Whatever system you use, you will need to incorporate online volunteers into your recordkeeping.

We are adamant that you not create a system for tracking online volunteers separate from your tracking of onsite volunteers! Whatever you track for current, onsite volunteers—the assignments they handle, the number of hours they contribute, their available skills and time, or anything else—should also be tracked for online volunteers. You may need to adapt the way that you collect data from online volunteers. For instance, someone working remotely cannot sign a check-in sheet placed at the entrance of your facility. But you can still use the same database software to input and track data about online volunteers as you do onsite volunteers.

Volunteer management database software varies widely,[2] so it is difficult to offer blanket advice on

> ### Volunteer Tracking System
>
> If you are completely new to volunteer involvement, whether onsite or online, you will need a system to capture all key volunteer information (name, postal and e-mail addresses, telephone number, skills, interests, etc.) and to track volunteer activities/accomplishments. For fewer than 50 online volunteers, a series of spreadsheets may be enough, but eventually you will have to graduate to a more sophisticated program. You can build a system using a database program you can customize (FileMaker Pro, OpenOffice Base, LibreOffice, NeoOffice Database, Microsoft Access, etc.) or buy a package designed specifically as a volunteer management database. For a comprehensive list of volunteer management software, see http://www.coyotecommunications.com/tech/volmanage.html.

how to adapt any software system for online volunteers. We can caution against creating all data fields based on the premise that service is done onsite (such as collecting dates, times, and places where volunteer service is provided) or on the premise that all volunteers work in defined shifts. In addition, you have to consider how you will track progress and activity in volunteer projects. If you are already using project management software, for instance, you will need to adapt it to show what different volunteers are doing with regard to each project.

Planning how to adapt your current system for online volunteers is part of fully integrating virtual volunteering into your organization and getting everyone on board to think of online volunteers as being as real as onsite volunteers. It may mean involving your fundraising staff in discussions, since you may share the same donor-tracking software for both volunteers (time donors) and financial contributors.

Basic Internet Tools

Since the publication of the first *Virtual Volunteering Guidebook*, there have been big changes regarding networking technology tools. The first *Guidebook* dealt strictly with written communications with online volunteers via desktop and laptop computers.

Now tools that bring people face-to-face over the Internet are much more common, and the use of cell phones, smartphones and other handheld technologies permeates our lives in a way that was hardly imaginable not too long ago.

In this *Guidebook*, we try to strike a balance between assuming readers are familiar with Internet tools, services, and platforms and explaining absolutely every tool in great depth. Just as we direct newcomers to volunteer management to resources designed to teach the basics, we do the same for technology. If you are lost in the discussion of any technical element, or want to learn more, please make use of the books and Web sites listed in the Virtual Volunteering Wiki.

Nevertheless, as this chapter is about preparing to start or expand virtual volunteering, we identify the range of available tools for working online with volunteers. We simply list and describe them here; in later chapters we select specific ones to cover in greater depth.

We need to group these tools into categories in order to talk about them more broadly. We might have chosen categories such as text-based tools versus video- and audio-based tools, for instance. Instead, we divided this networking technology into *asynchronous* and *synchronous* tools.

Asynchronous Tools

People using an asynchronous tool do not have to be online at the same time in order to interact with each other. Asynchronous tools include:

- E-mail, e-mail-based newsletters, and e-mail-based communities (discussion groups)

- Web-based communities (discussion groups or bulletin boards), such as Yahoo! Groups or Google Groups

- Blogs (Web logs, online diaries/journals)

- Podcasts (audio recordings)

- Online recorded video (recorded video available anytime for viewing)

- Collaborative online work spaces, such as Google Docs, where multiple people can work on the same documents, spreadsheets, and presentations; share a calendar; and so on

- Wikis (collaborative work spaces for large documents that track edits and editors; the most well known is Wikipedia)

- Online social networking tools such as Facebook, Google+, MySpace, or Change.org

- Photo-sharing sites with online social networking capabilities, such as Flickr

Synchronous Tools

With synchronous or real-time tools, users *do* have to be online *at the same time* in order to interact with each other or to get the most out of the online activity. These include:

- Instant messaging

- Chat rooms

- Live audio or video chats via a computer, such as via Skype, iVisit, Google Talk, Google+ Hangouts, or Yahoo! Messenger

- Live blogging (published as an event happens, by someone witnessing the event, and inviting comments while the event is still happening)

- Web conferencing/webinars (with platforms such as WebEx, ReadyTalk, or Adobe Acrobat Connect), allowing everyone to see a slide show presentation or workspace at the same time while hearing the speaker live either through a telephone conference call or by using voice-over-Internet protocol (VoIP) and being able to interact

- Avatar-based platforms such as Second Life (an avatar is a graphic representation of yourself, which can be anything from a human image to a pink elephant; this will be discussed in chapter 7)

- Micro-blogging and live blogging, such as with Twitter (also discussed in depth in chapter 7)

Note that these tools are often used together. For instance, people may participate in a group online audio conference (teleconference) but submit their questions for discussion via a text-based chat room.

Basic Online Communication

Once upon a time—meaning only 15 years ago!—we dealt with the subject of online communications primarily in terms of how to interact with volunteers in virtual assignments only, since it was assumed that only a few onsite volunteers would have Internet access. Flash forward to today and it is obvious that the world has changed dramatically. The Internet is how we communicate with everyone (at work and at play, with family and strangers) and Internet tools have become as seamlessly integrated into daily life as postal mail and the old-style telephone used to be. This development led to the merging of online and onsite volunteering, which is our driving contention in this Last *Virtual Volunteering Guidebook*.

The following discussion is imperative for working with volunteers in cyberspace, but learning these basics will also make *all* your online communications more effective and will give you new ideas for strengthening your work with volunteers onsite. Win-win.

The Myth of "They Do Not Have Internet Access"

Do not let anyone use the excuse that "most of our volunteers are seniors" or "most of our volunteers are low-income" to assume that some or most volunteers do not have e-mail addresses, smartphones, or access to the Internet. The only way to know for sure is to routinely *ask* everyone on all application forms and periodic surveys.

In 2009, a report from the Pew Internet & American Life Project[3] said that 45 percent of American seniors were online, up from just 26 percent in 2005; by 2012, the same study announced that the number had increased to 53 percent. That report said that 74 percent of Internet users age 64 and older send and receive e-mail. In 2010, that project reported that online social networking use among Internet users age 50 and older nearly doubled, from 22 percent in April 2009 to 42 percent in May 2010.[4]

Search the keywords *Internet use among the homeless* on Google, or have a look at people posting to Yahoo! Answers, and you will discover that a large percentage of younger homeless people have e-mail addresses and access the Internet through public libraries and technology centers set up at homeless shelters.

This is not to say that there are not millions of people in the United States and certainly around the world without Internet access or e-mail. There is still a "digital divide," though it grows smaller every year. But assumptions about "that group does not have e-mail" often turn out to be partially or wholly incorrect, and this concern will keep diminishing over time.

In fact, as Internet access becomes more universal, it will also have an impact on the way we deliver future services to clients, who also will be online. This, in circular fashion, will further change volunteer roles. Here is just one possible example: in 10 or more years, homebound seniors are going to be older Baby Boomers who will have been communicating by Internet for dozens of years. So instead of telephone reassurance projects or even once-a-week personal visiting, volunteers may assist multiple seniors to meet together over the Internet using their webcams. "Isolation" will be more a matter of choice than either geography or health.

No matter the communication medium, *the written word remains essential.* Even when using audio and video, text-based communication still plays a primary role in online interactions. To work well with volunteers online, you must be comfortable communicating via the written word.

E-mail and More

Your organization should already ask for e-mail addresses on your volunteer application form, as well as additional online contact information such as Skype, iVisit, or IM addresses. Fields for this information should be added to whatever database you use to track all the other facts about your volunteer corps. You should also consider:

- *E-mail may not be the best way to get in touch with all volunteers.* Some people are still more easily reached via a phone call, while others will respond immediately only to cell phone text messages or to messages received via the most popular online social networking site of the day (at the time of this book's publication, that is Facebook). So you may want to add a line to your volunteer application for "How do you prefer to be contacted online?" with a choice of e-mail, phone call to cell

phone, text to cell phone, Facebook account, instant message, and so on. However, note that this can change, especially as Internet applications come and go.

- *Periodically—every six months or so—verify volunteers' e-mail addresses and other online contact information, as these are notoriously in flux.* People change their e-mail addresses often or change jobs or Internet providers, and their online contact information becomes out of date. Also, someone without an e-mail address when first applying to be a volunteer will probably obtain one later. So keep asking for updated info or for volunteers to update their information themselves (many software programs and online platforms allow volunteers to do this).

- *Give all volunteers the e-mail addresses of the VRM and any other employees or volunteer leaders they work with, and encouraged them to contact these colleagues via e-mail as needed.* Your organization should also establish a standard for replying to volunteers, such as a commitment to respond to all e-mails within three business days (72 hours) of receipt. However, note that people in their 30s or younger expect a response even more quickly than that.

Online Communities

You may well already be a member of an online community, also known as an online forum, online discussion group, bulletin board, or message board.[5] If not, we recommend that you join one to understand its potential in working with volunteers. When you enroll in a group—and it is almost always free to do so—you begin to receive or get granted access to messages or postings from other members of the community (you usually can choose whether to view these messages on the Web or via your e-mail). When you or someone else responds to any message, that response is seen by everyone else in the group.

You are not required to reply to queries or points raised in an online community; you can simply *lurk* (the term for reading the exchanges but not adding to them) and read what others say. For some communities, all you will want to be is a lurker. For others you will definitely want to participate and ask questions, respond to questions from members, make comments and observations, and perhaps even engage in a debate. We identify online communities for VRMs in the Virtual Volunteering Wiki.

In addition to joining online communities focused on VRMs, you should consider joining communities that do not relate to volunteer management but do relate to a particular demographic. For instance, look for an online forum relating to something you personally find *very* interesting: a hobby, sports activity, television show, rock band, whatever. Watch how different people interact and express feelings. Note how sarcasm may be common in one community and completely misunderstood and inappropriate in another. Note how different age groups communicate. Note how people try to calm arguments or address criticism—or even forbid them altogether. And note how, sadly, there are a few people who seem to want to only make others angry; the term for these sorts is *trolls*, and you have probably encountered them at lots of onsite meetings as well!

Reading posts in online communities, and eventually joining in, cultivates your skills in communicating online. As you improve, you will be laying the groundwork for expanding your use of the Internet to support *all* volunteers, onsite and online. This will also prepare you for creating an online community

for your organization's volunteers, if you do not have one already.

Starting an Online Forum for Volunteers

If you already interact with volunteers via e-mail, and you already lurk on an existing online forum or community, then you are ready to start an online forum for your organization's current volunteers. We strongly believe that *this is a fundamental step in implementing virtual volunteering* and increasingly for working with *all* volunteers. An online forum for volunteers will be referenced throughout the rest of this *Guidebook*.

An online forum allows an organization to make announcements easily to all volunteers at once and, conversely, enables volunteers to interact with employees and each other, to get suggestions and feedback, and to ask questions and more at any time that is convenient. In addition to message threads, most forum platforms also permit members to upload document files, pictures, and other materials for the rest of the group to see, and also maintain the history of past exchanges in a searchable archive. An online forum can serve as a written record of participation, concerns, trends, and issues for volunteers. It is a natural extension of onsite interactions among volunteers and employees. And the good news is that many of your options for hosting an online forum are *free* of cost.

We encourage you to select a platform that allows users to choose message delivery methods and functionalities that are best for them. Two popular platforms are Yahoo! Groups and Google Groups—both are free and allow you to have complete privacy for your online communications. You can also search TechSoup for additional free online group options. As we write this edition of the *Guidebook*, Facebook and LinkedIn have created group options that are increasingly popular, and even newer platforms will surface in the future.

For online volunteers, this electronic forum will be an important way to feel connected to your organization and to a larger corps of volunteers. Anyone in a virtual assignment should automatically be given access to the online community. Participation in online exchanges should be listed as one of the responsibilities in each virtual volunteer position description.

A Successful Online Forum

Your goal is to make the online community something that offers essential information, is frequently updated, and is both useful and welcoming to online volunteers. Online forums connect your online volunteers to information routinely shared with onsite volunteers, since you can post electronic versions of memos, newsletters, announcements about events, policy changes, and new volunteering opportunities currently communicated in other ways.

A successful online community needs:

- *Participation.* You may initially need to be intentional about asking certain volunteers to post. We return to this issue of encouraging group exchange in chapter 12 on working with online volunteers.

- *People to fill the roles of facilitator, administrator, and moderator.*

  - *Facilitator:* keeps the community focused, posts items to generate useful discussions, reminds participants of the ground rules or topics for discussion, and sometimes steps in to calm nerves when arguments get out of control.

  - *Administrator:* helps with technical issues/problems, deletes/adds members, and archives the conversations.

  - *Moderator:* filters content by reading it before it is posted and keeps out improper posts (jokes, advertising, insults, etc.).

    The VRM, another employee, or an online volunteer can fill all three of these roles. Or you can have different people in different roles, or you can have multiple people in each role.

- *Forum guidelines.* These should be based on your organization's policies and procedures regarding confidentiality, sexual harassment, and discrimination.

- *Support from the VRM.* If you are not the VRM, you will need to convince your VRM

that creating an online forum for all volunteers is a great idea. Assure the VRM that you will take care of setting up and supervising the community, and encourage the VRM to mention the forum in regular communications with volunteers and to participate in the community as well.

Applying This to All Volunteers

Although you may be thinking that an online forum is especially useful for volunteers working virtually, the real goal is to establish one overall forum for all volunteers. Which begs the question: Should you make joining your online community mandatory for all volunteers?

The answer depends on your organization's culture or business needs, but recognize that you may lose some volunteers who are not willing to agree to a mandatory requirement. Most traditional organizations that have lots of volunteers find that it is best to introduce an online community as an option rather than a requirement, while newer organizations

---

Lawyers Without Borders

Christina Storm, founder and president of Lawyers Without Borders, noted the importance of her organization's online community for volunteers in an interview via e-mail:

Our virtual community of volunteers is very tight and very dependent upon the computer for communication. They make a point of speaking via telephone periodically so we can get to know each other better. They have submitted photos which we share online so we can put a face to a name. We have a newsletter that features the online volunteers and is a communication tool to let them know about each other, so they have a sense of belonging. We even convert many in-office volunteers and interns to virtual volunteers when their time with us is over.

get no resistance at all to such a requirement. It may be tempting to sign everyone up and offer them the opportunity to opt out, but for-profit companies who have tried this over the years have ended up with customer backlash and even some negative press.

Again, the key is to provide volunteers information through the community that is essential, making it something that they feel they *must* be a part of, even as lurkers. For onsite volunteers to value an online community and log in to it regularly, it must provide at least something that cannot be found anywhere else. That is one benefit of electronically posting all printed-on-paper materials to the community archives: all volunteers will know where they can find the latest versions of all important documents, refresher information from past training, and any notices predating their first day with you. So it is a great resource for both new and longtime volunteers.

Use your creativity to offer materials of interest to volunteers. You can post: announcements about the results of onsite events that your volunteers may have helped to coordinate; links to newspaper articles about the organization; the text of a recent speech by your executive director; links to photos of volunteers in action—all items that your volunteers might miss if not for their online forum. Frequently encourage volunteers to post about challenges they face, resources they find particularly helpful, and their volunteering experiences in general. Remember to thank every volunteer who posts to your online forum. Altogether, this encourages volunteers to help other volunteers using the forum.

Refer to the forum regularly in onsite events and meetings ("I hope you all have had a chance to see the debate that is happening on the online forum about the best method for reporting . . .") and via your volunteer newsletter. Also, *the VRM, as well as other employees or core volunteer staff supporting and involving volunteers, must participate in this online community for it to be successful.* Volunteers must know that employees and other volunteers value the forum enough to use it as well.

Such an online forum can be kept private, with only vetted volunteers allowed to join (to post and to read messages). Volunteers who have been dismissed from the organization should be removed from the forum. But consider allowing volunteers who are

> ### Volunteers Will Talk Online with or without You
>
> If you do not start an online forum for your organization's volunteers, they may start one on their own! You may search Yahoo! Groups or Facebook pages for the name of your organization to see if any volunteers are discussing their experiences without official endorsement. An organization has no control and little influence over such an independent forum, outside of having a staff member join to make sure that the organization's point of view is represented, confidential information is not published, and the organization's policies are not violated—and, if they are, taking appropriate action against the offending volunteer (who can remain on the independent online forum, even after he or she has been let go by your organization).

taking a pause or retiring from volunteering to stay on the forum; it keeps them involved in your organization and perhaps lead them to come back. Further, these experienced folks can help new volunteers via the forum, becoming online volunteers without even knowing that is what they are!

Cyber Deputies

There is not enough time in the day to do absolutely everything you could do online with volunteers.

Involving volunteers to help with online communications is a great way to delegate the work and to show just how much you value the volunteers' contributions. More than a decade ago, a friend of Susan's coined the phrase *cyber deputy* to refer to volunteers who handle online communications and support roles, whether virtually or onsite. Cyber deputies can: facilitate your online community; guide online volunteering candidates through the application process; answer inquiries sent to the main e-mail address for volunteer involvement; review all photos from volunteers before they are posted to a photo-sharing Web site; and perform any of hundreds of other management and administrative tasks.

A caution about working with cyber deputies: most online volunteers expect the VRM or the person in charge of a particular project to be actively engaged with them, including answering their e-mails and participating in the volunteers' online community. Cyber deputies should not create a level of bureaucracy that allows the VRM or other managers to avoid having to interact regularly with others online. If you want volunteers to use an online tool, the employees who work with volunteers must use that online tool as well and not delegate their online interactions entirely to cyber deputies. Also, make sure cyber deputies document what they are doing and how they are doing it; when such a volunteer leaves, having a written record of the volunteer's passwords and protocols will help another volunteer to step into that role immediately.

Solidifying the Organization's Commitment

All of the advice here should, we hope, get your organization to embrace virtual volunteering and make all of the necessary adjustments to fully integrate online volunteers. No matter how confident you may feel at this point, however, you need to clarify the organization's commitment to effective volunteer involvement in general and to virtual volunteering in particular.

A good way to do this is to create a flowchart that chart shows exactly how *any* volunteering assignment comes to fruition, including how long each step should take:

- Who creates a volunteering assignment

- How this assignment comes to the volunteer resources manager

- Who recruits and when recruitment happens in the process

- Who tracks and follows up on all expressions of interest from potential volunteers for an assignment

- Who screens potential volunteers and when screening happens in the process

- Who matches volunteers to assignments (unless volunteers self-match to assignments; see chapter 4 for more information) and when matching takes place

- Who accepts or rejects a volunteer for an assignment and when this step takes place

- At what point the volunteer actually starts undertaking the project

Here's an example of a flowchart regarding the volunteer intake process:

Volunteer Intake Process

You need to chart all of the various steps that happen from the time an assignment is defined and a volunteer is recruited to the time a volunteer is officially given an assignment, and what happens after the assignment is completed. Review your volunteer management flowchart and add any notes necessary to alter or adapt the process for virtual volunteering. The flowchart should remain largely the same for both onsite and online volunteers, with most adjustments made in wording. Indeed, some steps will be online rather than onsite (such as the new volunteer orientation).

Work together with paid staff and leadership volunteers to create or update this flowchart, and ensure that everyone gets a copy of the final draft. The flowchart ensures that staff understand that virtual volunteering will now be fully integrated into the organization's overall volunteer involvement, providing clear expectations about everyone's responsibilities regarding virtual volunteering at your organization.

NOTES

1. For more information on anti-virus/malware software, go to the TechSoup Global Web site, http://www.techsoup.org, and do a keyword search.

2. For a comprehensive list of volunteer management software, see http://www.coyotecommunications.com/tech/volmanage.html.

3. Sydney Jones and Susannah Fox, *Generations Online 2009* (Philadelphia: Pew Research Center, 2009) <http://pewresearch.org/pubs/1093/generations-online>.

4. Mary Madden, *Older Adults and Social Media.* (Philadelphia: Pew Research Center, 2010) <http://www.pewinternet.org/Reports/2010/Older-Adults-and-Social-Media.aspx>; Kathryn Zickuhr and Mary Madden, *Older Adults and Internet Use* (Philadelphia: Pew Research Center, 2012) <http://www.pewinternet.org/Reports/2012/Older-adults-and-internet-use.aspx>.

5. Some people mistakenly call all e-mail-based discussion groups "listservs." In fact, LISTSERV is a particular brand of software and a trademarked term. Just as Xerox does not want its name used for copies made on other company's copiers, or Kleenex does not want its name used for a tissue that its company did not produce, the folks behind the LISTSERV software get testy over misuse of its name.

Diana Cocoru, online volunteer coordinator, Kabissa-Space for Change in Africa, whose mission is "to help African civil society organizations to put Information and Communication Technology (ICT) to work for the benefit of their communities."

Chapter 3
Designing Virtual Volunteering Assignments

A basic premise of volunteer management is this: What you ask a volunteer to do is fundamental to the success of everything that comes next with that volunteer and the task to be done. Designing the right assignments for volunteers is therefore crucial, whether the work is done onsite or online. Without well-crafted, well-written volunteering assignments, you cannot recruit the best people, provide the necessary training and support, or accomplish goals. In this chapter we concentrate on developing virtual volunteering roles, recognizing that the generic principles of volunteer management fully apply.

Be Open to What Online Volunteers Can Do

We are about to discuss a range of virtual volunteering activities with varying levels of responsibility, required time commitments, and access to confidential or proprietary information. Even if you are your organization's champion of virtual volunteering, you may discover that you—yes, YOU—are resistant to some of our ideas, ready to balk at giving online volunteers high-responsibility roles with access to confidential or proprietary information.

If this description fits you, remember that:

- Employees undertake these roles at organizations, and a paycheck does not guarantee qualifications, the fulfillment of commitments, or a promise regarding confidentiality. You have systems in place that ensure employees meet these requirements, and you should adapt these systems for volunteers as well, onsite or online.

- Onsite volunteers undertake such roles at thousands of organizations. Many organizations reserve high-responsibility, even high-profile, roles specifically for volunteers and report great success. Consider the board members of all nonprofit organizations or the first responders of disaster relief organizations like the American Red Cross. Some organizations are run entirely by volunteers, also with great success. Why would online volunteers be any less reliable than such onsite volunteers?

- The key to assuring confidentiality is training: explain exactly what and how information is to be protected, and emphasize the importance of confidentiality, both professionally and legally. Chapter 5 provides more information about confidentiality concerns, and chapter 8 further reviews how to ensure safety in an online volunteering project.

Other staff members may also be uncomfortable with the degree of delegation virtual volunteering tasks require. It is often a challenge to get staff to identify meaningful volunteer roles for real-world, onsite volunteers, let alone for those who will serve online. The question "How could volunteers help you?" often produces blank stares or comments such as, "What I need done would take too long to explain to a volunteer" or "No volunteer is capable of doing the things that I need done."[1] These sorts of responses imply skepticism that a volunteer might come with expertise or skills.

We suggest that you do not even mention volunteers when you begin to discuss virtual volunteering tasks. Instead, focus on *what needs to be done*. Ask questions such as:

- What do our clients (or you) need or wish our organization was doing now but is not, because we lack the funds and resources to do so?

- What do you wish people could see or know about our work that would help them realize how valuable this organization is to the community/mission we serve?

- If you could get a grant to hire a consultant with a particular area of expertise to help you with a part of your job for two months, what kind of consultant would you hire? What project would you ask this consultant to work on?

- What expertise or skills would benefit the community/mission we serve but are not offered by current staff members?

- What tasks are you responsible for right now that you wish you could delegate to another qualified person so you could spend more time on other essential responsibilities?

The discussion that results from these kinds of questions will identify things that are necessary and important but not being done now, along with some wish-list items that would be nice to get done. Then, and only then, can you lead the discussion toward the next question: "If we recruited the right, qualified volunteers, which of these tasks might you delegate to them?" Finally, ask a follow-up question: "And which of these roles might be productively— even more effectively—done by the right, qualified volunteer *online*?"

Remember to lead by example: How do *you* involve online volunteers in high-responsibility roles? As advisers? As short-term project managers? As managers of other online volunteers? How many of your online volunteers are highly skilled and highly trained and using these skills as a part of volunteering to support you?

The critical concept here is that no activity is *inherently* a volunteer or an employee role; it all depends on finding the most qualified person to do the task. Once again, if the task can be done by a human, it can be done by a volunteer. And if a task can be done by a volunteer, there is an excellent chance that at least some of it might be accomplished through online service.

Virtual Volunteering Assignments Requiring a Little Bit of Time

Most people talk about their volunteering in terms of the work they do or the roles they take on:

- *I'm a trail maintenance volunteer with the state park.*

- *I'm a board member at the ballet company.*

- *I help out once a month at the senior center computer lab.*

Volunteers often have no idea that many VRMs divide up traditional volunteering roles by specific terms like *highly-skilled volunteers* and *episodic volunteering* and that VRMs have heated debates regarding how these terms are used. Volunteers see themselves simply as volunteers, and that is how they talk about themselves.

It is the same for virtual volunteering. There are a lot of labels for the different types of tasks that online volunteers undertake, and there is no universal agreement on the boundaries between these different types. But to online volunteers, they are simply *volunteers,* and what they do is *volunteering.*

However, because this chapter is mainly directed at organizations creating the best ways to deliver services, we recognize that designing work for online volunteers requires defining those roles. To that end, we categorize virtual volunteering activities by task duration and by the level of responsibility the online volunteer assumes or the expertise the volunteer provides. We offer labels that describe these different types of virtual volunteering activities, noting that our definitions are not set in stone and are frequently debated. What is most important to remember is that we are talking about *volunteers,* period. As noted in the preface, we named this book *The* Last *Virtual Volunteering Guidebook* because we want this to be the last volunteer management guidebook that separates out the discussion of virtual volunteering from all of the volunteering happening at an organization. When discussions about online volunteers happen, we hope they do not get bogged down in labels!

Byte-Sized Assignments or Micro-volunteering

Back in the 1990s, Jayne coined the phrase *byte-sized volunteering*, her label for short-term online volunteering tasks that could be completed in just a few minutes and did not require any ongoing commitment. While the practice has been around for many years and has enjoyed a surge of popularity recently, Jayne's original term has been replaced by a far more popular label: *micro-volunteering.*

The proliferation of smartphones has led to a huge surge in the popularity of micro-volunteering among volunteers. The term is used to describe virtual volunteering tasks that have these characteristics:

- Do not take long to complete: perhaps a few minutes or hours over one day, a few days, or two weeks

- Do not involve high security or handling of proprietary data

- Are important, but not immediately critical (as in, if they do not get done within the next two weeks, it will not bring your organization to a screeching halt)

- Can be done by just one person, rather than needing a team

Here are some examples:

- Compiling a list of blogs relating to a specific topic

- Identifying which groups on Flickr or another photo-sharing Web site your organization might want to sometimes post photos to, in order to get the word about your work and events

- Setting up an account on an online social networking site for an organization, such as Facebook, Google+, MySpace, Twitter, or Change.org

- Analyzing information on a spreadsheet and offering a short narrative on what the data mean

- Editing a podcast (cutting out background noise or silence, adding introduction music, etc.)

- Testing a Web site to make sure it works on a variety of computers and Web browsers, even smartphones, and identifying any problems so that IT staff can take action to make a site more accessible

- Editing a press release, newsletter article, or new Web site section

- Compiling a list of online communities relating to a particular field of expertise, a specific topic, a specific geographic area, etc.

- Finding free online training materials for whatever software tool your office is learning to use

- Answering questions for a day about accounting software on an online forum as questions come in

- Going through a set of photographs and writing brief descriptions and keywords to help a library catalog ephemera that would otherwise remain inaccessible to the public

Mike Bright, founder of HelpfromHome.org, a UK micro-volunteering site, with the tagline *Volunteer in Your Pyjamas*

Some micro-assignments are more complex in nature, will take longer, and require volunteers with certain expertise. Some examples:

- Translating one Web page, a flyer, or a short brochure into another language

- Gathering information on one topic (identifying all nonprofit organizations in one specific city that are focused on children, finding conferences in the next six months focused on human resources management, finding samples of volunteer policies online, finding samples of company social networking policies online, etc.)

- Designing an online graphic

- Doing a Web search to seek out resources and activities that are needed for clients in a specific geographic location (summer camps, vocational training, child care, government programs to help a particular group of people, etc.)

- Checking grant proposal submission guidelines on the Web sites of various potential funders, such as foundations or corporations

- Creating a new Web page (putting up a newsletter article as a new Web page, for instance)

- Researching which Web sites link to your organization's site, and researching which sites should link to your organization's Web site but do not currently

- Adding new tags to your photos already uploaded on a photo-sharing site to ensure they will come up on a search of certain keywords

You can see that these tasks are concise and volunteers could work on them in just a few minutes, a few hours in a day, or just a few hours over a few days. You can and should establish deadlines for such assignments and require a mid-assignment report if the deadline is a week or more after the assignment is given.

Micro-volunteering assignments are a great way both to introduce virtual volunteering to your organization and to provide a trial run for new online volunteers. That said, there is no need to use any term such as *micro-volunteering* or *virtual volunteering* if you think people might find such labels intimidating; you can simply recruit *volunteers* to do *online* assignments and leave out the jargon altogether!

Trial Runs

A micro-volunteering assignment is great for a new online volunteer because it introduces you to each other. You will learn quickly what it is like to work with the new volunteer and see if the volunteer honors a commitment, communicates well online, has the necessary attention to detail, or any other factor. In return, the new online volunteer will learn about your organization and begin to feel a part of it. If you have proper support and recognition, the volunteer should feel motivated to ask for another virtual assignment—or, at the very least, to talk positively about your organization to others.

A volunteer could complete one of these assignments and then walk away and never volunteer with your organization again. That is OK, so long as the result is helpful. And if things do not work out as hoped with the volunteer, this initial trial run offers a point to halt the volunteer's involvement without either of you feeling the effort has been wasted.

Crowdsourcing

Crowdsourcing is a form of virtual volunteering as old as the Internet itself (which makes it more than 30 years old). It is often called *distributed problem solving* or branded as micro-volunteering. We define crowdsourcing as a task or question offered up online to anyone who would like to take it on, where the organization does little or no screening of contributors, and the names of contributors and their contributions may not be tracked. Crowdsourcing can be as simple as posting, "How would you handle the following situation . . . ?" to an online community of volunteer resources managers or asking your online community of volunteers, "How could we improve our online volunteer orientation?" With crowdsourcing, you can ask advice from anyone, such as posting this question to a discussion forum for human resources managers: "Would anyone be willing to share their company's dress code? We're looking for ideas."

Micro-volunteering in Practice

Bpeace is a U.S.-based nonprofit that recruits professionals to help entrepreneurs in countries emerging from war, like Rwanda and Afghanistan. Many Bpeace volunteers contribute their service online and are a mix of short-term and long-term contributors, including people who take on micro-volunteering assignments.

Each Bpeace entrepreneur is assigned an online volunteer consultant called an advocate, who either has a background in the business the entrepreneur wants to pursue or has experience in the country where the entrepreneur is based. This advocate is a long-term online volunteer who contributes several hours of time each week over many weeks or months. The entrepreneur tells the advocate what knowledge is needed, and the advocate finds or produces easy-to-access materials that provide that knowledge. The advocate may, in turn, create micro-volunteering assignments, so shorter-term online volunteers can contribute advice based on expertise the advocate does not have.

An example: A businessman in Afghanistan, who wanted to start an office- and home-cleaning business, told his advocate that he needed guidance in developing a business plan, including a marketing plan. The advocate did research over a few weeks to develop an outline for the plan and then found representatives of cleaning companies willing to spend just an hour or two reviewing the outline and offering suggestions based on their own small businesses—in other words, very short-term, focused volunteering around their area of expertise. The advocate used these micro contributions to create a robust, practical guide for starting a cleaning business that took into consideration the realities of conditions in Afghanistan as well as the expertise of two successful small businesspeople. The advocate volunteered for several hours over several weeks; the cleaning company representatives volunteered for just an hour or two each, and then they were done with their online volunteering contributions.

Toni Maloney, co-founder and CEO, notes:

It took us a while to realize that Bpeace members pulse in and out of being active and that's not any reflection on their interest in Bpeace, or our ability to keep them engaged. At any point in time, one-third of our membership is active, meaning truly investing time in a project. And that one-third is constantly shifting because our members have full lives—families, careers, other interests. When we reached this realization, we designed projects differently—breaking them down into manageable bites with clear beginning, middle and ends on short time lines.

Crowdsourcing is not just for discussion questions; it can also include more complex tasks that anyone is invited to complete or contribute to. There are many well-known projects relying on this sort of communal virtual volunteering, such as:

- In the free open-source software (FOSS) movement, *anyone* can participate, at any time, in helping to write the code for these software products.

- Wikipedia is an online encyclopedia that anyone can edit at any time.

- Clickworkers was a small NASA project begun in 2001 that engaged online volunteers in scientifically-related tasks that required just a person's perception and common sense, but not scientific training, like identifying craters on Mars in photos the project posted online. Clickworkers participated whenever and for however long they chose.[2]

- People from various locations can create a map of information (text info or photos) using their cell phones, smartphones, or tablets. For the 2012 moth census in Northern

Ireland, people were asked to report sightings of rare moth species and the information was used to create an online map. There are many similar efforts via Crowdmap.com.

- NetSquared, an initiative of TechSoup Global, invites anyone to view proposed tech-networking projects listed on its site, post questions and thoughts about these proposals, and vote on the ones they believe will have the most potential for social impact. Most of the projects relate to cell phones and smart-phones used in community-empowerment or humanitarian efforts. Partners for its project proposal competitions have included USAID, Microsoft, and Yahoo!

Crowdsourcing can involve people who are not a part of your organization—such as anyone visiting your Web site or on an online discussion group run by another organization—or it can be reserved only for vetted volunteers on your internal online discussion group. If you make crowdsourcing activities available to people outside your vetted volunteers, you might want to explore ways to capture their key contact information so you can provide personalized follow-up regarding the project or issue to which they contributed, a note of thanks, and information about more in-depth volunteering. If people have a positive experience, you may turn some of them into longer-term online volunteers!

On-Call Expertise

A special category of virtual volunteering (and also a part of the micro-volunteering subcategory) is service offered by highly-skilled professionals or experts who make themselves available to answer questions online as required. So the volunteering is byte sized but repeats sporadically over time. Such on-call advice can be on any and all subjects, from legal or medical to sales techniques or hip-hop music. For example:

- Being the on-call expert for the human resources manager to help write a sexual harassment policy
- Answering quick questions from clinical or counseling staff regarding psychiatric/behavior patterns of specific clients

- Reviewing all press releases and outreach strategies developed by the marketing staff
- Consulting on a proposed strategic plan for a new client service
- Developing an online outreach strategy

The key to success in this type of technical assistance or expert advice is specific, clear questions from employees or volunteers to the expert who has agreed to assist. No expert wants to take time out of a busy day to have an unfocused, live discussion via instant messaging, live audio, live video, or even the telephone with a person who is not sure what advice he or she is looking for. Avoid open-ended and vague questions, and show the expert that you value his or her time by being focused on the specific task or issue for which you need advice.

YouthNet's "Agony Aunties"

YouthNet is the UK's leading online charity providing advice, information, and support to young people aged 16 to 25. It provides non-judgmental support and information on everything from sex and exam stress to debt and drugs on TheSite.org through the efforts of hundreds of peer volunteers.

According to YouthNet: "Our straight-talking emotional support is available 24 hours a day. Chat about any issue on our moderated discussion boards and live chat room, browse over 2000 articles and videos by professional journalists, or ask a question—we'll give you a personalised answer within three working days."

Because of the often sensitive or specific nature of the questions received, it is vital that YouthNet assure the validity of replies provided by more generalist volunteers. So they have recruited a network of professional psychiatrists, psychologists, physicians, and more who are available online to help the responding volunteers give the best advice. In the office, YouthNet refers to these on-call volunteer experts as "agony aunties," the British expression for "advice-to-the-lovelorn" newspaper columnists.

Spontaneous Online Volunteers

When a big news story or a natural disaster strikes, hundreds and even thousands of people may contact organizations to offer help, including potential online volunteers. Any organization could suddenly be swamped with e-mails and phone calls from people who want to volunteer onsite or online.

How you deal with these spontaneous online volunteering candidates will depend on how directly involved your organization is with the crisis or hot issue at hand. All the best practices of emergency response volunteer management onsite apply, of course, and the key is preparing in advance to cope with many offers of help. See chapter 7 for suggestions on how to respond to spontaneous volunteers, as well as a list of possible activities they might take on to benefit your organization in a crisis situation.

Other Short-Term Online Supporters

There are additional ways that people can support an organization online. They can:

- Enter shopping sites by first going to an organization's Web site and clicking in through a special link, thereby assuring a cash donation to that cause.

- Change their social media avatars to your organization's logo on a certain day to create awareness about your organization's work.

- Share your organization's Facebook status update with friends.

Is this virtual volunteering? Consider the offline versions of these activities:

- A person chooses to buy cookies through your organization, rather than going directly to a store, so that your organization gets a percentage of the profits.

- A person wears a t-shirt with your organization's logo to a family reunion.

Are these volunteers? We offer a big, definite *maybe*. How wide you cast your virtual volunteering or even your micro-volunteering net is entirely up to you.

Virtual Volunteering Assignments That Require a Greater Time Commitment

A number of the short assignments just mentioned clearly can expand in time and complexity if both the volunteer and you are interested. Besides, virtual volunteering assignments should not be limited to low-responsibility tasks. Even in this age of overwhelming information, longer work hours, and so much competition for attention and time, there are many people who want to make a more substantial commitment to an organization than a quickie volunteering assignment and are willing to provide the time needed for a high-responsibility role. These higher-commitment, higher-responsibility tasks can involve the handling of some confidential or proprietary data.

At least some volunteers who have proven themselves reliable with short-term tasks will want to progress further. You need to identify more advanced assignments before volunteers start asking for them so that you can place people into roles quickly, while they are enthusiastic.

Longer-term tasks will probably be more critical to the organization than micro assignments. They may still only require a few hours a week by a volunteer, but they also will require a much longer-term commitment than just a couple of weeks, as well as regular reporting regarding progress and challenges. A task may have a timeline of weeks or months, but the volunteer should always have an agreed-to end date, at which time the volunteer can decide to continue for, say, another three months or move on. This way, a volunteer does not quit suddenly and leave an important task unfinished—and you have benchmarks at which to give recognition and thanks.

Longer-term, higher-responsibility roles could include:

- Translating an entire chapter or publication (something longer than a page) into another language

- Proofreading the work of other volunteers who are writing or translating various documents

- Developing an entire new section of a Web site or an entire new Web site

- Designing a database

- Preparing a proposal, a new brochure, an entire newsletter, or other printed publication

- Developing an online workshop

- Moderating or facilitating an online forum hosted by the organization

- Monitoring other organizations' online communities and bringing up discussions or debates there relating to your organization to the appropriate staff for review or response

- Monitoring Internet media outlets and bringing any articles relating to the organization and its mission to the appropriate staff

- Producing material and managing activities on one or all of the organization's online social networking accounts, such as Facebook, MySpace, Twitter, or Change.org

- Creating an online tutorial so that employees and volunteers can understand how to use a shared online workspace (Google Docs/ Google Drive, Basecamp, Minigroup, or Microsoft SharePoint) to work together on documents, spreadsheets, and presentations; share a calendar; and otherwise work together online

- Brainstorming with a group online regarding a particular challenge faced by the organization or a proposed new activity

- Creating and editing a video and/or a podcast (or a series of these)

- Leading, facilitating, or moderating a live online event, such as a webinar

- Create captions for an online video (so that it can be understood by people with hearing impairments or people who are not native English speakers)

- Conducting the initial screening and online orientation of new online volunteers

- Responding to e-mail inquiries regarding an organization's volunteer involvement (acting as a cyber deputy, as discussed in chapter 2)

- Conducting a survey of all online volunteers and creating a report that analyzes the results and keeps feedback anonymous

In chapter 8, we look in-depth at virtual volunteering assignments working directly with your organization's clients or the public on your behalf. By definition, such roles will be more long-term and involve greater expertise and responsibility.

Technical Assistance/Pro Bono Service

As noted earlier with on-call service, some online volunteers are highly skilled in a particular field and donate services for which they are otherwise paid. A more intensive role for such experts usually focuses on one specific project for an organization and has all the characteristics of a paid consultancy. In fact, this sort of volunteering is often called *pro bono work* rather than volunteering, but the consultants are still volunteers!

These online volunteers are recruited for their existing expertise and, by design, may be far more skilled and credentialed in their specialty than anyone at your organization. However, just because someone has professional skills, it does not necessarily follow that s/he knows how to be a consultant, advisor, or trainer, yet that is exactly what is necessary to be of greatest help. There is a world of difference between doing a task and assisting or training others to do it. Therefore, your screening and matching process should ascertain whether or not the volunteer needs some instruction in how to consult or advise. In chapters 4 and 5 we look more carefully at some of the special considerations posed by pro bono volunteers, whether offline or on.

Volunteer-Generated Assignments

Everything we have talked about so far has been from the perspective that volunteering assignments are generated by the organization's staff. However, volunteers are also excellent resources for creating new service opportunities, for themselves or for new recruits.

Ask volunteers via all of your communications methods (your volunteer newsletter, onsite volunteer meetings, and online forum for volunteers) if they have ideas to help your organization's clients, support the staff in their work, or promote your mission—and how volunteers might be a part of filling those needs. Ask them if they have specific skills or expertise that they are not yet using on your behalf but would like to share. Invite their ideas frequently—your goal should be for everyone in your organization to look for virtual volunteering tasks.

For a proposed volunteering assignment idea to be accepted, it has to be of value to the organization. Each assignment should relate somehow to current work or client needs and be tied to the responsibilities of a current staff member. That staff member will have to decide whether or not the assignment is worthwhile and if the staff member is willing to work with the volunteer.

Putting It in Writing

A key to success in all volunteer management is making expectations clear. It is therefore fundamentally important to put any volunteer role *in writing*. You are not just delegating a task—you are delegating responsibility. In the online article "Giving It Away: The Art of Delegation," Paul Lemberg notes that when delegating you must "communicate precise conditions of satisfaction . . . Time frame, outcomes, budget constraints, etc.; all must be spelled out. Anything less creates conditions for failure. It is like the old story about basketball—without nets the players do not know where to shoot the ball."[3]

The written assignment description, at least part of which will be used for volunteer recruitment, should include:

- A *title* for the volunteer role. As Susan frequently reminds people, the label "volunteer" is not a title; it is a pay category that does not explain what this unpaid person is doing! So select an appropriate title: *Online Community Facilitator, Researcher, Grant Writer, Online Mentor to a Middle School Student*

- The *scope* or subject matter of the assignment

- The *volunteer's contact person* at the organization. Which person will: supervise the volunteer in this assignment; supply all materials needed; evaluate the volunteer's service at the end or at key points during the assignment, etc.

- A *detailed description* of what the volunteer will do in this assignment

- *Reporting requirements.* Is the volunteer required to report on progress every week? Meet online or via phone with the key staff contact every two weeks?

- An explanation of *why this assignment is important* to the organization and the mission it serves (critical to recruitment)

- A list of expected *deliverables* (in other words, what success in the assignment will look like)

- A description of *skills, experience, and core competencies* the assignment requires of the volunteer

- A description of *hardware and software* required for this assignment. For instance, must the volunteer have a broadband or wireless Internet connection? An account already set up on iVisit or Skype or Google Talk? Use only a computer that is password protected so that organizational materials used by the volunteer could not be accessed by anyone else? Have a digital camera or a camera on a cell phone or smartphone?

- A description of any *screening* the volunteer will have to go through. Will employment listed on a resume be verified? Will references be contacted? Is a criminal background check required and, if so, who will be responsible for paying for this?

- Details about *monitoring* that will happen during an assignment. For instance, if the volunteer works directly with clients, will all online exchanges be archived on the organization's servers? Will all exchanges be reviewed by a staff person?

- A description of any *training*, beyond the standard online orientation for all new online volunteers, that is provided to accepted candidates and how this training will be delivered

- The number of *hours* a day, a week, or a month this assignment requires

- The *commitment* required for the assignment (two weeks? a month? three months? six months?)

- The *time frame*. Does this assignment need to start in the next two weeks? Anytime before the end of the year?

All of the above are vital to a position description for any volunteer, but you can see some of the elements unique to a virtual role. On pages 39 and 40 are two examples of written virtual volunteering assignment descriptions that put our recommendations into practice.

Detailed, written volunteering assignments like these examples allow potential candidates to determine whether or not they are qualified for a position, if their availability matches what is needed, and other details to help them decide if they are interested in doing the service.

Different volunteers will be attracted to different assignments, depending on their skills, interests, and availability. Having a diversity of assignments makes your organization more attractive to a variety of different types of people with different interests and work styles. It will also make your organization more accessible for people with disabilities but who have areas of expertise that your organization could put to good use. Organizational accessibility is discussed in detail in chapter 9.

Diversity in assignments comes from asking for ideas from a wide range of staff members and volunteers from different areas of your organization. In truth, there are endless ways to involve online volunteers, and this chapter has only presented the basic categories of online work for you to consider.

Skill Level Needed

You may be wondering about the level of skill assumed necessary for these assignments. Yes, the assignments we just suggested require some degree of expertise, but remember two things: 1) the vast majority of people will not claim expertise they actually do not have, and 2) you will know almost immediately if someone is telling the truth about possessing specific skills. For instance, if someone says that he or she can convert text into .html for a Web page, you will find out in just a few days whether or not this is true. It is very hard to fake skills when it comes to online service. That said, you will still want the online volunteer's work to be evaluated. If someone has translated text into another language, you will want a native speaker to review the work and verify that it is correct; if someone has created a page for your Web site, your webmaster can assess whether the markup was done correctly or not.

Notes

1. Adapted from Karen Lawson, "How to Delegate Effectively," Lawson Consulting Group, 2002–13 <http://www.lawsoncg.com/lcgi-article_delegate.htm>.
2. You can read more about this now defunct project by going to www.archive.org and typing in this URL: clickworkers.arc.nasa.gov (choose the earliest version of the site available).
3. Paul Lemberg, "Giving It Away—The Art of Delegation," Talkbiz, 1998 <http://www.talkbiz.com/digest/emt17.html>.

Sample Virtual Volunteering Position Descriptions

Example 1:

Title: Online Researcher

Scope of assignment: Research universities in the United States, Canada, and the United Kingdom with undergraduate and graduate degrees in folklore studies.

Requesting manager: Dr. Emma Beasley

Description: This volunteer will use the Internet to compile a list of universities with undergraduate and graduate degrees in folklore studies—the traditional art, literature, knowledge, and practice that is disseminated largely through oral communication and behavioral example. The volunteer should not contact any of these universities; rather, the volunteer should compile the needed information and provide it to the manager. At the end of the assignment, the volunteer will be asked to complete a survey about his or her experience. The volunteer will also be asked to join a private online forum for all volunteers.

Reporting requirements: The volunteer is expected to report in via email to the responsible manager one week after being granted this assignment and every seven days thereafter until the assignment is completed. If the assignment lasts for longer than two weeks, a meeting by phone or iVisit will need to take place between the volunteer and the manager.

Importance of this assignment: Our organization has field staff working with small, rural, isolated communities throughout North America and the UK regarding health issues and gender empowerment. We need better contact with university programs that are focused on folklore studies in order to access information we may need about a particular community, to recruit field staff from among those studying folklore at the university level, and perhaps even to invite university staff to consult with us on some projects.

Deliverables: The finished product would be a list of these universities, with the name of the university, the name of the program, the city, state and country where such is located, and the Web site for each program.

Needed skills: The volunteer will need to enjoy using Internet search engines and reading text online, have excellent attention to detail, and respect deadlines and commitments.

Needed equipment: The volunteer will need reliable Internet access. It would be appreciated if the volunteer had a webcam and an iVisit account, but this is not absolutely necessary.

Screening: Candidates for this assignment will be interviewed by the requesting manager by either e-mail, phone, or iVisit.

Monitoring: There will be no direct supervision of the volunteer during this assignment.

Training: None required.

Time commitment for this assignment: At least two hours a week for four weeks.

Time frame: This assignment needs to be completed by the end of October.

Example 2:

Title: Community Forum Moderator

Scope of assignment: Moderate and provide technical assistance for the online community for volunteers.

Requesting manager: Jay Denton

Description: This volunteer will:

- Confirm with the volunteer resources manager that those requesting to join the forum are volunteers with the organization, then approve new members
- Delete members, as directed by the volunteer resources manager
- Work directly with members who express a need for guidance regarding using the forum tools
- Withdraw improper posts, such as advertising or off-topic jokes, and send these to the volunteer resources manager for appropriate action
- Remind members, as needed, where to find resources on the forum, such as the policies and procedures
- Create a monthly report regarding forum use (how many members, how membership numbers compare with previous months, number of postings from volunteers and how this compares with previous months, what percentage of membership is posting, etc.)

Reporting requirements: The volunteer is expected to report in via email to the volunteer resources manager once a week, as well as once a month via phone or Skype.

Importance of this assignment: The online forum for volunteers is a fundamentally important tool at our organization. This is an ongoing discussion by volunteers regarding their service to our organization, and a place where they can seek support as needed. A moderator will greatly improve this group as a tool for both volunteers and staff.

Deliverables: Monthly reporting will confirm that the volunteer is engaged in the requested actions. The volunteer will also be asked to participate in surveys to evaluate the organization's support of virtual volunteering activities.

Needed skills: The volunteer will need to already be a member of Google Groups and already understand all of the moderation tools, as no training will be provided. The volunteer should be experienced in participating in online communities. This moderator should also have already volunteered onsite at our organization in some way.

Needed equipment: The volunteer will need reliable Internet access. Having a webcam and a Skype account would be appreciated, but this is not absolutely necessary.

Screening: Candidates for this assignment will be interviewed by the requesting manager by phone or Skype. The candidate's name will also be searched for online, and any profiles he or she may have will be reviewed.

Time commitment for this assignment: At least two hours every other day, for four months. At the end of the assignment, the manager and the volunteer can decide to extend the time commitment further, with a new end date.

Chapter 4
Interviewing and Screening Online Volunteers

Having now described what it is you want online volunteers to do, you might expect the next step to be recruiting them. But you are not yet ready to invite anyone to join your virtual volunteering ranks—until you have done all the planning and set up all your procedures to engage them properly. Rest assured we will get to the important subject of recruitment in a later chapter. But first let's discuss the next cornerstone topic: creating an interviewing and screening process for new online volunteers.

Every organization will have different interviewing and screening methods based on what services volunteers provide and its workplace culture. Even for volunteers working onsite, the issues involved in volunteering for a beach cleanup or simple clerical work are not the same as issues involved in volunteering to tutor young children or manage an organization's computer systems.

The same is true for online volunteers. Your screening approach will be different for a volunteer designing a Web page than for one creating a private online area where your staff and clients will interact and the online volunteer will have far more access to client contact and other confidential information.

The Realities of Cyberspace Immediacy

We have continually emphasized that managing online volunteers calls for the same approaches as managing traditional, onsite volunteers. But there *are* some differences. One of these differences that most affects screening and matching to virtual volunteering assignments is *speed*.

Cyberspace generates a sense of immediacy. The majority of people who express interest in a virtual volunteering opportunity want to get started right away. In this chapter, we suggest ways to manage applications and screening to address both the issues of immediacy and screening out those who express interest in virtual volunteering before considering the very real commitment required.

This cyberspace immediacy has a very big downside that affects the placement of new online volunteers into assignments: giving work too soon to brand-new volunteers. People often fire off an e-mail or fill out a short expression of interest on a volunteer recruitment Web site, saying they want to volunteer virtually before they *really* think about the time and commitment online volunteering takes. Asking candidates to read a bit of information and to respond to even just a few questions quickly screens these people out—meaning they withdraw before they receive an assignment, rather than after the assignment has been given, when you are already counting on the volunteer to get the assignment done.

Consider the following experiences of three seasoned VRMs and how they used a simple screening procedure, a few intake questions, and an online application to slow down the process and provide better results.

Jayne shared this observation during the Virtual Volunteering Project in the late 1990s, regarding her work with online volunteers:

A mistake I made early on was giving assignments to people as soon as they expressed interest via email; the result was that most assignments did not get done, or I gave out the same assignment to more than one volunteer, assuming that at least one of them wouldn't complete the work. To remedy this, I now direct all potential volunteers to an online application. Completing this application is mandatory for being an online volunteer with this project. If a volunteer cannot complete this simple form, could they really commit the time and attention necessary for an online assignment?

The answers to this form are sent to my email address. Upon receipt and review of this form, I send an email that serves as an online orientation. It provides a very brief history of the Virtual Volunteering Project, details on what the volunteer is committing to by signing up to volunteer with the Project, how assignment progress is tracked, and reporting requirements. Only when the volunteer responds to this orientation is he or she given an assignment.

The online application and orientation have dramatically cut down on the number of people who email interest in volunteering but whom I never hear from again after I make the first assignment—I call them "virtual no-shows." When I first began, about 75% of the people who said they wanted to volunteer online with this Project were never heard from again after that first email. Now, more than 50% complete the assignments, and about half of those ask for a second assignment. This process has also put me in a much better position to match volunteers with appropriate assignments, and cut way down on the amount of time I spend tracking assignment progress.[1]

Christina Storm, founder and president of Lawyers Without Borders, echoed this experience with her organization's first online volunteers:

I was fortunate early on to get a volunteer who designed an intake form, expression of interest and volunteer registration protocol at another Internet site we maintained. We made our volunteers go through so many hoops that we knew those who completed the process were committed volunteers. Ours is an international organization and it relies upon committed volunteers around the world for its effectiveness . . . We have drawn interesting, committed volunteers who we would have never otherwise attracted to our organization and who have made substantial contributions to the organization. One of our largest and most focused projects came to us from an early online volunteer who ended up being employed in Liberia. The experience has

confirmed our commitment to being global in our perspective, recruitment and work.[2]

Laurie Moy is another experienced virtual volunteering manager, mostly through Pearls of Africa, a nonprofit she started that involves online volunteers to support people with disabilities in Africa. Laurie has seen firsthand the importance of a rigorous application process for online volunteers:

When we started out, we would give an assignment to anyone who was interested. But once we made our application process more rigorous, we saw several things happen: the quality of the work turned in improved, the turnover of volunteers went down, and we got to know our volunteers so much better. It made us respect the work that needed to be done, and it caused them to take pride and ownership in their assignments.[3]

The recommendations from Jayne, Christina, and Laurie are balanced between making the procedure as rapid and easy as possible for new volunteers to get started right away and screening out people who cannot make the very real time commitment needed for online volunteering. As we show in the rest of this chapter, implementing the process requires back and forth between the volunteer resources manager (VRM) or recruiter and the new volunteer, with certain steps to be completed by both parties. But note that these steps can be completed quickly. Depending on how you set up your protocols, these steps could even happen all on the same day the volunteer applies. It is possible for a new online volunteer to become engaged in an assignment within an hour of expressing interest, depending on the nature of the task, the screening required, and the staff's availability to interact with the new volunteer. However, because it is important not to skip any of the screening and orientation steps, it usually takes at least a few days for a new online volunteer to complete screening and get started on an assignment.

This way of working with online volunteers may affect your screening and matching of volunteers for *onsite* assignments as well; many people today who want to provide volunteering service onsite also want speedy access to volunteering and expect immediate responses to their expressions of interest.

Online Volunteer Application Form

We advocated strongly (in chapter 2) for having a designated area on your organization's Web site for volunteering, and we hope you were successful. Once you have created volunteer position descriptions (described in chapter 3), you should post them to your designated volunteer Web pages to allow prospective applicants to consider if you offer anything of interest to them. Next, whether for onsite or online volunteering, a volunteer application form should be available on your Web site. You should give *all* potential volunteers the option to fill out the form before they come onsite for an interview or go through an online orientation, saving everyone a great deal of time. The volunteer application form can be:

- A document that a potential volunteer downloads to his or her own device, completes electronically, and returns to the organization as an attachment via e-mail

- A document that a potential volunteer downloads to his or her own device, prints out, fills out offline, and either postal mails or faxes back to the organization or scans into his or her computer and sends back as an attachment via e-mail

- An online form that the volunteer candidate fills out online and then clicks *submit* or *send* to submit the information electronically to the organization (If you use this method, consider also sending a copy of the information to the candidate's own e-mail address automatically.)

If your organization does not have a volunteer application (and, therefore, does not currently involve onsite volunteers):

- Ask staff who have worked with volunteers at other organizations to provide volunteer application forms from those previous experiences (if possible) to adapt for your organization's use.

- Review "The Volunteer Application Form," an article by Susan J. Ellis and Katherine Noyes Campbell, available online on the Energize, Inc. Web site.[4]

- Type the words "volunteer application form" (without quotes) into your favorite online search engine, and a range of forms will be displayed.

Work with your IT staff or recruit someone knowledgeable from your existing volunteers to set up such an online application. Someone on your board of directors may work at a company with a large IT staff and may be willing to donate an employee's time to your organization to set up this online application with all the features you need.

You should also post any policies and procedures you feel are vital for any volunteer, but certainly for an online volunteer, to know and accept in advance.

You may use third-party Web sites, such as VolunteerMatch or the UN's Online Volunteering service, to recruit volunteers (we discuss this in detail in chapter 11). But please note that many organizations require volunteers who apply via these third-party services to also fill out the organization's official volunteer application and, depending on the nature of the assignment, to sign some sort of legal waiver or an acknowledgement that they have read their specific volunteer policies and procedures.

Legal Waivers

In addition to the application form, you may need candidates to sign a legal waiver or an agreement stating they have read and agree to the policies of the organization and the requirements of the assignment in which they have expressed interest. These forms need to be available online for volunteers to complete remotely, even if you want to require that they be handed over in person.

If original documents and real signatures are needed, ask the volunteer to print out the signature page, sign it, and send it to your organization via postal mail. (Be sure to provide the postal address of where such copies must be sent so that a volunteer does not have to go looking for it online.) Do *not* ask for original documents and real signatures unless you absolutely require them; an e-mail from the volunteer agreeing to the policies of the organization and the requirements of the assignment is often all that is needed—provided that you date and store such an e-mail exchange. Many people are also able to make a PDF out of a document and then sign it digitally. Consider whether you can accept that as an alternative to a paper signature.

If proof of identification is needed, ask the volunteer to scan his or her driver's license, ID card with photo, or passport photo page into his or her computer and send the file to you as an e-mail attachment or to make a photocopy that can then be faxed or sent to you via regular postal mail.

Some online volunteering roles may be attractive to people under 18; for these minors, most organizations require signed parental permission to volunteer. You may have to ascertain whether or not an online volunteer applicant is a minor, a topic we discuss fully later in this chapter.

Application Addenda for Virtual Volunteering

As we have pointed out, you should already be asking for Internet-related information, such as e-mail address, IM address/platform, etc., on your general application form for *any* volunteer. You might also want to ask all applicants about their computer and Internet skills, even if they are going to provide service onsite; this information can help you know what scope of tech skills and knowledge you have among all volunteers. On the next page is a sample addendum you can attach to the regular volunteer application form, designed specifically to help you pinpoint the knowledge base of a prospective online volunteer. Of course, you may have to keep adding more items as the Internet and mobile technologies change and grow.

In addition, for people applying to become online volunteers, you may want to ask more questions, such as:

- Where is the computer or device you will use for volunteering with our organization? Is it at home, at work, or at a public space? Is it with you at all times, because it is a smartphone, PDA, or tablet?

- How many hours a day do you have access to this computer or device?

- Do you know how to zip/unzip or stuff/unstuff a file?

- Are the files on your computer or mobile device password protected?

- Do you have anti-virus software on your computer or mobile device, and do you update it at least monthly?

- If you are using a laptop or PDA/smartphone for your service as an online volunteer, how often does this laptop or PDA/smartphone leave your home or workplace?

- How often do you back up your data on your computer, smartphone, or mobile device?

- Who else has access to the computer, smartphone, PDA, or tablet you will use for your service as an online volunteer?

You can include these questions as a separate form online or attach them to the regular application form. These questions set a tone with the volunteer, implying that you need his or her equipment to be reliable as a part of his or her service.

Getting to Know Applicants

For some online assignments, in addition to assessing the volunteer candidate's level of tech literacy, you will also want to screen the volunteer for certain qualities, even his or her attitude. You do not have to settle for getting to know a potential online volunteer purely by text communication. In fact, the applicant as well as the organization may welcome the opportunity for more verbal or visual contact.

Conduct an Interview

Don't forget the telephone! It remains an excellent way of conducting a remote interview. Even better, today you can use various online tools like Skype, iVisit, Google Talk, or Yahoo! Messenger—all free!—to hold a conversation and even to see each other via webcam. Having a verbal chat (as opposed to a text chat) may be a good compromise between an applicant coming to you physically and communicating solely via e-mail. Hearing someone's voice gives you an impression of how the person presents himself or herself in person and allows you to gauge level of energy and ability to express thoughts.

Sample Addendum for Online Volunteering Application

On a scale of 1–5, with 1 being a complete novice and 5 being an absolute expert, please rate your knowledge of and experience with these electronic and Internet tools:

___ Word processing

___ Spreadsheets

___ Databases

___ Digital artwork/graphics software

___ Sending, receiving, and managing e-mail

___ Online discussion groups (via e-mail or the Web)

___ Using the Internet for research/finding information

___ Building a web page

___ Building an entire web site

___ Producing/managing a blog

___ Live blogging

___ Micro-blogging (such as via Twitter)

___ Instant messaging

___ Chat rooms (text-based)

___ Internet voice or live video software, such as Skype, iVisit or Google Talk (for *either* live audio or video conferencing)

___ Podcasts (*listening to online audio from a variety of sources would rate a 3; producing and uploading a podcast would rate a 4 or 5*)

___ Sharing photos via a third-party site that has an online social networking component, such as Flickr

___ Online recorded video (*watching online videos from a variety of different sources would rate a 3; producing, converting, and uploading a video would rate a 4 or 5*)

___ Collaborative work spaces, such as via Google Docs/Google Drive, Basecamp, Minigroups, or Microsoft SharePoint

___ Online social networking tools such as Facebook

___ Online professional networking tools such as LinkedIn or Plaxo

___ Web conferencing (such as WebEx, ReadyTalk, or Adobe Connect) allowing everyone to see a slide show presentation at the same time

___ Second Life and other avatar-based platforms

However, keep in mind that some people express themselves far better in writing than they do on the phone or have accents or speech impediments that could affect your perception of their volunteering abilities. Others simply do not like to talk on the phone, preferring face-to-face communication, and this affects their ability to sound confident via voice-only communication.

In short, audio communication may provide you with a higher comfort level in working with people unseen, but be aware that there are a range of factors that can adversely affect how an otherwise terrific candidate for volunteering presents himself or herself verbally.

No matter how you conduct the interview, you might consider asking the applicant questions that:

- Propose hypothetical situations: "How would you handle a client that was angry with you for any reason?"

- Ask the volunteer to share a story about when he or she faced a particular situation: "Tell me about a positive customer service experience, whether you were providing the service or you were the customer."

- Uncover a candidate's hobbies (not just what they are, but how the volunteer originally got involved in them, why the volunteer stays involved, etc.) to give you an idea about the volunteer's attitudes and character.

The answers may give you a sense of the person's integrity, passion, attitudes, and commitment.

Check Credentials

At workshops regarding virtual volunteering, people will frequently ask us, "How do you know someone who wants to volunteer online is *really* who they say they are and can really do what they say they want to do as a volunteer?" We respond, "How do you know

Infinite Family

Infinite Family is a U.S.- and South Africa–based nonprofit organization that connects orphans and vulnerable children in South Africa with mentors in both countries, as well as other countries, using video and text-based messages via a secure Internet site. The South African teens have few, if any, adult role models and few people in their lives encouraging them to pursue education or careers. Dana Gold, program director at Infinite Family, talks about the kind of online volunteer her organization seeks:

Volunteering online at Infinite Family requires a certain kind of tech skills and it requires a certain kind of person. And for our type of online mentoring that's international, it means seeking an even smaller market of people, people who are very open-minded, who see themselves as citizens of the world, and who are willing to invest the time needed to make a relationship work, and understand that these kids live in very fluid situations, in situations very different from the mentor.

Infinite Family requires new candidates to complete a very brief online application and a brief phone interview to start. Candidates that pass this initial screening then undergo a criminal background check. If this is passed, candidates are then asked to view a series of online training videos. Gold estimates that half of the candidates drop out over the course of this process—and she considers this a good thing.

We make it so easy to go through the entire process. We don't even give you a time schedule to finish the online training. But people often realize they don't have time to watch the videos, and if they don't have time, then they wouldn't have time for our kids. These steps are not road blocks. They are weeders out. And we need to weed people out. Our kids are too precious for anything less!

someone who wants to volunteer at your organization, who walks through the door, is *really* who they say they are, and can really do what they say they want to do as a volunteer?" Laying eyes on someone in the same room as you does not confirm her or his credibility!

You can check an online applicant's credentials in a number of ways. If you need confirmation that a candidate can design a Web page, ask for samples of his or her work. If you need confirmation that a candidate who wants to translate a document into Spanish is actually fluent in the language, find a native speaker to interview that candidate in Spanish. If you need confirmation that a candidate really did work at such-and-such company listed on the application form, call such-and-such company to verify it. In short: do all the same things with new online volunteering candidates that you do with new onsite volunteering candidates and, for that matter, new employees.

If appropriate for the assignment under consideration, ask the applicant for references and *follow up on them.*

Legal Screening Requirements

If an online volunteer is going to have access to an organization's client, proprietary, or other confidential information, or if an online volunteer is going to have direct interaction with clients, you will most likely have a legal obligation to apply specific screening methods just as for anyone else who undertakes any of these tasks. That may include requiring an online volunteer to undergo a criminal background check, live in the same city as your organization, or come into your organization's facility for part of this process. You can explain these processes in advance to would-be online volunteers and stay firm in carrying them out.

Paying to Volunteer Online?

It is not uncommon for organizations to require volunteers to pay for the criminal background check that is performed on each new candidate or to purchase standard uniforms, with exceptions made for people with low or no incomes. There are also organizations that require, or strongly encourage, paid membership by online volunteers. Bpeace, highlighted in the last chapter, is one example, for which CEO Toni Maloney notes:

Dues contribute only about 5% to our operating budget, but having our volunteers pay membership dues helps demonstrate to grant makers and other larger donors that our members are serious and understand that there are costs associated with supporting volunteers. This includes the percentage of staff time it takes to communicate and support several dozen volunteers working at any given moment. Dues help defray costs [so that] money from grants can go to many other areas of direct support to entrepreneurs in Afghanistan and Rwanda. Our volunteers are investors, in every sense of the word, and we treat them as such![5]

Using the Web to Learn More about a Candidate

Privacy, while a legal right, has been turned on its head in this day and age of public information online. It has become commonplace for employers to "check out" possible new hires by seeing what is available about them online and we often do this personally to vet contractors and blind dates. So one of the tools at your disposal for learning more about virtual volunteering applicants is to type the candidate's name into your favorite search engine and look for the candidate's name on online social networking sites such as Facebook to see what you can learn from existing public postings made by or about the applicant. However, be sure you put a note in the position description or on the volunteer application form, from the start, that you will do this kind of screening, so a person will know *before* he or she applies.

But if you are going to explore what's posted on social media, understand the social rules. Do *not* exclude a person you have screened online because he or she:

- Is politically active . . . *unless* the activity is clearly in conflict with the mission of your organization, such as a potential volunteer campaigning against gun control on his or her blog while, at the same time, applying to your anti-handgun organization to be its online marketing person.

- Posts opinions online . . . *unless* these are irrational and/or personal attacks ("I hate the mayor; she's fat and stupid"), are slanderous to a person or organization ("the local zoo is slaughtering monkeys and selling the meat to the local butcher"—which you know is actually not true), or are in conflict with your organization's work, as above.

- Posts personal photos to public spaces . . . *unless* you feel these would be inappropriate for viewing by your clients (such as a potential volunteer who would lead your online marketing campaign against teen drinking posting photos of herself passed out from too much alcohol).

You are not looking for perfect angels or for people with whom you are in complete agreement in terms of politics or values. Rather, you are looking for *clearly outrageous* material that is obviously in conflict with the role the volunteer will fill with your organization. If you do find material that you believe could be used by the public or the press to put your organization in a bad light, talk with the volunteering candidate first about what you saw online. Make sure it really *is* the candidate (many people have the same names!), and hear the candidate's point of view before making a decision. Again, this level of screening is only for volunteering assignments that warrant such special attention.

Much more on ensuring safety in virtual volunteering programs can be found in chapter 8. For more about the basics of screening in volunteer management, see our list of recommended volunteer management resources in appendix B.

Negotiating the Role

Use the written volunteer position description during the interview with a prospective online volunteer. It will guide you in expressing expectations in a clear and consistent way. Most important, it will allow the candidate to ask questions, commit to doing the work, or decide that the role is not right for him or her.

Once a volunteering candidate reviews the assignment descriptions, she or he may say: "I can do everything but such-and-such part of this assignment." If this is feasible given what you really need to have done, work with the candidate to accommodate this preference. Perhaps the assignment can be broken up, with different volunteers taking on different tasks but still completing all the work. On the other hand, do not compromise without good reason. Remain committed to what you most need the volunteer to do, even if that means this particular applicant will not be able to fill the role and you need to keep looking.

Setting the Initial Time Commitment

Be honest about the amount of time it will take to complete a short-term project or what can be accomplished in an ongoing assignment during a specified time period. You and the volunteer can mutually identify a point at which the online volunteer can choose to end his or her role or can renew for another agreed-to period of time. The initial commitment for an ongoing high-responsibility role could be three months or six months after the start of the assignment, but do not make it any longer than a year because you want to be able to do periodic assessments. You (and the volunteer) may *hope* for a mutually-beneficial relationship lasting for years, but there is no way to guarantee that. Better to commit in manageable increments of time and allow you both to get acquainted and to evolve your loyalty.

As the end-of-commitment date approaches, both the manager and the volunteer can assess what the volunteer has completed, re-evaluate the volunteer's expectations and availability, and decide how best to proceed. If both agree for the volunteer to continue, then mutually determine a new period of commitment; again, we recommend not more than six months. This allows you to have another positive conversation with the volunteer then and keep motivation high. Conversely, it gives volunteers a point at which they can resign with plenty of notice for you to recruit a new person before they leave.

It's a Two-Way Street!

Notice that the organization is making a commitment of its own when offering a virtual volunteering assignment. You are committing to provide online volunteers with all of the information and support they need to undertake this assignment, to be available to them for support, to read and respond to their progress reports, and to acknowledge their contributions.

Do not *assume* that a particular volunteer will stay in a role for many years. While it may indeed happen that an online volunteer remains with your organization for a long time, requiring that the volunteer *renew* his or her commitment regularly will reduce the likelihood that the volunteer will leave suddenly, with no one to fill the role. This method also shows the volunteer that you do not take him or her for granted. It could also result in a volunteer taking a break rather than quitting altogether.

Candidates Self-Screening Out—and In

Your goal in any volunteer recruitment is to be welcoming and appealing to the right candidates, while helping others to determine for themselves not to apply in the first place or not to move forward into an assignment. In other words, you want to provide enough information to help people *screen themselves out* of volunteering with your organization, which stops them from wasting their time as well as cutting down the amount of time the organization spends with candidates who turn out not to be appropriate for an assignment.

Most of the tools we explain in this book allow someone to increase their enthusiasm for the virtual volunteering role or to move on:

- A detailed task description that lays out expectations clearly.

- An online application process that requires the volunteer to be detailed about his or her qualifications and availability for a specific assignment, and the completion of a self-evaluation regarding online volunteering readiness.

- An online orientation (see next chapter) that clearly communicates policies and procedures, links to important online material a new volunteer must read before getting started, and provides a way for volunteers to state that they have read such and agree to follow the policies. (Some organizations require that an applicant complete the orientation before making a final determination on both sides that the placement should happen; others first accept the volunteer and then offer the orientation as the initial step into the assignment.)

- An overall system that blends these steps in such a way that the recruiter knows quickly whether or not a candidate communicates well online, in a timely manner.

The good news is that much of this process can be automated so that the recruiter does not start working with a potential volunteer directly until the candidate has completed certain steps. For instance, consider this possible sequence of actions for moving an interested person into virtual volunteering at your organization:

- A candidate sees interesting information about the volunteer position on your organization's Web site and contacts you as instructed, perhaps by completing the online application form you have made available.

  - Alternatively, a candidate finds a notice of a volunteer assignment for your organization at a volunteer recruitment Web site such as VolunteerMatch and fills out an expression of interest at that site. You, the recruiter, receive an e-mail with the expression of interest and whatever information the candidate has filled out on that Web site's short form.

- You respond promptly (the quicker the better!) by thanking the candidate for expressing interest and sending a more detailed version of the virtual volunteering position description. You ask the volunteer for written confirmation within a set period (perhaps 48 hours or two business days) that he or she has read the expectations in full and that this is, indeed, an assignment the applicant is interested in. Note that it is a lot easier for a candidate to *say* he or she responds quickly to e-mail than to demonstrate it. The step of asking for a prompt reply helps you screen out people who are not committed to timely communications.

- Once you receive the confirmation from the candidate, you (and the person who will work directly with this volunteer, if it is not you) decide if this is enough information to accept the volunteer and start the online orientation, or if the volunteer should move on through other screening steps such as filling out your organization's official volunteer application form, having a personal interview, and/or completing any other screening requirement such as a background check. The person who will work directly with this volunteer (who created the assignment in the first place) decides when and if the volunteer should be accepted for the assignment. Then the candidate goes through the online orientation.

- After the volunteer orientation, the person who will work with this volunteer begins immediate communications, providing all support materials that are needed for the assignment and giving the volunteer the chance to ask questions, whether by e-mail or telephone. Then volunteer service commences.

Because the virtual environment is one of immediacy, it is important to move the interviewing and screening process forward as quickly as possible. We are not suggesting speed over quality; do what is necessary to ensure you select the best volunteers. Just recognize that the longer the time between screening steps for volunteering candidates, the more likely you are to lose the candidate.

All of this above sounds like a lot of activity that would take a lot of time, but for the byte-sized tasks we recommend as introductory assignments, it really can all happen in the span of *one* work day, even just an hour or two, at least assuming an online application that the volunteer submits electronically. Of course, for high-responsibility roles or direct client service activities, more screening will be needed and therefore more time. If you must conduct background checks, for example, you cannot control how long it will take to get a report back. When there is a delay, keep in communication with the candidate to maintain enthusiasm.

Sometimes candidates will ask to take longer to go through the online orientation or to read through the full assignment description and all associated materials. They may ask for more time because of

their work style or because of a disability that requires them to spend more time going through materials at a slower pace. They may not give you a reason for the request. If this request for a slower pace can be accommodated, by all means agree. If it cannot, explain why to the candidate. Refrain from asking why this extra time is needed unless you feel that further explanation is warranted. What is important is to see if the person meets the deadline he or she requested for returning the necessary response.

Once again, each step of the process offers a chance for a candidate to withdraw from an assignment before ever getting started, and you can *expect at least half to do so* (compare this with your statistics for people who express interest in onsite opportunities with your organization and you will find it is quite similar). These are also chances for you to see if the candidate communicates well via the written word.

Special Screening Situations

The application and screening process we have been discussing here will work with a wide variety of prospective volunteers, but there are always special situations. Again, these occur all the time with onsite volunteers and, if you have developed systems for accommodating special cases already, you can simply adapt them to online service.

Four types of applicants deserve consideration here: court-ordered and other mandated service, students fulfilling academic requirements, young people under age 18, and expert volunteers.

Court-Ordered and Other Mandated Service

These days, organizations can find talent from many sources in the community, including a number of forms of *mandated* service, in which the volunteer is giving time to fulfill a requirement imposed by a third party. One large category is court-ordered service, in which a person is ordered to do "community service," either as an alternative sentence to jail or a fine or as part of probation or parole. There are welfare-to-work programs, public housing lease agreements, and even corporate disability leave policies that all provide an option to do community service as an alternative to some other requirement, such as finding a paying job. A growing number of school districts require students to do a certain number of hours of community service in order to graduate (which is only one variation of how students may come to you, so we will deal with them in the following section).

While there is ongoing debate about labeling such service as *volunteering*, there are good reasons to include mandated service in any discussion of working with volunteers. That's because they are not paid by the organizations they serve, have many characteristics of other volunteers (such as helping part-time, needing to be oriented to the work of the organization, deserving appreciation for what they accomplish, etc.), often take on exactly the same tasks as other volunteers, and have many talents to offer. The best mandated service programs allow the person to choose where to complete the required hours, so you can expect the applicant to have some basic interest in your work. It is entirely possible that someone who has a satisfying mandated service experience will remain with you by choice as a volunteer for much longer than the original time required.

Many people seeking placement for mandated service will telephone to see if you will consider their application, or you may first be contacted by an official of the referring agency. Others may apply on their own through the normal procedure for any volunteer but will need to tell you about their requirement at some point. That's because all mandated community service hours must be *documented* and attested to by you to show an official of the mandating court or agency that the person has fulfilled his or her service requirement. Get the details of this reporting process *before* the service begins. The documentation is generally determined by the sending authority, such as a judge. Your organization may be requested to send a letter through the postal mail stating the number of hours the volunteer completed and in what time frame. It may be an official sign-in sheet that someone at your organization must initial every time the volunteer provides service.

It is also advisable to request the applicant to get permission immediately from his or her official liaison, in writing, to perform community service *online*. Unfortunately, many mandatory service programs do not yet recognize online service as *real* volunteering, often because they have never heard of it. It would be a shame if the person provided

several virtual volunteering hours only to have them refused by the institution mandating the service. Offer to write a letter to the liaison on the person's behalf, as appropriate, to validate your organization and describe the kinds of things online volunteers do. Explain how the volunteer's work will be reviewed and how you determine and verify hours contributed.

For court-ordered service, you have the right to know what offense was committed before accepting the candidate, although whether it is appropriate for you to *screen* on the nature of the person's offense will depend largely on the type of online tasks you are going to have this person perform—which is exactly the same consideration for assigning someone to an onsite role. It may be that online service is best for someone committing a crime causing bodily harm, for example, because it does not put the person into direct contact with others. But if the offense is connected in some way to your work, you might be more cautious; a domestic violence shelter, for example, would want to make sure the applicant's offense does not relate to any type of actual or threatened violence.

What if someone is sentenced to community service for hacking into a secured government computer system? You might legitimately be concerned that he or she will do the same to your system or not want to offer temptation. On the other hand, you may think: "This person really knows computers, so I'm going to involve them in a particularly challenging online task for which we do not have the expertise!" Being careful, of course, not to provide access to client or other confidential data.

There *is* an opportunity for fraud in mandatory service performed over the Internet—namely, how do you know if the person who has been mandated to perform service is actually performing the service, and not that person's parent, sibling, roommate, friend, etc.?[6] If the court or other agency requires verification to ensure the person completing the online service really is the person who is supposed to be, it is the *volunteer's* responsibility, not the organization's, to provide it. You can, however, make some suggestions. For example, the person might provide his or her service via a public library computer and ask a library staff person to check the volunteer's identification and sign the person's time sheet to verify time spent online. Then the volunteer's staff contact can further sign to validate that the assigned service was performed.

Students Fulfilling an Academic Requirement

Many schools—at every level from primary grades through graduate school—are mandating that students fulfill a minimum number of hours of community service in order to graduate or to get course credit. Some universities are also requiring that admission applications include community service experience. If the service students seek relates to coursework, it is often called *service-learning* or *curriculum-based service*, because it is meant to allow students to apply what they learned in the classroom to the real world outside. If the experience is meant to last over several weeks or months, it may be labeled an *internship*.

You may want to add something to the volunteer application form inquiring whether the assignment is being sought to fulfill an academic requirement. This will alert you to asking for more information, such as the learning objectives the student hopes to meet. It might also affect the amount of time the student has available to volunteer with you and therefore direct you to the type of activity you should assign. However, do not assume that every student will disappear at the end of the semester. Discuss whether the student wants to accept an assignment *until it is completed*, even if that happens after the semester is over. Just because a class has ended does not mean your organization's needs have, too. Some students will be happy to know their work is valued and not just something made up as homework.

Also discuss whether you will have to provide some kind of verification to the school or instructor as to the hours students contributed and what they did as volunteers in your organization. Again, do this *before* the service begins and determine what kind of documentation they will need. If necessary, request they get permission immediately from the teacher or school administrator, in writing, that their requirement can be met through online service. For internships, ask if you will need to meet with faculty or to produce an end-of-service evaluation or report about the student's performance.

Applicants under Age 18

Many teens enjoy online volunteering because they are judged by the quality of their work rather than assumed limits of their age or their youthful appearance. There are some highly qualified teens out there who can perform online tasks very well (we have worked with many) and you may be cheating your organization out of a lot of great talent and resources if you arbitrarily refuse applicants younger than 18.

Look at online discussion groups and bulletin boards for teens, and you will see an endless number of messages from young people who want to volunteer, for a range of reasons.[7] Some have the same motivations as any other volunteer: to extend their onsite volunteering, to make a difference, to have something to show on a résumé, etc. Some teens want to volunteer online because they do not have a way to get to onsite volunteering opportunities that are farther than walking distance for them or because the organization that they wanted to help does not allow volunteers under 18 years of age onsite.

You may wonder whether child labor laws restrict volunteering by minors, or at least for those under the age of 14, which is the most common milestone at which a young person can work part-time for pay. The answer is that legislation speaks only about the *employment* of minors and does not limit unpaid service—though, of course, you should always check the law in your jurisdiction. On the other hand, it is simply smart to avoid assigning young volunteers to anything you would be prohibited from paying them to do, such as working with heavy equipment. In this respect, *online* volunteering poses no problems![8]

Teens are likely to be completely comfortable online and have technology-based experience that organizations can apply to many of the possible virtual volunteering assignments already discussed. They can also serve as a focus group for other teens, such as giving you advice about a brochure or Web area your organization wants to use to target teens.

Generally, it is inappropriate to ask volunteer applicants their birth date or age, unless you need to do so for legal reasons. However, it is entirely appropriate to ask, "Are you under (or over) the age of 18?" If you ask this question on your application form, be sure to note that applicants under 18 are welcomed to volunteer and will *not* be prevented from participating because of their age.

For an applicant who indicates s/he is under 18, send a parental consent form for the parent or guardian to sign to give permission for the teen to volunteer, and have information on this form for the parent or guardian to know how to access online information about your organization and how it involves volunteers, including policies and procedures and the contact information for the VRM. For a three-hour task, this may not be worth the effort, but for a 20-hour task over two months, it is probably useful to have documentation on file that the parents know what is going on.

To find samples of permission slips, go to your favorite online search engine and type in: *parental permission slip.*

Expert Volunteers

Expert volunteers may be recruited for highly-specialized projects or tasks, or they may offer their pro bono services, unasked, to an organization.

It may not always be appropriate to say yes to donated services. The services offered may not be what you want or really need. There may be large costs to your agency to maintain or support whatever the expert volunteer wants to create for your organization. Or, what the volunteer is proposing may not fit with your organization's mission. When an online volunteer—or even a group of online volunteers (such as a department within a corporation)—approaches you about donating a service, do some internal evaluation about what is being proposed. Consider what you think your own staff and resource commitment will need to be to make the offered pro bono service truly worthwhile.

A volunteer resources manager on CyberVPM cautioned:

It's a common problem that well-intentioned, but frankly ignorantly conceived assistance actually makes the lives of the [nonprofit] staff more difficult and hinders our ability to do work that corresponds with our mission. [Often] we're so darn busy being grateful for something that isn't inherently helpful. The reward is more in the doing, so finding something that's inherently a benefit means working with the agency in question and carefully designing and planning a response that is consistent with the needs.[9]

Setting the Tone Early

The steps we have outlined in this chapter not only screen out people who do not understand the very real commitment of virtual volunteering; they are also the building blocks for retaining online volunteers over a long period—months, even years, instead of just a few weeks.

You want new online volunteers to get a sense quickly of the seriousness with which your organization views virtual volunteering assignments, as well as a sense of how much the organization values volunteers in general. Along with feeling welcomed by the organization and confident in beginning the work, online volunteers will know there is nothing virtual about the deadlines and outcomes of their assignments and the seriousness of their service.

Notes

1. The full archive of the original Virtual Volunteering Project is still available at http://www.coyotecommunications.com/vv/vvvols/screen.shtml.
2. Excerpted from e-mail exchanges between Christina Storm and Jayne Cravens from 2007 to 2009.
3. Excerpted from e-mail exchanges between Laurie Moy and Jayne Cravens from 2007 to 2009.
4. Susan J. Ellis and Katherine Noyes Campbell, *Proof Positive: Developing Significant Volunteer Recordkeeping Systems*, 21st century edition (Philadelphia: Energize, Inc., 2003). Excerpt available at http://www.energizeinc.com/art/apro.html.
5. Excerpted from e-mail exchanges between Toni Maloney and Jayne Cravens from 2007 to 2009.
6. Note that we say there is an *opportunity* for fraud; in the more than 20 years the authors have been researching and promoting virtual volunteering, they have never heard of this happening.
7. The Community Service board on Yahoo! Answers is not focused specifically on teen use, but, indeed, they make up the largest number of users, and the most frequently-asked question on the board is a version of "where can I volunteer?"—including, "where can I volunteer *online?*"
8. For more on the legal aspects of volunteering by minors, see Susan J. Ellis, Anne Weisbord, and Katherine H. Noyes, *Children as Volunteers: Preparing for Community Service* (Philadelphia: Energize, Inc., 2003).
9. Author unknown, circa 2009. <http://groups.yahoo.com/group/cybervpm>.

Volunteer computer programmers and Web developers
collaborated intensively at
the 2013 "Hackathon dla
e-wolontariatu," in Warsaw,
Poland.

Chapter 5
Orienting and Training Online Volunteers

By this point you have laid the essential groundwork for success with online volunteers. You have:

- Adapted existing policies and procedures for onsite volunteers to apply equally to virtual assignments.

- Designed a range of volunteer assignments that can be completed online.

- Developed an area of your organization's Web site that provides full information about volunteers, including position descriptions for any open volunteer role onsite or online and a posting of all important policies and procedures a volunteer should understand in advance.

- Provided a way for interested people to apply online or through forms they can download from the Web site.

With individual applicants, you have:

- Received whatever documents you requested to conduct appropriate screening and possible background checks, including acknowledgement that the applicant has read and agreed to the policies.

- Proceeded far enough into the process that both you and the applicant know you want to continue moving toward accepting the person as an online volunteer.

If you are unsure of any of these elements, we encourage you to read the previous chapters that introduce them all. Otherwise, we assume you are ready for the next step: preparing the new volunteer to make a final commitment and to begin the volunteer work.

New Volunteer Orientation

No matter how skilled they may be in the work they have agreed to do, all new volunteers need an orientation to your organization (or, as our British colleagues call it, *induction*). This includes an explanation of the organization's mission, goals, service focus, and value to the community—and the rules for all volunteers. New volunteers thereby learn to understand the organization and put their contributions into the context of the larger organization. This can include basic information, such as the history of the organization, a description of the clients served and the services provided, funding sources, and more. It should also include key "need-to-know" facts such as policies on confidentiality, risk management and safety procedures, chain of command for decision making, and so on.

You need to find a balance between overwhelming new volunteers with too many details and keeping them in the dark. Of course, you have the ability online to highlight key information on the Web site and then provide links to lengthier details that someone can choose to explore or not.

Beyond facts, an orientation sets the tone for the working relationship you want to establish with volunteers. It is possible to be welcoming, even humorous, and still convey serious intent.

For online volunteers who will do most or all of their service remotely, the orientation emphasizes that your organization and its work are real and that online service is a valued part of achieving your organization's mission. It is an opportunity to express your expectations and also to extend a warm welcome. This helps motivate volunteers to complete the activity they have undertaken and starts them on the road toward becoming longer-term supporters and even financial donors.

At an onsite volunteer orientation, volunteers are often asked to sign a statement saying they have read and agree to the policies of the organization and the requirements of the assignments they wish to pursue. The orientation leader may say, "Let's take a few minutes for you all to read these materials before you sign the document saying you have read and agree to them," and then observe to make sure new volunteers are, indeed, reading the materials. Note that this cannot happen online; sending materials via e-mail or putting them up on a Web site is no guarantee that a volunteer has reviewed them. If this is a concern, develop a short quiz, a specific follow-up e-mail, or an interactive session for the new online volunteer with questions or conversation points that will let you know whether or not the volunteer has reviewed all necessary material.

Real-world single days of service such as a riverside cleanup become more successful by explaining to volunteers why they are picking up trash, why the organization has undertaken this activity, and how to stay safe during the event. Similarly, even if a new online volunteer will do a very brief assignment—such as proofreading a two-page document or testing a new online tool—that volunteer should receive some sort of formal welcome and orientation taking only a few minutes, not hours. It could be just a short narrative and a few questions that confirm the candidate understands what he or she is going to do and why. But this simple orientation and screening process will ensure micro-volunteering tasks are completed and you do not spend valuable time re-assigning these tasks again and again, hoping someone *eventually* completes them.

Moving from Onsite to Online Presentation

Whatever you currently make available onsite at new volunteer orientations needs to be available online, either publicly on your organization's Web site or via your private online forum for volunteers (see chapter 2). That means posting policies and procedures, staff lists, tip sheets, work sheets, all forms, and handbooks. Current onsite volunteers as well as new online volunteers will appreciate this because everyone may need to reference these materials in the course of their service. You may find that placing your orientation materials online

The EPA's Volunteer Monitoring Program

A good example of making traditional volunteering materials available online for those volunteering virtually is the Web site for the Volunteer Monitoring Program of the U.S. government's Environmental Protection Agency (EPA).[1] This is an umbrella site for the many locally-based programs that mobilize and train volunteers in pollution prevention and monitoring. These volunteers monitor various environments and report on water quality, build awareness of pollution problems, help clean up problem sites, and provide data that is used by decision makers at all levels of government. EPA-produced support materials for these remote volunteers are all available electronically.

cuts down on the amount of time all new volunteers need to spend with you in person for the orientation process; you may decide to give onsite volunteers the option to do some of their orientation activities online, too.

Online Video Orientation

Do you have a video that new volunteers watch at the onsite orientation for your organization? Get it converted to an online format and put it online! An online volunteer can even help with this conversion. If it is appropriate for this video to be public, you can upload it for free to online sites like YouTube or Vimeo and give new online volunteers the Web address. Your traditional, onsite volunteers may appreciate this as well; some will probably want to re-watch the video.

Developing orientation materials for online volunteers may give you the incentive to create a brand new video (or video series) for all volunteers, or you can produce something specifically for online volunteers (Infinite Family's online volunteer video is described in chapter 4). This video can be quite simple and made with resources you probably already have; almost all new laptops and tablets, regardless of operating system, come with a built in webcam and software to record videos. If you are just entering the world of online video, visit "Creating a Video Lecture" on Wikiversity[2] for the step-by-step basics of creating a video and posting it online. You might also visit OnlineVideo.net for more in-depth tutorials about producing videos for the Web.

Here are three examples of online videos for new volunteers. They were created for volunteers working onsite but will help you think about how you might approach online video orientations especially for virtual volunteering. More examples are listed on the Virtual Volunteering Wiki.

- Volunteer Orientation for World Relief Durham, http://vimeo.com/67855979

- Safe Sanctuaries Training (for reducing the risk of child abuse in churches) by Missouri United Methodists,[3] http://vimeo.com/35632870

- Parent Volunteer Orientation 2012–2013 by the Clinton Township (New Jersey) School District, http://vimeo.com/51937171

Once again, remember that online video is not accessible for people who do not have very fast Internet connections or relatively new hardware and software, or for people with some disabilities, such as hearing impairments. Online video should not contain any information that is not replicated in written materials and available to volunteers. If at all possible, create closed-captioning for any online video your organization produces; this not only helps people with hearing impairments but also helps people who may not be fluent in English. This is yet another task with which online volunteers could help!

The Case for Putting All *Your Volunteering Information Online*

We are often taken aback at the reluctance of VRMs or other staff to put most of their volunteering information online for anyone to see, including: volunteer policies and procedures; a list of tasks volunteers undertake; requirements for new volunteers; details about reporting requirements for volunteers, etc.

Some VRMs say they fear such information will scare potential volunteers away. On the other hand,

perhaps it is best to scare some potential volunteers away before they get to your interview or orientation and discover that the requirements are more than they can handle or that volunteering at your organization is just not a good match for them.

But in reality, not every potential volunteer candidate is going to read all of the information right away—they will only read just enough to convince themselves that volunteering with your organization is right for them or not. Putting pertinent information online not only demonstrates transparency; it also shows just how seriously your organization views volunteer service.

Real-Life Examples of Effective Orientation

The Aid Workers Network (AWN) is a British-based registered charity and an entirely virtual organization; it has no physical office space. AWN provides an online forum for professionals working in aid, relief and development work in Third World and transitional countries, and links to several dozen blogs by such workers. All of AWN staff are volunteers and everyone works remotely. On pages 58–60 we present excerpts, used with permission, from AWN's online volunteering orientation. All new volunteers must read the orientation documents and acknowledge having done so via e-mail. Note how the point of contact at AWN could determine whether or not a new volunteer has read the orientation (and you will not know unless you also read the entire message!).

Another example of an online orientation comes from Sidelines, a nonprofit organization that provides international support for women and families experiencing complicated pregnancies and premature births. The organization matches women experiencing a high-risk pregnancy with volunteers who have personally experienced the same condition. Online volunteers were added to the support services in the late 1990s. On pages 61–62 , we present excerpts from Sidelines' online orientation for its "Email Volunteers."

But Sidelines does not stop there. After orienting new online volunteers, they provide online training, too. In an e-mail interview, Nancy Veeneman, Sidelines' online director, noted:

Sample Online Orientation from Aid Workers Network

On behalf of the volunteers who make up the leadership of AWN, thank you for your application to volunteer online with the Aid Workers Network. AWN has no paid staff; everyone who helps to maintain AWN does so as a volunteer.

The next step is for you to go through the AWN volunteer orientation process via email (which you are doing now, as you read).

You need to read this email *carefully.* This orientation communicates to you the expectations of online volunteers. There are several directions to be followed in this email, and one of the ways that I know that you have read the email is if you take the actions asked for in this email.

If you do not have time to read this document, then you *probably* do not have time to volunteer with AWN.

I promise that all emails from me are NOT this long.

*******Please save this email for future reference.********

Your Commitments in Volunteering with AWN

1. You should already be registered on the AWN site (http://www.aidworkers.net). If you have not registered, please do so now.

    You may NOT volunteer with AWN unless you are registered on our Web site.

2. You must also have **regular** access to:
    - a computer
    - your own email account
    - the Internet, both via email and the Web
        If you will not have access to these resources during the next two months, please let me know in your response to this email.

3. While volunteering with the AWN:
    - You are responsible for your own equipment and its maintenance.
    - Equipment to be used by you during this assignment should be fully operational.
    - AWN cannot reimburse you for any expenses associated with this assignment without prior written approval from AWN. (We do not anticipate any costs being associated with assignments, but if you come across such a possible cost, please let us know and wait for approval before you make ANY purchase.)
    - You are expected to complete any assignments by the deadline date. There is nothing "virtual" about assignment deadlines. Your work is often going to be used in conjunction with something that someone else is working on, and if your part isn't done on time, it can hold up other activities. If you cannot complete the assignment, you are expected to notify the volunteer at AWN with whom you have been working at your earliest possible convenience.

■ While actively engaged in an assignment, you are expected to answer all emails from your main AWN contact person within 72 hours (three business days) of receipt (weekends and holidays excluded).

■ Please correspond with AWN at all times via only the email address you used to apply to volunteer originally. If you need to change this address, please let us know. But we ask you to use only ONE email address in your correspondence with us.

■ Please always use your full name in your emails to AWN; the volunteer resources manager cannot always tell who you are based only on your email address or your first name.

■ Computer virus protection for your own computer is YOUR responsibility. You should have anti-virus software on your computer, and understand how this software operates. Most AWN community members make efforts to ensure their files are virus-free, but please be aware that some may not.

■ Material produced by volunteers for the AWN, including graphics materials, Web page designs, narratives, research, compilations, instructional texts, etc., becomes the property of the Aid Workers Network upon submission.

■ Volunteers should receive written positions before representing the organization online, such as when sending an email to others or posting a message to an online bulletin board. Unless you have written permission to do so, do not speak as a representative of AWN, online or onsite with others.

■ AWN rarely works with confidential information. However, we ask that you not distribute emails or documents relating to AWN to others, unless you have received permission from AWN. You are welcomed to share URLs of resources on the AWN Web site with anyone, however.

■ Please keep passwords that give you access to any part of the AWN Web site confidential. If you think your password has been compromised, change it immediately and contact the AWN webmaster.

■ If you receive an inquiry from the press regarding AWN, please forward the inquiry to your primary AWN contact immediately; please do not speak on behalf of AWN to the press unless you have been given permission to do so.

■ You should back up the files of your computer AT LEAST once a month. For added safety, when you are working on an AWN assignment, copy your work to an external drive or CD and store this backup in a safe place. Please save completed tasks on your computer or a disk for at least 60 days after you submit the assignment to AWN.

■ Your name will NOT be sold, traded or given to any other organization because of your status as an online volunteer with AWN.

■ You are expected to keep track of how many hours you contribute to AWN as a volunteer. Estimates are fine.

■ You may be asked to complete a survey about your volunteering experience with AWN.

■ Violation of policies by a volunteer may result in the dismissal of that volunteer.

Reporting In

This is how I know if you've read this orientation: whether or not you follow the reporting instructions that are listed here and will be listed again in the details of your first assignment:

For assignments that last longer than two weeks, please report in via email to Jayne Cravens (jc@coyotecommunications.com) on the 1st and the 15th of **every** month (only while you are actually working on an assignment). In this email, please note:

- Your full name (I cannot always tell who you are based on your email address)
- What assignment you are working on
- How many hours you've worked on this assignment (even if it is none)
- What percentage of the assignment is left to do (are you half done? 75% done? have you even started?) and how "on track" you feel (do you think you will meet the deadline date?)
- Any problems/obstacles you've encountered in completing this assignment, or any comments or opinions in general you would like to make about the assignment (love it, hate it, learning a lot, what you are learning, etc.).

When you complete an assignment, you should also email Jayne to say:

- What assignment you finished
- How many hours you worked on this assignment
- What tools or resources you found most helpful in completing this assignment
- Any problems/obstacles you encountered in completing this assignment, or any comments in general you would like to make about the assignment (loved it, hated it, learned a lot, etc.).

Ending Your Volunteer Role

You can cease volunteering with AWN upon the completion of any volunteer assignment, or when you are not currently engaged in an assignment. We ask that you please complete any assignment for which you have signed up; we really are counting on you. But, if after completing an assignment, you need to withdraw, we will understand. Please notify AWN by email if you are going to stop or take a break in volunteering, and say why you are stopping (so we can make adjustments in our program, as needed). We encourage you to keep participating in the AWN forum regardless of your volunteering status with AWN.

One final thing: if you have the technology to do so, please view the Aid Workers Network welcome video, which is about five minutes long and reinforces several of the points in this written orientation: http://www.youtube.com/watch?v=3ONOteVSgug

And that completes your orientation! Whew!

Please reply to this email with 72 hours (three business days, excluding weekends or holidays), noting that you have read through it, that you are registered on AWN (if I do not know you, please note that I will check to make sure this is so) and that you feel that you are ready to begin . . . or please let me know of any questions/concerns you may have. If you were able to watch the video, please note that in your reply as well. And once I've heard from you, I will send you more details about the assignment for which you signed up.

Sample Online Volunteer Orientation from Sidelines

What Is An Email Volunteer?

A Sidelines email volunteer supports women and their families online by communicating via email, online chats, and instant messages. Email volunteers are trained by the same process as phone volunteers.

Volunteering from a home or work computer is different than working onsite with an organization for many obvious reasons: there's usually more flexibility in the use of your time, a greater degree of independence. For some, these differences make virtual volunteering ideal; these same reasons can make it difficult for others.

Setting you own schedule is one of the chief joys of virtual volunteering. However, there's nothing virtual about the commitment you are making.

You can be both an email and a local phone volunteer. That is up to you. Sidelines has a policy of no more than 2 moms per volunteer whether that be email, phone, or a combination of both. Please review our Volunteering Locally for Sidelines page.

I Want To Be An Email Volunteer. Am I Ready?

Before you volunteer to help Sidelines via the Internet, consider the following to determine if you are ready:

- Do you have regular, ongoing access to the Internet?
  If access is only from work on certain days, let us know. We can work around your schedule if needed. If your access is only 1 or 2 days per week, we may have to wait until you have more access to you email. Let us know! Ideally, you would have email access daily.
- Do you know how to communicate well via the written word?
  You don't have to be an English major! :-) But you do need to know how to convey empathy and feelings to high-risk moms.
- Are you comfortable working on your own, without direct supervision?
  The Group Coordinator is always available for consultation—for problems or questions that may arise.
- Are you self-motivated?
- Do you have a set time each day when you can send email to your patient referral? (That can be any time day or night.)
- Do you answer your emails quickly (no more than 48 hours after receipt)?
  This is VERY important. We rely on volunteers to check their mail to take patient referrals, and the patient referrals rely on you to respond to their emails.

If you answered "No" to any of the above questions, or had difficulty answering some of the questions, perhaps you are not ready for volunteering virtually. Still, you never know until you try!

Many times new or prospective volunteers ask: "What if I become too busy to be a volunteer?" We know that moms are busy people! So each time we have a patient referral for you, we'll ask you if it's okay for you to support her at that time. If you continually turn down patient referrals, we will probably take you off our active list until you are ready to volunteer again.

We encourage volunteers to let us know if they will not be available to support patient referrals due to vacation, family situations, etc.

If you are currently pregnant: We *can train you* while you are pregnant. But, once you are trained you cannot support someone until AFTER you deliver. Sidelines has a strict policy about not matching pregnant moms with each other.[4]

Our training is done online through a guided system of materials broken down into sections that are easier for the potential volunteer to study. This also allows the user to do the training at their own pace which is very important when one considers that the potential volunteer usually has a new baby. Sidelines uses a contract system . . . The potential volunteer must acknowledge each section of the contract before she (or he!) is allowed to become an active volunteer. Several of these sections include specifics about their training. Finally, we do have a system to remove volunteers who do not follow their contract agreement. Our Group Coordinators monitor this closely.

Other organizations also follow best practices in online orientation and training. For example, the Young Adult Library Services Association extensively involves online volunteers from among its members, including as bloggers for the organization. They post their blogging guidelines online,[5] so potential blog volunteers know exactly what they are agreeing to before signing up. MentorPlace is an online volunteering mentoring program that brings together IBM employees and students to focus together on activities that help with the students' academic work and career goals. MentorPlace has posted extensive training and support materials for mentors, students, and teachers on their Web site.[6] You can find many more examples, and we present more about online mentoring in chapter 8.

Volunteer Handbooks and Instruction Sheets

In addition to providing an orientation and listing the policies, procedures, and key contact information for volunteers, some organizations also produce a volunteer handbook. This handbook can be for every volunteer or for specific volunteer roles, such as volunteer mentors who work onsite with children. Will your online volunteers need a special handbook? Maybe.

You will recruit many online volunteers based on the training and expertise they already have for the roles you need to fill. For instance, an online volunteer designing your Web site should be chosen because he or she already knows how to do the work, just as the volunteer moderating an online community should be recruited for his or her experience in moderating and facilitating such an online forum. So, beyond preparatory materials on your Web site and access to your online forum for volunteers, such skilled volunteers probably do not also need a tailored handbook or manual.

However, those online volunteers who engage in roles that are central to meeting your organization's mission—such as working one-on-one with your clients or with the public—may indeed need both training and a tailored handbook to support their service. For instance, they may need advice on *netiquette* (online culture and accepted manners); how to handle various scenarios online (such as a hostile client); where to find online resources a client may need; and so on. The development of such a specialized online volunteering handbook that addresses these concerns requires a great deal of employee and volunteer time and research in order to identify what these online volunteers will likely need to know. Also, it should be a perpetual work-in-progress, with volunteers frequently asked to submit suggestions to improve the handbook.

While creating an entire handbook may not be necessary, it is likely that some written *instructions*

> **A New Chapter 12**
>
> One of the many new features in this second edition of this *Guidebook* is a new chapter 12, written especially for online volunteers themselves. Perhaps you will want to share some or all of those materials with new online volunteers, to help them know what they are getting into. We have given you a self-evaluation for new online volunteers, tips for online volunteers to work successfully with an organization, and special advice for those who provide expert assistance to an organization, such as a pro bono consultant. This might be the start of your own organization's online volunteering handbook.

will be very useful for many situations and assignments. Perhaps a two-page checklist would be helpful for a specific volunteer role, where all of the steps of the activity are listed in sequence and a volunteer is encouraged to check off tasks as finished. A completed checklist can double as a report if you leave space for "date completed" and "comments" next to each item. In the same vein, a page of frequently-asked questions (FAQs) and answers about some aspect of online service can be helpful to volunteers in the same position. A series of such instruction sheets can be kept up to date by encouraging volunteers to suggest changes and additions based on their experiences. The latest versions should always be available online for easy access by everyone.

The Online Volunteer's Point of Contact

Regardless of who recruits new online volunteers and brings them on board, it is critical that each volunteer create a one-to-one relationship with a staff member or a leadership volunteer at the front line of the project when it is time to begin work. All of these people are also *leaders of volunteers*, regardless of their job titles. Each person is the primary point of contact at the organization for the volunteers working virtually and, in the best-case scenario, should be the person who initiated or fully defined the online volunteering assignment in support of the volunteer's work.

It is imperative that this point of contact is ready to move quickly in communicating with new online volunteers. The VRM should remind this manager of this need.

Training Online Volunteers

As we previously discussed, orientation should be similar for all volunteers regardless of the assignment, the roles they will undertake, or their qualifications. But training should be tailored to each situation.

Was a volunteer recruited for specific existing expertise or skills needed to accomplish the assigned activity? Note that it is quite possible that a volunteer may come to you with *more* expertise than that of the paid staff—especially if you have recruited highly-skilled or pro bono volunteers. In those cases, you still have the right to request that work be completed according to your needs, rules, or standards, but "training" becomes more of a process of guiding the volunteer in how to *adapt* existing skills to what is needed in your setting. This may mean a short discussion about ways things must be done and why, or perhaps a chance to review previous examples of work done the way your organization prefers. After that, the point of contact can assign a small task, review it, and move forward as a coach to the volunteer.

On the other hand, you may have recruited a volunteer for his or her interest in and willingness to learn the work, not because of any previous experience (assuming, of course, that the assignment can be done by a generalist rather than a specialist). In that case, the supervisor or point of contact will have to determine what needs to be taught, in what sequence, so that the volunteer can start working as quickly as possible and build the necessary skills over time. *How* this training is accomplished needs to be strategized, but rarely will it be the same for every volunteer. Just as with onsite volunteers, learning can come from such techniques as:

- A live, formal training session, either one-to-one or in a group, in which someone teaches and demonstrates what has to be done. This can be onsite, or it can be shared by telephone, webinar, or other Web conference.

- Videos or Flash presentations created in advance and viewed by the individual volunteer, followed by discussion with the supervisor. As mentioned before, it is possible to quiz new volunteers on whether or not they have learned important material.

- Written documents: articles, reports, samples.

- A buddy system, in which the newcomer shadows an experienced volunteer to observe what is being done. For online service, this might mean receiving copies of e-mails or joining in on a work-related conference call.

Training should also be adapted to the learning style of each volunteer. Some people love to read and can almost teach themselves. Others much prefer hearing the information. And so on.

Special Training Issues

There are several aspects of online service that need special attention in the training process.

Confidentiality and Privacy

Throughout this book, we review simple measures an organization can employ to ensure the safety of all participants in a virtual volunteering program (particularly in chapter 8, where we focus on online volunteers working directly with clients).

Issues of confidentiality, privacy, and security are already present at your organization, regardless of whether or not you involve online volunteers. You should already have policies that address these important issues for your current employees and onsite volunteers, as well as your clients. This is important for any organization, whether or not you serve vulnerable populations (children, the elderly, people with disabilities, the seriously ill) who deserve special protection. Similarly, volunteers also deserve the protection that comes from policies and procedures relating to confidentiality, privacy, and security.

In truth, we have found that many concerns expressed about confidentiality are a smokescreen put up by staff who are resistant to volunteer involvement—online or offline. To counter, you can point out that confidentiality is not guaranteed by having an employee complete an activity (they can gossip, too) or by requiring that the work be done in the office next to you. More than anything else,

maintaining confidentiality is a matter of clear delineation of what information is private and then training everyone to adhere to the rules.

It's obviously important to incorporate a discussion of confidentiality in any volunteer training curriculum. For instance, what do you mean when you talk about *confidentiality*? It is more than not revealing a client's name; it is not revealing *any* information that would allow someone to guess the identity of the individual involved. And it is more than not revealing client information to the public; in fact, not all staff, paid or volunteer, should be privy to all client information. Some organizations believe that the number of employees is confidential. Many domestic violence shelters do not have any online information about where their shelters are physically located. Your organization needs to define what it considers confidential and why, and explain this clearly to all staff, paid or volunteer, onsite or online.

You may be especially concerned about maintaining the confidentiality of information that volunteers may access as part of their online service. This may require policies regarding whether and how to keep your organization's information on a volunteer's computer. There are several possible scenarios to consider, because online volunteers may be using:

- Computers at their place of work, which may mean that files and communications relating to your organization end up archived on the volunteer's company's backup system.

- Computers at home that may be shared with other household members.

- Public-access computers, such as those at the public library, which obviously are used by many unknown people. Not only can online work be observed by passersby, but material created by the online volunteer could possibly remain accessible to subsequent users. Also, many public computers have no *save* function enabled.

- Portable laptop computers or smartphones that could be more easily lost or stolen than a desktop computer always in place.

Before you let these scenarios scare you, consider that much of what online volunteers will do for your organization will *not* be confidential. So it should not be of great concern that a corporation's backup system has a draft copy of your organization's new Web site or if a volunteer's smartphone gets stolen.

Even so, you should always rate an online volunteering assignment in terms of the need for confidentiality and security, and communicate with an online volunteer beforehand regarding any such concerns. You should also develop a process for dealing with confidential materials that makes sense for each situation. For example, you might require volunteers to *password protect* all files and e-mails connected to their work for your organization. Or you may ask volunteers to never use a public-access computer for the purpose of logging into a private discussion forum, to ensure that no confidential information gets downloaded. Let common sense and constant discussions with volunteers guide you.

Any procedures you ask online volunteers to follow should be the same as those you ask (or would ask) onsite volunteers to follow. Any documents you ask volunteers to sign should mirror what is also asked in writing of paid employees. An onsite volunteer is not inherently more trustworthy than an offsite volunteer, any more than an employee is inherently more trustworthy than a volunteer.

We repeat: Confidentiality is a training issue. Your organization's policies must be clear regarding confidentiality, and these policies must be regularly communicated. You can learn more about how to structure and follow confidentiality policies and procedures for volunteers in general through the various resources listed in appendix B and in the Virtual Volunteering Wiki.

The Volunteer's E-mail Address

Do you want volunteers to engage with clients, professional contacts, or other volunteers using their own e-mail address? Or will you give them a specific address issued by the organization (stefan@ourtown nonprofit.org)?

Volunteers may prefer using their own e-mail address because that seems easier to them. But there are ways to set up the volunteer's mailbox that make it comparatively simple to use a separate address. And some volunteers will like to identify publicly with your domain name.

Conversely, your organization may be reluctant to give volunteers individual e-mail addresses with its domain name, because that implies the volunteer is an official representative of the organization. Note: If volunteers are e-mailing people outside of your organization as part of the work necessary to fulfill assignments you give them, they *are* representing the organization!

There are clearly no hard-and-fast rules on this subject. But you can determine what approach to take based on the demands of the assignment you give the online volunteer. If the online volunteer's work mainly requires interaction with staff or other volunteers, then using a personal e-mail address is fine. But an organizational e-mail address has more importance for volunteers who work with clients and the public, who manage other volunteers, or who are engaged in high-responsibility roles within your organization. It will allow these volunteers to easily separate what they do as part of their volunteering from all other personal or business e-mail exchanges—so it will always be clear and easy to tell, online, when the person is speaking as a volunteer and when the person is speaking as a private individual apart from the organization's volunteer assignment. It is also easy to discontinue an e-mail address once a volunteer ends a role at your organization.

In summary: Develop policies to define which volunteers are eligible for an organizational e-mail address, including how and when the right to use the address ends. Then train each new volunteer about these policies.

Addressing Online Volunteers' Concerns with Written Agreements

Note that online volunteers are also taking a leap of faith concerning you and your organization when they engage in virtual volunteering. How does someone online know that your organization is credible or that it even really exists? If a potential online volunteer is geographically distant and will never visit your facility, do not be surprised if the volunteer asks some background questions about your organization's funding, history, and mission.

Because of the two-sided nature of possible concerns, you may want to develop written agreements to be signed by both the online volunteer and whoever will be their liaison at your organization. Such agreements may include:

- Confidentiality of the volunteer's name, e-mail address, and other contact information. Who will have access to this information? Will it ever be shared with another organization?

- How the volunteer should represent himself or herself to the public or your clients as a representative of your organization: In what circumstances? Should the volunteer have a designated title? Have a signature line that gives contact information for your headquarters? Use the organization's logo?

- Appropriate public credit for the virtual service provided, including who owns the copyright on work produced during the assignment.

- The right to access to a staff liaison for questions and feedback, matched by a commitment from the volunteer to communicate and report regularly.

- Assurance on both sides of up-to-date virus and anti-malware protection on all office and personal computers used.

Volunteer Experts

We have focused attention on recruiting skilled or pro bono volunteers who already have expertise in the content of the work to be done. However, just because someone has professional skills, it does not necessarily follow that the person knows how to be a consultant, advisor, or trainer. Yet volunteers often find themselves in such roles. There is a world of difference between doing a task and assisting or training others to do it. Therefore, your screening and matching process should ascertain whether or not the volunteer needs some instruction in how to consult or advise, and then provide some.

Problems can also arise in situations when the volunteer does not fully understand the needs or the resources of the organization or is working with a system or technology that the volunteer understands quite well but the staff liaison does not. Never assume that someone is aware of how nonprofits and government units differ from a for-profit business—from size of budgets to how decisions are made. So talk about the goals and possible constraints of the consultancy, especially the time involved in finding new funding or going through an approval process that might need to wait for the next board meeting. We've already recommended drawing up a written agreement describing each pro bono assignment, which is a great opportunity to go over such issues with each volunteer.

Many nonprofits become frustrated with companies or consultants providing donated services. Why? Because the for-profit side feels that the nonprofit should be satisfied with whatever service is provided, whenever it is provided. "After all, it's *free*." This is an unhealthy and potentially disastrous attitude on the part of the person or company donating service. The nonprofit organization or NGO needs to set the tone early with volunteers of any kind, and that includes expert online volunteers. No matter how expert the volunteer is, he or she needs to go through your organization's online volunteer orientation and know the policies and procedures regarding how your organization operates. This lets the volunteer immediately know that you have a system regarding volunteer service—a system to which the volunteer needs to adhere. It encourages the volunteer to treat your organization as a serious customer with a *real* business that includes *real* deadlines and expectations—and very real consequences for not meeting those.

Training Paid Staff

In chapter 2 we addressed the possibility that paid staff might resist working with online volunteers. Before you deal with this problem, make sure you provide training to your staff on how to work with *any* volunteers! Unfortunately, too many people go through extensive formal education and earn advanced degrees without ever hearing a word about partnering with volunteers. So training in how to supervise or liaison with volunteers will be helpful for relationships between everyone, whether onsite or online. Here we want to focus on possible training needs helpful to the introduction of virtual volunteering.

Staff will more quickly embrace virtual volunteering if they already feel comfortable using computer and Internet tools and if they see virtual volunteering as a natural expansion of volunteering at your organization. But they will want to know where they can get answers to questions and concerns about both virtual volunteering and tech tools. Consider holding a series of short (less than one hour) workshops on:

- Virtual volunteering, its history, and what it looks like at other organizations

- Supervising someone remotely via e-mail and the realities of text-based communications (the different styles of communicating online)

- Instant messaging as a communication tool. If possible, set up the workshop so that you can have an instant messaging session with a current volunteer that most of the staff knows but who is offsite at the time.

- Audio or video conferencing via Skype, iVisit, Google Talk, etc. Again, set up the workshop so that you can have a conversation, with sound and webcam, with a familiar volunteer offsite.

- Participating in the online volunteer community—how a staff member can help it be effective

- Virtual volunteering basics: how to identify tasks that could be done, how to write a virtual volunteering opportunity, how to work with a new online volunteer, and so on

You could use the individual chapters and sections of this book as a source of ideas for your workshops and to create slide presentations.

One person does not have to do all of these workshops alone. For instance, you could invite a knowledgeable employee or volunteer to run the session on managing e-mail or using instant messaging.

If you are the VRM, you will most definitely want to present the virtual volunteering introduction workshop, as well as the sessions on the basic elements of involving online volunteers, such as writing a virtual volunteering opportunity. You will want to stress again and again that the practicalities of managing volunteers virtually are not vastly different from managing people onsite.

If you are not the VRM, but you are the primary champion for virtual volunteering at your organization, you should work together with the VRM, keeping that person involved in planning and assisting with all of your training activities. Remember that your goal is not to create a different track of volunteer involvement; virtual volunteering is *real* volunteering and should be a part of your organization's existing volunteer engagement efforts.

Apart from designated training sessions, reinforce how you want staff to be supportive of volunteers at other opportunities:

- Thank a staff member for posting to the volunteers' online forum

- Bring up something that has been discussed on the volunteers' online forum at a staff meeting

- Laud staff members who are already working with volunteers online

- Talk about your use of instant messaging and live audio and video tools to work with volunteers

Timing

When should you offer formal staff training regarding virtual volunteering? Should it happen before or after you initiate a virtual volunteering pilot project or simultaneously? That is a question only you can answer. Every organization is different and adopts new practices in different ways. Your organization's own unique culture and internal politics will influence whatever you attempt. For some organizations, it may be easier to start with small introductions of virtual volunteering activities, without a formal announcement, in order to avoid potential fears or hostilities. For others, custom and protocol may dictate that the introduction be quite formal, with a written proposal, slide show presentation, etc.

NOTES

1. EPA Volunteer Monitoring Program <http://www.epa
   .gov/owow/monitoring/volunteer/epasvmp.html>.
2. "Creating a Video Lecture" on Wikiversity, accessed July
   2013　<http://en.wikiversity.org/wiki/Creating_a_video
   _lecture>.
3. The Missouri Conference Web site, accessed July 2013
   <http://www.moumethodist.org/pages/detail/930>.
4. Downloaded June 2009 from http://www.sidelines.org/
   volunteer/volunteer-virtually/.
5. Linda W. Braun, "Blogger Guidelines," post to the Young
   Adult Library Services Association Blog, July 1, 2008, and
   updated by the YALSA board of directors, March 2011
   <http://yalsa.ala.org/blog/blogger-guidelines/>.
6. MentorPlace Training Resources <http://ibm.mentorplace
   .epals.org/Strategies.htm>.

Chapter 6

Basic Techniques for Working Online with Volunteers

What Everyone Should Know

Have You Read the Chapters before This One?

We know that many readers of this book are actually not going to read the entire book and will jump directly to the sections they feel they need most. That is fine! However, if you are having difficulties with virtual volunteering and you have come directly to this chapter looking for help, you might consider reading the previous chapters as well. You may find that your problems are addressed by more effectively preparing the foundation for your efforts.

Until now, we have emphasized that managing volunteers virtually is not vastly different from managing volunteers onsite. In this chapter, however, we look at a few key differences.

While it is a generalization, online volunteers tend to be more independent than onsite volunteers. This is particularly true for those online volunteers who are supporting staff rather than working with clients. Therefore, anyone working with online volunteers, particularly those working on project-specific assignments with a definite start and end date, should avoid supervising with the *steamroller approach* and telling volunteers exactly how to do work. A much better option is the *snowplow approach* that allows the manager to be the enabler of the volunteers' service. In truth, even with volunteers onsite, it is better to *partner* than to *supervise*.

For many short-term, online volunteering assignments, including micro-volunteering tasks, staff will manage volunteers by results rather than by process. How a volunteer accomplishes the work is not as important as ending up with the desired result. By contrast, staff will manage the volunteer for *both* results and process for online volunteering

assignments that are ongoing over several months, where the volunteer takes on a role rather than a specific project. Each person serving as a point of contact for online volunteers should be a facilitator who provides assistance, support and guidance. That does not mean giving the online volunteer the go-ahead for an assignment and keeping your fingers crossed that the volunteer sends something back by the deadline date that meets your needs. Rather, the manager ought to stay in touch regularly and convey attentiveness to the online volunteers' needs and contributions.

Another distinction of online interactions with volunteers is that most can be recorded. E-mails to and from volunteers are easily archived. Instant messaging, chat room conversations, webinars, and even live audio and video sessions can be recorded and archived as well. This is a blessing in that it makes it easy to find out who said what and when, but it has a downside: it means all of your own words are logged forever, including words you might regret later.

A Designated Contact

Regardless of the type of virtual assignment, every online volunteer needs a primary contact at the organization. This must be someone who understands the work being undertaken, so it usually is the person who requested the help in the first place, who might be in any staff position. The volunteer resources manager (VRM) may be involved in recruiting, screening, and maintaining records on the volunteer, but training and day-to-day contact have to be with someone familiar with the work to be done.

If the designated contact has not worked with onsite volunteers before supervising an online volunteer, some training might be in order, or at least some monitoring in the early stages of the partnership.

Developing Relationships with Online Volunteers

The traditional physical work environment for organizations includes external motivational and inspirational prompts for onsite volunteers: posters in the lobby of goals and achievements, someone excitedly walking into a room to give good news, and the camaraderie of group interaction around the coffeepot. Online volunteers also need to feel in touch and in tune with the organization, and it is the role of the designated contact person to maintain their interest and enthusiasm, despite physical separation.

Here are some ways to keep online volunteers engaged:[1]

- *Answer e-mails and questions from online volunteers quickly.* The 72-hour turnaround goal for all e-mails is really important here (and note that, for some projects, 72 hours is too long for a response!). Even if you just say, "Got your message and will respond tomorrow," the point is to make the volunteer feel at the top of your agenda.

- *Give clear directions* to volunteers on how to find important information and resources as part of their assignment. For instance, is there a special online database that has information that applies to your organization or the assignment but might not surface via commonly used search engines? Are there particular online publications that might be difficult to find by someone not already familiar with your organization's work? Is there certain jargon you and others working in your particular field know well but a volunteer might not recognize?

- *Schedule regular contact.* All volunteers need to talk regularly with their contact person to assess needs, give feedback, and discuss problems, and such staff need to communicate advice on performance. Quick telephone "meetings" are really useful, or use one of the many online phone services such as Skype or Google Hangouts. You can also use instant messaging. Apart from setting a time to text chat, when you see that a volunteer is online,

you can send a quick "How are things going?" message.

- *Ask for and follow up on regular reports.* You need to be kept informed about what the volunteer is doing; this requirement should be stated in the position description and reinforced on an ongoing basis. When a volunteer adheres to the reporting schedule, it shows the volunteer's ongoing commitment; when you acknowledge those reports, you demonstrate that you care about the work being done. More about reports in a moment.

- *Be patient, be supportive, and remember that not every task is right for every volunteer.* The better your screening, orientation, and supervising processes, the less chance there is for misunderstandings or incomplete assignments. It is okay to give a volunteer the option to choose a different assignment if the volunteer seems to be struggling with the current task.

- *Use your online community for volunteers liberally.* Post text from internal office memos; announcements about upcoming events; the results of onsite events; links to newspaper articles about the organization; the text of a recent speech by your executive director; links to photos of staff, volunteers, or clients in action; or anything else of interest. Frequently encourage volunteers to post about challenges they are facing, resources they find particularly helpful, and their volunteering experiences in general—and thank every volunteer who posts to your online forum.

- *Put online volunteers on your postal mailing list*, along with your onsite volunteers. Online volunteers should receive the same paper mailings that other supporters receive. Even in this age of electronic communications, it is often still exciting to receive something via postal mail. Consider sending a postcard via postal mail once or twice a year, particularly for online volunteers who are geographically remote from your organization and may never come onsite. It is an inexpensive but very personal touch that remote volunteers appreciate.

- *Send the same invitations and thank you notes* that you send to onsite volunteers, if at all possible. Even if online volunteers are much too far away to participate in an onsite event, they will appreciate being included on the guest list anyway—and you'll never know if they might make the effort to attend.

- *Be open with volunteers about problems and challenges.* If you think a live conversation would be a more comfortable way to talk about an uncomfortable subject, schedule a live online audio or video session or pick up the phone. Treat volunteers with the honesty that you would want as a volunteer yourself.

- *Require participation by online volunteers in surveys.* This requirement should be stated in your full task description for an online volunteer. Report on survey findings via your online forum for volunteers.

- *Fine-tune and tailor your communication-sand management style* as different situations require. Perhaps you find that you need to send more e-mails to volunteers to keep them better informed or perhaps to send *less,* to keep them from feeling overwhelmed. Adapt to those volunteers who prefer talking on IM and to others who prefer a message via Facebook. While you will certainly find methods and strategies that work over the long term, you also need to be in tune with your volunteers so that you know when an adjustment in communications or management is needed.

- *Celebrate successes.* Acknowledge benchmark accomplishments as they occur, without waiting for the final product. This can be done via a "way-to-go!" e-mail or a posting for all to see on your online forum for volunteers.

All of these activities reinforce the importance of online service and go a long way toward successful and efficient completion of work.

Real-Life Examples

To illuminate the principles just described, three of the organizations we have already introduced make them work daily.

LibriVox creates audio versions of public-domain books and distributes them free on its Web site. *All* LibriVox volunteers are remote. "We have no other actual presence (no office or anything) except in the homes of volunteers,"[2] says Hugh McGuire, founder of the organization. LibriVox uses several different tools to enable hundreds of volunteers to stay in contact:

- An online forum/bulletin board,[3] which McGuire calls "the most important communication tool we have, and all our project management/organization, etc. happens here."

- A blog

- Podcasts (audio recordings). This is not just the output of volunteer contributions; they are also used for internal purposes. Most LibriVox volunteers use the free software, Audacity, to make recordings.

- A wiki that provides guidelines for volunteers producing audios

- Instant messaging for in-depth help sessions

- Calls on Skype, both for in-depth help sessions and for interviews that will become part of future podcasts

- Custom software tools for project management and volunteer management

Sidelines, already introduced as providing international support for women and families experiencing complicated pregnancies and premature births, again demonstrates good volunteer management practice. In an e-mail interview, Nancy Veeneman, Sidelines' online Director, noted:

All [online] volunteers are required to keep email to and from clients for a minimum of six months after the client delivers [her baby]. Phone support volunteers use a log sheet that is also kept for six months after the client has delivered. There is also a check-and-balance system in place that we use to contact the client to be sure that her support is meeting her needs. If necessary they are assigned a new volunteer or an additional one to cover additional complications.

Pearls of Africa supports people with disabilities in Africa. Founder Laurie Moy has strong feelings about the importance of deadlines for online volunteers, no matter how long or short their task or role:

Setting rigid deadlines is so important! There is so much going on in our volunteers' lives, and some are able to set their own deadlines and get work turned in with a short turnaround. But in most cases we found that without a deadline, the task lost priority. We didn't want volunteers who would do the work when they got around to it—we take the work seriously, and one way of conveying that (and making our own work flow moving) is to set clear and strict deadlines.

Note how many of these suggestions for managing and supporting online volunteers are related to encouraging them to report in regularly and keep contact persons up to date about what they are doing, challenges they are facing, etc. Reporting requirements should be detailed for online volunteers during the new volunteer orientation and in the task description, with reminders sent out occasionally as well.

Developing a Great Reporting Process

Many people cringe at the thought of requiring or submitting reports, yet these are an essential tool for keeping work on track. You don't need to use the word *report* all the time; call it *regular feedback, progress status,* or simply *keeping in touch.*

Make reporting simple and even rewarding by creating specific forms and a procedure to complete them on a regular basis. Keeping in mind that no one has time to write long e-mails (and the last thing you need are more e-mails!), develop a short, standard set of questions that an online volunteer can answer concisely. Reports can be returned to you via e-mail, via a private Web-based form that allows each volunteer to log in to report on progress, or via an online project management or collaboration tool.[4]

Here are possible items to include in whatever reporting system you use:

- The volunteer's full name, since it is not always obvious from an e-mail address

- The volunteer's current assignment or project (because the manager may be working with multiple volunteers and may not be able to remember instantly what each person is working on)

- How many hours the volunteer has worked on this assignment to date or in the period reported on (even if the answer is "none")

- What percentage of the assignment is left to do (Is the volunteer half done? 75 percent done? Even started?), followed by something that indicates whether the volunteer feels on track, such as "Do you think you will meet the deadline date?"

- Any problems or obstacles encountered in completing the assignment

- Any help, support, or resources needed from the organization to complete the work

- Comments or opinions in general the volunteer would like to make about the assignment (love it, hate it, learning a lot, what has been learned)

- What the online volunteer's next steps will be

You can ask currently-engaged volunteers to send in this report every two weeks—say, on the first and third Mondays of the month—and post a reminder to the online volunteer forum about when reports are due. Keep track of who is and is not reporting in, and follow up accordingly. New volunteers may need frequent reminders before they learn that reporting really is as important as you have stressed in their orientation and in the written task assignment.

Reply to progress reports immediately, even if you only acknowledge receipt. Let volunteers know that their needs are important to you and that you are carefully listening to what they say. Include something in your reply that lets a volunteer know you really did read the e-mail, rather than repeating a standardized form-letter reply each time. Most important, follow up on anything the volunteer identifies as a need for help or resources.

If a volunteer does not report in as agreed, e-mail or call to check on progress. Do this the *very first time* you don't receive a report; otherwise, you convey the attitude that it doesn't matter whether or not the volunteer complies with this requirement. You really do need to know what online volunteers have been doing and want to offer support—and you have made the process easy enough to expect each volunteer to report in. *You don't have to be negative.* Use a tone such as "I was looking for your report due last Friday. I truly am interested in how things are going with your assignment, so please submit the form now or let's schedule a call to talk about things." For most volunteers, you'll only have to take this action once.

Balance formal reporting with informal reporting and checking in. If you see a volunteer online while you are both logged into the same platform (MySpace, Facebook, Skype, Google Hangouts, instant messaging, whatever), you can say, "Hey, how are you? How are things going? Thanks for that last report!" But do not be too pushy—a volunteer who is online may not, at that exact moment, be interested in communicating about volunteer assignments and may dread logging on if it means hearing from you *every* time.

We recognize that finding the right balance for the frequency and length of messages can be tricky—and even impossible. What some people perceive as over-communication can be seen by others as under-communication. So ask volunteers: "Are you receiving enough messages, with enough details?" Expect some conflicting answers, and know that you will not be able to please everyone.

Also, beware of the complaint that there are "too many meetings," online or onsite. The real complaint may be that online meetings are not efficient, not well run, and not results oriented.If online meetings are valuable to participants, volunteers will feel they are necessary and will attend. Be honest in assessing what you do in these meetings and make them more meaningful or appealing to attend.

Communicating Online

In chapter 2, we examine the many different ways to communicate online and give some advice for dealing with the flood of e-mail messages (from many different sources) and cell phone texts. We urge you to go back and review this information if you are still struggling with the basics of electronic messaging, an increasingly essential way to communicate with all volunteers, all the time. In chapter 12, we also givespecific recommendations to individual online volunteers, as it takes two to tango.

We return to this topic in this chapter because, when working virtually, written communication is a critical component of supervision. Onsite volunteers give and receive all sorts of visual cues during conversations with their supervisors or liaisons that are missing in e-mail or text messages. So everyone needs to pay closer attention when "whipping out" an e-mail, if that is going to be the only time in maybe a week that direct contact is made.

Different Online Writing Styles

E-mail, texting, and posting to any online site all require writing ability. But everyone has his or her own style and comfort level with the written word. For instance, some people:

- Write messages exactly as they talk, using punctuation (!!!), text symbols, or graphics representing their mood or facial expression (what are called *emoticons*, such as ;-) to indicate a wink), just as they might use lots of facial expressions when they are talking.

- Express themselves formally, using the standards of a printed *business* letter.

- Use online jargon or abbreviations that may be common among their peer group but rare outside of it (like writing "LOL," for "Laugh Out Loud," in response to a comment they think is funny).

- Write short and to the point, while others write long, detailed paragraphs, even when instant messaging.

- Send lots of messages all the time.

- Interpret silence as approval, but others perceive it as disapproval.

- Will e-mail you and then call on the phone, as they are not absolutely certain about e-mail communication and need to hear an approving voice.

- Post frequently to online communities. Others post occasionally, and many will just lurk and never post at all—or will send questions or comments directly to you instead of to the entire membership.

- May misinterpret intent or tone based only on the way they perceive the message to be written, not what the message actually says. This is true particularly of those who are new to the Internet or do not frequently use e-mail or online communities. For instance, one-word answers to questions may be interpreted as the respondent being angry or even rude.

- See all questions as personal attacks or as signs that the person asking the questions does not like them or trust them. (We discuss how to handle online criticism in chapter 10.)

- Write messages littered with punctuation, spelling, and sentence structure errors (despite being quite respected in their professional field) but are very articulate on the phone or speaking in front of an audience.

- Are not completely aware of all the things they can do with their e-mail software, such as formatting options, creating a signature, setting the default to reply to the sender only rather than to everyone, filtering messages automatically into folders, etc.

- Become *documenters*, who keep resending the full text of all previous messages in the thread, even after numerous responses. Others are *snippers,* who concisely remove so much of the text in the original e-mail that it can be hard to figure out what they are responding or referring to. (This may come from a difference in e-mail systems or the person's technical know-how, or may simply be a personal or cultural preference.)

Before you feel overwhelmed regarding these many different styles of online communication, consider all of the different ways that people communicate face-to-face: some make direct eye contact while others look away; some use their hands as they talk, while others stay quite still; some are proactive in starting a conversation or expressing an opinion, while others will not do so unless directly asked; some people have an accent, speak a dialect, or have a speech impediment, and the way you listen and respond to them raises or lowers their comfort level.

In other words, you already adjust your style when you communicate with different employees and volunteers onsite. The same will be true online.

Communicating with Young Volunteers

Most teenagers and twenty-somethings in the U.S. and other industrialized countries have used

---

Communicating with Volunteers via E-mail

Penny Leisch, formerly with the Arizona Pioneers' Home Volunteers Association,[5] offered this advice to the Virtual Volunteering Project for communicating with volunteers via e-mail:

People interpret written words based on their experiences, culture and education. Some people are very literal, good readers and very good listeners. Other people need the same information repeated several times before they assimilate everything . . .

Online volunteers may come from a variety of cultures and my everyday terms can mean something totally different to them. For instance, in Australia a 'downy' is what we call a comforter or bed cover in the U.S. I can usually tell when there is a cultural difference by the physical structure of the written grammar. I've learned to watch for these types of indicators . . .

The language I use is simple. I avoid technical terms and e-mail abbreviations unless I've worked with the person enough to know they will understand my references.

electronic communication all their lives and are "digital natives." These days, most send messages to family and friends for personal and social reasons via social networking on Facebook or Twitter or send text messages on their phone, rather than by e-mail.[6] They also may use texting shorthand that is often unintelligible to the uninitiated (OMG![7]).

As with adults, a teen's capability as an online volunteer depends on the teen's online skills. For instance, a young person may be a whiz at using Google+ to post updates about his or her life but may have such poor grammar and spelling that the teen would not be a good candidate to manage any of your organization's online profiles. Teens may be more prone to express interest in an online volunteering assignment but not really be qualified; if you follow the screening and orientation recommendations we have made in earlier chapters, you should be able to identify someone who may actually not be skilled enough for a particular assignment.

In addition, teens may need more frequent training and follow-up on your organization's Internet-related policies than older online volunteers. Because they have grown up with Internet technology and social networking, teens do not always understand the reasons for social boundaries online. Remind them about your policies, guidelines, and protocols regarding posting information about the organization and its clients, sharing photos, making information public about fellow volunteers, etc., and tell them more than once why these policies are necessary. Teens also may need more frequent reminders about the importance of deadlines; their online volunteering with your organization may be their first-ever work experience, and they may not understand that there is nothing virtual about online commitments and deadlines.

Teens and young adults are notorious for not checking or responding to their e-mails. If you want to communicate with young online volunteers mainly by e-mail, discuss this in orientation and training. Explain why this is *your* preferred method of exchange of information and that it is a chance for them to learn and practice a universal work skill. Ask volunteers to commit to checking their e-mail boxes, say, twice a week. Promise to send a text message alert whenever there is an e-mail that needs the teens' attention. And every once in a while, you can engage in a live chat or some other form of online exchange. We look at these options next.

Using Real-Time Communications

There is warmth in IM (instant messaging). I feel closer to the person on the other end of the computer. I can get emotional, they can get emotional. It just feels so much more personal. It gives me the chance to be myself, even to be more creative online . . . Email is, to me, something formal. It is for long, official things. It is static. It has its place, of course. But IM is informal. I use it with "my" people in the field. I write them and, if they are available, they write back immediately. They may say, "I cannot write right now" and that's fine, because it is an immediate response. I may email someone and not hear from them for days, and think, gee, are they ignoring me?

—Alexandra Haglund-Petitbo,
formerly with the United Nations
Information Technology Service (UNITeS)
at United Nations Volunteers

Online chats, instant messaging, live audio and video conferencing, tweeting and more have all become common tools for many organizations to hold online meetings with remote staff, including volunteers. These tools also allow online volunteers to interact with clients, or each other, or have live events where volunteers listen to or watch a featured speaker or guest.

These forms of real-time, synchronous communications add a different dimension to the remote volunteer experience.[8] For instance, one-on-one instant messaging between a volunteer and staff member can often solve problems more quickly than an e-mail-only exchange. Some feel the nature of real-time communications adds a feeling of informality, spontaneity, and friendliness that is missing from e-mail (which can have the tone of a formal business letter or internal memo, even when that is not the desired effect) or even blogging (which can feel like a newspaper or magazine article, again, even when that is not the desired effect).

The dialogue from written real-time communications is easily (and often automatically) archived for later reference. Video conferencing puts human voices and faces to online volunteers. Live, instantaneous interactions, together with e-mail and other asynchronous tools, can help strengthen the bonds among participants and build community.

It is impossible to list every conceivable use of synchronous tools with or by online volunteers, and we are not going to try. While we share ideas for how volunteers could use these tools in their service, please do not take these ideas as a blueprint for what your organization should be doing. Not every tool is appropriate for every organization, and there is not enough time in the day for you to use every online tool, even if that were the sole focus of your responsibilities. But we can present some general advice for different ways of interacting in real time online.

Instant Messaging

If you have a Yahoo!, Google, or Windows Live account, then you already have an instant messaging (IM) account that will work across all three of those platforms; you just need to download the appropriate software from these sites to get started. If you do not already have such an account, get one by going to any of these three platforms. Again, these are all *cross* platform, meaning that users of any of the three systems can send instant messages to each other.

An account on Skype, iVisit, MySpace, Google+, Facebook, ormost any other online social networking or video conferencing tool will also give you an instant message account, though not all of these are cross platform with other IM software; each is intended to be used only with your other friends who have the same service.

An instant messaging account allows volunteers to see when you are online and, therefore, potentially available for a quick question. Once you have an account on Yahoo!, Google, or Windows Live and have downloaded the proper software, send an e-mail to a few volunteers, or even to all, and let them know your instant message ID and the service you are using (if it matters). Welcome them to add you to their IM address books and to IM you any time they see you online. Then log into your account daily and see which volunteers contact you.

In the beginning, you might receive several messages, and these can feel like interruptions, as they will pop onto your screen any time you are logged in to your account. However, the conversations will probably be quite short and, as the newness wears off, you will stop receiving so many random "Hello!" messages from volunteers. If you are experiencing a particularly busy period and do not want to be interrupted, simply log off your account, or choose the feature that allows you to appear to be offline when you really are not.

Over the next several weeks, even months, make a commitment to log in to your IM account regularly. See how you like it, see how your volunteers use it (or do not use it), and consider what role IM might eventually play in your organization. If you have teenagers or young adults among your organization's volunteers (or, for that matter, clients), you may find that they prefer IM communication. As we noted in the previous section, some organizations have found that their youngest volunteers tend to ignore e-mail in favor of IM or cell phone text messaging. Consider using IM to alert younger volunteers that you have sent them an important e-mail to which you would like a reply. And consider ways that volunteers could use IM to talk to each other, to employees at your organization, or even with clients of your organization.

Share your instant messaging ID and the platform you use with all volunteers and, if you want to be able to see when volunteers are online, you need to add their IM addresses to your platform's address book as well. You also need to remember to turn this tool off, or to change your status to *busy*, if you do not wish to be interrupted. Think of it as the same as when you put a *do not disturb* sign on your closed office door. Then be sure to turn this tool back on or to change your status later!

You can easily bring a chat to a close: "It's been great chatting with you. Thanks! Now I need to get back to some other work. Goodbye!"

Web Conferencing

You can use Web conferencing to deliver some or all of your volunteer orientation and training. Live online presentations are successful for the same reasons as a successful onsite, face-to-face presentation: they start on time, they deliver information in a lively way, and they respect the time of attendees by providing only the most essential information.

Create an account on an audio and video conferencing tool, such as WebEx or Skype, or use the audio or video chat tool that comes with Yahoo! Messenger or Google Talk/Google+ Hangouts. The software is easy to download and, again, is free, but you will need a microphone and speakers on your computer, or a headset with a built-in microphone on whatever device you are using, to present on either of these platforms. A webcam is helpful, if you want a user to be able to see you as well as to hear you, but is not absolutely necessary.

Once you have set up your preferred system, send an e-mail to a few or all volunteers, letting them know your user platform and account name. Ask them to send you their account names as well, if they use the same service. For all those that respond, set up a date and time to have a test conversation, either just via audio (which will be like a conference call, but with the added bonus of also having a private chat room where everyone participating can send text messages during the meeting) or with video as well (though this will work only one-on-one, not with a group, unless you are willing to pay a fee).

Try these test audio and video sessions more than once. See how you like communicating this way, see how volunteers like it (or don't), and consider what role live audio and video might eventually play in your organization. As you use these audio and video tools, consider ways that volunteers could use this easy and free electronic form of contact to talk to each other, to employees at your organization, or even with clients of your organization. And if you do any international projects, contact through voice-over-Internet protocol—also known as Internet phone calls—truly makes the globe smaller, allowing for immediate contact with anyone using the same service, at *no cost*.

Be aware that you can involve volunteers in an audio or video conference even if they do not have a computer. Many online phone technologies, such as Skype or Google Talk, give you the option of contacting someone via a landline telephone number anywhere in the world. You have to initiate the call (the volunteer cannot call in directly), but once connected, the person using a phone can hear everyone else and vice versa. Be aware that there is usually a charge for calling a landline phone from your computer, but the cost is extremely low—even to call an international number.

It can be tempting to multi-task when you are on a phone call, online or via your telephone, such as reading e-mail as the other person talks. Try not to do that, as the person on the other end of the line,

volunteer or not, can usually tell if you are truly listening. One of the advantages of live video is that you will probably be much more focused on the person you are speaking with than if you were on audio only!

Experimenting with Advanced Internet Tools

Instant messaging and audio/video conferencing tools are enough to get you started on a more advanced tech-use track without becoming overwhelmed. Using these tools will also build your capacity to use more advanced tools, which will be referenced throughout coming chapters.

In experimenting with Internet tools, remember that some of your current volunteers will be limited from participating because of their lack of tech literacy or tech comfort, lack of fast Internet access, lack of language literacy in general, or a disability that does not allow them to use a certain tool. E-mail and Web-based communities are accessible for everyone, including people with sight impairments, so long as participants are literate; more advanced tools such as live audio or video may not be accessible for some of your volunteers. Experiment with various ways of communicating and encourage volunteers to do so as well, but also assure volunteers that you will not switch to using high-tech tools exclusively. You will add them to the growing exchange options but not use them to substitute entirely for current ways of communicating. These tools should make everyone more accessible to each other, not less!

We discuss more about accessibility in virtual volunteering throughout this book, and it is the specific focus of chapter 9.

Some More Ideas

Here are some additional ideas to get you thinking about ways to use synchronous communication tools with volunteers:

- Use instant messaging, live audio or video, or Web conferencing for special, one-time events, such as featuring a special guest speaker, or for regularly scheduled events, such as an online meeting held on the first Tuesday of every month.

- Use a chat room to make a major announcement to volunteers and give volunteers the opportunity to express emotion, provide immediate feedback, and ask questions that can be immediately answered.

- Use a video conference to introduce a new staff member to volunteers, allowing for a more visual, lively introduction than just sending out an e-mail.

- Use a video conference as a way for remote volunteers and clients to ask questions of a featured expert in a particular subject or field or to meet online with the executive director of an agency.

- Allow remote volunteers to view a live online broadcast of a major event by your organization and to have a simultaneous online conversation about what they are viewing.

You can use some tools together at the same time. For example, many people on conference calls engage in simultaneous instant messaging with each other, creating an easy way for the call moderator to immediately see questions everyone may have or trends in participant reactions.

The more your employees and volunteers are experienced in using these tools, the greater the chance that an online event using these tools will be successful. Staff may need training in order to get started, as well as prompts by more experienced online volunteers.

Some Possible Issues

As with everything else, there are downsides to using synchronous communication tools. Many or all require users to:

- Be at their computers all at the same time—and that takes away one of the primary attractions of working remotely for staff and online volunteers. By contrast, asynchronous e-mail and e-mail-based or Web-based communities allow users to participate, ask questions, provide feedback, etc. at any time of the day or week, as often as they want.

- Think and react immediately. Many people instead want time to reflect, consider, and craft a response carefully.

- Have the same software or operating systems or the latest hardware and operating systems. Not everyone has these! By requiring remote staff and online volunteers to have these tools, you will be excluding at least some people.

- Organize strong facilitation to keep the conversation going or to keep it from spiraling out of control. A lot of pre-planning is also often necessary to get all of the participants together at the same time, set the agenda, make sure everyone understands the agenda and protocol before the meeting, etc. This can be time-intensive, and many organizations lack both the time and expertise to undertake these steps.

- Have an excellent understanding of how the technology works and a high comfort level in using it. If a volunteer has a bad experience trying to use one of these tools for the first time, he or she is going to be very reluctant to try it again in the future.

- Control numbers. Having 1,000 people on a text-based asynchronous online discussion group is usually not overwhelming, because only a small percentage of the members may actually post frequently—the rest will lurk or post infrequently—and members will not all post at the same time. Also, people can easily ignore messages they do not want to read. Having 1,000 people on a *live* chat, however, can quickly become overwhelming, because most of the participants will try to engage in conversation.

Note as well that *onsite* participants with laptops or smartphones can become so engrossed in a simultaneous chat online that they do not interact with the people right next to them or ask questions of whoever is presenting! Help everyone to engage to the fullest.

Experiment with synchronous communication tools in informal situations, again and again, before you commit to their regular use. Your goal is to find a tool that works for everyone, is inclusive, and is popular and pervasive among volunteers.

The key to successful use of synchronous online tools is having a concrete reason for using them and expressing this reason clearly and effectively to potential participants. What do you want the volunteers to value about the real-time encounter and what do you want to happen as a result?

Survey Tools and Online Scheduling

In the old days, leaders of volunteer efforts were limited by small or nonexistent budgets from communicating frequently or managing efficiently. Today the Web provides so many tools that are easy to use, work effectively, and are *free*. And there is so much potential for newer gizmos, apps, and special sites. Two examples of these newer available tools are online surveying and online scheduling.

Want to get volunteers to evaluate a training session or special event? Need to reach agreement on anything from a new policy to the colors of your logo? The easiest way to get such comments or input from volunteers is with an online survey. Two of the most popular sites are SurveyMonkey and Survey-Gizmo, both of which offer free access for creating and running small surveys and reasonably-priced memberships for more complex surveys and greater numbers of respondents.

Use your imagination for ways to employ online surveys. In an *e-Volunteerism* article, "SurveyMonkey Changed My Life: A Volunteer Manager's Perspective," Laura Hamilton, volunteer manager at George House Trust, the largest HIV social care charity in the northwest of England, described seeking a way to schedule and manage volunteer rotations. She stumbled upon SurveyMonkey: "Whilst exploring how it worked, it struck me that with a bit of tweaking, we could set up a form which, rather than collecting feedback or evaluation data, would allow people to tell us their availability and sign up for shifts."[9]

Which brings us to a set of online tools that seem to be growing in number recently: sites dedicated to letting volunteers develop their own schedules. VolunteerSpot and OrgAction are but two examples. Such tools are especially useful for all-volunteer organizations needing to coordinate the wide variety of times their members are available to do service.

Finally, you will find many uses, volunteer management-related and other, for sites and

> ### Reminder about the
> ### Virtual Volunteering Wiki
>
> This chapter talks about a lot of different online interactive tools, far beyond just e-mail and Web pages. But just as it is not possible to list or review every organization engaged in virtual volunteering, it is also impossible to list every online interactive tool available for working with volunteers. Please visit the Virtual Volunteering Wiki (virtualvolunteering.wikispaces.com), where we list the many resources that have contributed to our learning and keep a more up-to-date list of tools than we could in a traditional printed publication.

smartphone apps that allow people to determine a meeting time convenient to all, such as Doodle or ScheduleOnce. These tools are being developed regularly; a good way to know what is available is to have online volunteers do this research for you or to review the TechSoup community forum for discussions regarding such tools.

Social Media Interconnectedness

Two terms that have been in vogue for a few years are *online social networking* and *Web 2.0* (meaning the "second incarnation" of the Web). But the Internet has *always* been touted as a place to exchange ideas and to create networks and communities that defy traditional community structures and hierarchies. Perhaps what is happening now is that many people are realizing for the first time that the Internet is an ongoing series of very human conversations and human-to-human, rather than computer-to-computer, connections.

What's relatively new about social networking sites is that they allow people to identify their *offline* friends and connections to everyone with whom they interact online. So, in principle (depending on how you have configured your privacy settings), your friends, family members, professional colleagues, and others are able to see everyone else with whom you associate. In turn, you are able to see the associations of your friends and connections as well—even to form your own associations with them directly, if you choose. You post status updates to these platforms, anything from "I am working on the annual report" to "I have to leave work now to go pick up my daughter from school," and anyone in your network can see this status update. At the time of writing, Facebook, Google+, Twitter, and MySpace are the four most popular online *social* networking sites, with LinkedIn and Plaxo being the two most popular online *professional* networking sites.

It's no surprise that online social networks have both an upside and a downside. They can be fantastic in helping online volunteers to become more to you—and each other—than just an e-mail address and lots of text. In exchange, you can give online volunteers a sense of your own personality by sharing things like online photos from your recent trip to Bali. But what are the boundaries between personal and private online activities, whether for yourself or for volunteers?

When you are posting your status to Facebook, are you representing your organization or your private self? Do you want volunteers to know that you are having your third beer at a pub downtown? Do you want them to know how you are voting in an upcoming election? Do you want them to know how cute you think a particular actor is? And do you want to know all the same information about them?

Other questions will soon surface. Is it appropriate for you to accept invitations from volunteers to connect to your individual profile on a social networking site? Is it appropriate to ask volunteers to use their online social networking profiles to talk about their volunteering activities?

We answer all these questions with a hearty *maybe*!

As we have noted in earlier chapters, your organization should have a written policy regarding how employees and volunteers should and should not engage as representatives of your organization online. This policy should include representations made via the latest Web 2.0 fads. Make it clear to volunteers, for instance, that while it is fine for them to highlight their role as volunteers for your organization in any online conversation, that does not make them *official representatives* of your organization, and they still must adhere to confidentiality rules. Give them examples of what is and is not appropriate to post online regarding their volunteering.

Acceptable posts by volunteers regarding their service could be:

- *It is a busy day here at the volunteer information booth!*

- *I just spent eight hours straight redesigning a logo for such-and-such organization!*

- *It's not easy to volunteer for such-and-such organization, but I think it's worth it.*

- *Jayne Cravens and/or Susan Ellis are fabulous!*

Unacceptable posts might be:

- *I think the volunteer orientation by such-and-such organization is long, boring, and stupid.* (Although you should encourage such honest, valid opinions to be shared directly with the organization instead.)

- *Here is where I will be today with all the Girl Scouts from Troop 1234567.*[10] (This violates Girl Scout policy regarding sharing information about the actual location of girls at non-public events.)

- *So-and-so is a stupid volunteer and I hate working with her.* (Personal attacks among volunteers should never be tolerated.)

Encourage volunteers to let you know of *any* comments or questions they see online regarding your organization—good and bad. Make it clear to volunteers that you are *not* trying to shut down dissent but want to deal with complaints and violations of your organization's policies in a timely manner.

Policy Considerations

Determine your policies regarding linking to volunteers on online networks, as well as for asking volunteers to use their online social networking profiles as a part of their volunteering. Specifically:

- Your organization's volunteers and staff may want to keep their online social networking activities separate from their professional and volunteering activities. Most employees and volunteers will be happy to include mention of their service to your organization on a professional networking site such as

LinkedIn or an issues-focused network such as Change.org, but do not *require* any volunteer or staff member to link to your organization via a *social* networking site such as Facebook, Google+, or MySpace. In the same vein, if you invite a volunteer or employee to become a friend online, include a note that you will not be offended if the invitation is declined.

- A volunteer may engage in or promote activities via the volunteer's online profile on a social networking platform that your organization does not wish to be associated with. Perhaps there are pictures of the volunteer on the site, or links to videos, that make you uncomfortable, even if these are not in violation of any policies or procedures. Keep in mind that volunteers may be engaging in *offline* activities your nonprofit would not necessarily want to be associated with either! (As an example, think about the messages on many t-shirts—and whether you provide suggestions for which should not be worn by volunteers and staff when connected to organization work.) Consider creating a policy regarding why your organization might refuse to link to a person's profile on a social networking site, and share this policy with volunteers. You could even ask for their help in drafting the policy; by involving them in the discussion, volunteers will have a sense of ownership of the rules.

- Staff members and volunteers may be asked to link to other employees and volunteers as "friends" on social networking sites, but they may not want to do so, at least not with everyone. We do not all define *friend* the same way. It is easier for an individual to turn down a link request on a professional networking site such as LinkedIn (with criteria that do not sound personal, such as, "I'm sorry, but I only link to people I have worked with directly") than it is to tell someone requesting to be friends on Facebook that he or she is "not really a friend." Employees who decline online friend invitations from volunteers or even other staff members may

end up hurting the feelings of co-workers. Encourage employees and volunteers to respect that some people may want to keep their social network activities separate from their work or volunteering relationships.

- Perhaps everyone needs to have two online social networking profiles: one for friends they socialize with and another for associates they know through work or volunteering.

There have never been absolute lines in our lives where work and volunteering end and social activities begin, of course. Similarly, this means there will always be gray areas when it comes to online interaction; people who work together do often become friends outside of work or volunteering, even without the Internet. Perhaps your organization needs to address this not so much through written policies but through frequent discussions about the issues. You want to create a culture where employees and volunteers are always being thoughtful about all of their online activities.

Virtual Volunteering Teams

To this point, we have spoken mainly about one-on-one relationships between a manager and an online volunteer, with each online volunteer working independently as an individual contributor. However, this is not the only type of virtual volunteering. Sometimes groups of online volunteers, and perhaps employees as well, work together as a team.

For instance, a group of online volunteers, with or without participating paid staff, may:

- Share the responsibilities of moderating an online community or online event.

- Work under the leadership of one volunteer to put together a new section of an organization's Web site or translate a large document from or into another language.

- Manage a shared online space or wiki, allowing everyone to make edits and comments on the development of a volunteer handbook, policies, a teaching manual to use with clients, etc.

- Develop software together that your organization will use or offer to others for use.

- Work together on producing a publication, a video, or an online tutorial.

These groups of online volunteers are called *virtual teams*, *dispersed teams*, or *dispersed working groups*. Whatever you call them, they present special challenges but also great opportunities.

Challenges and Advantages to a Virtual Team

Virtual volunteering teams tend not to last long; some go several weeks, some last several months, but few last for more than a year. They disperse when the project ends or when most of the original members move on to other projects. Being focused on a specific project with a set timetable helps limit unexpected drop-outs; people will fulfill tasks and then announce they would like to leave the team, rather than the other way around.

Managing any team is tricky even if all the members are onsite together. Managing a team that is dispersed and communicates only or mostly with online tools can be even trickier—although some managers prefer online work because it is so much easier to track the contribution and status of all team members. One advantage that virtual volunteering teams have over other kinds of work-based virtual teams is that the volunteers have all sought out involvement with the organization and the team. You don't have to convince the team members that working together is a good idea; they are already convinced, and that is why they volunteered.

A big challenge to success with a virtual team is establishing a sense of *team*, so that all members are working together, not individually, toward one ultimate goal: adhering to real deadlines and producing tangible outputs from each member.

Online teams of volunteers work best when they are focused on a specific project with a set starting and ending date, clearly defined criteria for success, identified milestones, and clearly assigned team member roles. Making virtual teams project based forces the team to focus quickly on meeting the deadline, as it is easier to identify what needs to be done, get going, and finish the tasks!

Repeated interactions and shared experiences are key in establishing a sense of team among online volunteers. An online team is most successful when it can move quickly from procedural messages to task-focused conversations. Trust is quickly established as team members fulfill their tasks, when action is taken, and when accomplishments, however small, are achieved and acknowledged by the team leader and other members.

Considering Who Should Be on the Team

As with any other volunteer activity, a clearly-defined project is the essential first step in creating an online team. The team leader, whether a staff member or online volunteer, should be involved in writing the team project description, identifying what skills or other requirements will be needed from team members, and selecting the members.

A good way to guarantee success among a virtual volunteering team is to ensure that its members are all veteran online volunteers—people who have already undertaken a successful assignment for your organization; are part of your organization's online community for volunteers; feel a sense of connection to the organization; and have a great deal of experience communicating online. Ideally, team members should already know each other, at least on a cursory level, from participating in your online forum for volunteers.

That said, a virtual team made up of brand-new online volunteers who do not know each other *can* work. The online volunteers that make up most of the services delivered by some of the organizations we have cited (LibriVox and Project Gutenberg/Distributed Proofreaders, for example) have usually never met each other face-to-face.

Virtual volunteering team members do not have to be geographically dispersed; they could all be in the same town but still interact primarily online. Such teams do not have to deal with time zone differences or, usually, language barriers. They all have at least their current city or region in common, and that can be enough to feel a connection to fellow online team members.

However, online teams may be in different time zones, which requires advance planning to select or rotate meeting times so that all members feel included. Individuals from different cultures may face challenges in communication and group dynamics. The team leader needs to be good at identifying and accommodating different styles based on nationality, and identify and head off potential conflicts and misunderstandings that can arise in text-based communication. Asynchronous tools such as e-mail give individuals more time to read messages and craft responses, and this is especially appealing to people who are not native speakers of your language. This can make cultural differences less noticeable and make team members more equal in communications.

Getting an Online Team Started

Once a team is formed, here are six immediate steps to take to get things moving:

1. The team leader should quickly introduce himself or herself to all the other members and ask all members to introduce themselves, too, via either synchronous or asynchronous communication. (See below for some tips on introductions.)

2. Share everyone's addresses for e-mail, IM, and live audio or video chat, plus other contact information.

3. Mutually develop a protocol for all team members to communicate with each other regularly and to report in about what they are doing, how they are feeling, challenges they are facing, etc. Clearly articulate expected response times and how messages should be acknowledged as received and read. The team leader can suggest a protocol, but you are likelier to get all team members on board if everyone has the chance to discuss exactly what they can expect from each other.

4. If an online workspace has not yet been selected, chose one immediately to allow everyone to collaborate on documents, spreadsheets and presentations, share a calendar, and otherwise work together online. There is a massive range of options for online shared work spaces, which we discuss throughout this book.

5. The team leader should seek a date for an initial live online meeting with all team members together and provide a way for all team members to provide input to that meeting.

6. Assign roles to each team member and determine immediate next steps to get to work on the assignment. By assigning discrete tasks to each team member, the work is shared appropriately, with each volunteer being comfortable with the assigned task, and there is no ambiguity among team members about what each of the others is doing. Some team members may be doing more than others in terms of time contributed, which is okay. Stress that each piece of the overall project is important and, therefore, every team member is important, regardless of the size of his or her role and contribution.

These steps should be done within the first or second week of a team's formation.

Introductions

The team leader should initiate team member introductions as soon as the members join—live (if all members can participate) or via e-mail or a short video that members can download on demand if everyone cannot be online at the same time. Keep introductions brief but friendly and social. For example:

An Online Team Forms a Nonprofit

In 2001, author Jayne Cravens recruited three online volunteers to moderate an online forum to broadcast live on the Internet during a larger event. The three online volunteers were several hundred miles apart from each other in three different time zones, had never met each other, and had never volunteered for Jayne before. The volunteers worked together to create a system to quickly process incoming messages sent to the live forum and, in the end, the event was a great success. These three online volunteers enjoyed their experience together so much that they stayed in touch online and even went on to form a nonprofit of their own: Afghans for Afghans.

Hi, my name is Ruth Morris. I live in Spottsville, Kentucky with my husband, two kids and three dogs. I'm a Web designer professionally, and I'm also a Girl Scout troop leader. I have profiles on both Facebook and LinkedIn if you would like to know more about me! I signed up to help develop this new online volunteering guidebook because I have volunteered online in the past many times and feel that I have a lot to contribute. Also, I really love Our Town Nonprofit Organization and want to help them in any way I can!

There is nothing wrong with developing and continuing social rapport along with task-oriented messages, and it can help very much with developing a sense of team. However, team leaders should be prepared to keep members from getting carried away. Social messages should not outnumber task-oriented messages, and forwarded e-mail jokes get annoying *very* quickly.

Communication Options

From the beginning, establish regular times and ways to communicate. In fact, you may want to put the meeting requirement into the task description ("members of the team will meet every Monday online via iVisit") so that you screen out those who would not be available at that time. Reporting requirements must also be clear (see next section).

There are many communications tools available for virtual volunteering teams, which is one of the things that helps with their success. In "The Psychology of Effective Business Communications in Geographically Dispersed Teams," Cisco Systems explains:

It is our belief that teams and individuals are most effective when they are presented with a range of communications options and clear information on which will be most effective at any given time. Knowing the communications preferences of your team members, and being able to see their status or 'presence' in advance of making contact can have a significant positive impact on the effectiveness of team working and knowledge sharing. Simple and instant access to a range of rich communications options that brings together text, voice and video allows individuals and groups to benefit

from much of the additional information that co-located teams take for granted.[11]

But which tool to use?

The nature of the task is an important factor in determining which communication media are best suited to the task's requirements. For example, during the first stages of a project, when relationship building is key, the use of richer media is important because of its high symbol variety and high immediacy of feedback. Conversely, when communication is more task-related, such as sharing guidelines and documents, leaner communication such as email is preferable due to its high rehearsability and high reprocessability.[12]

Use different tools for different occasions. Sometimes, a live audio or video conference, or even a live instant messaging session, might be called for to get something clarified or to re-energize the team, while e-mail or a private online forum with asynchronous messages might be better for routine communications. Free online platforms such as Yahoo! Groups or Google Groups allow a team leader to set up a private forum for team messages, share and archive files, and share a calendar.

In "Communication and Trust in Global Virtual Teams," authors Sirkka L. Jarvenpaa and Dorothy E. Leidner identified factors for success in virtual teams. Almost 10 years after publication, the authors' recommendations are still quite valid:

- *It is critical to engage in an open and thoughtful exchange of messages at the beginning of the team's existence.*

- *Not all individuals may be equally adept at handling the uncertainty and responsibilities inherent in virtual work. Managers should carefully choose individuals for virtual teamwork; such qualities as responsibility, dependability, independence, and self-sufficiency, while desirable even in face-to-face settings, are crucial to the viability of virtual teamwork.*

- *Participants should also have an awareness of the importance of their providing to the others timely and detailed accounts of the work they are doing. Likewise, participants must be aware of the need to provide thorough feedback on the contributions of the other members.*

- *Finally, participants should be aware that it is not the quantity, but the quality and predictability, of their communication that is most critical to the effective functioning of the team.*[13]

The Team Leader's Role

The team leader is, of course, crucial to ensuring productive interaction. Whether an employee or a volunteer, the team leader must keep team members focused on overall objectives and optimize each person's talents. A team leader also must:

- *Clearly communicate availability to team members and explain any delays in responding to team members.*

- *Express enthusiasm and optimism frequently.* A message saying "Great work, everyone!!!" really does have an impact on the motivation of team members.

- *Make suggestions and take the initiative when challenges arise.* A successful team leader will frequently ask for feedback and suggestions from team members but be ready to initiate action. Otherwise, a team leader will be stuck in the mire of waiting-for-someone-to-act that can frequently plague online teams.

- *Combat silence and team withdrawal.* Silence is deadly to a virtual team. If a member goes silent, it is up to the team leader to find out why. A personal e-mail to the unresponsive team member may not be enough to find out the reason behind the silence; perhaps it is time for a phone call. The ideal is to discuss and deal with whatever the problem is and reactivate the member. If the volunteer does withdraw, explain why this has happened to the rest of the team in a non-judgmental way, and seek the team's advice on how that volunteer might be replaced or the tasks could be divided among the remaining members.

- *Manage conflict.* Conflict can occur in virtual teams because people often feel more comfortable expressing a critical opinion online, particularly via text-based communications,

than they do onsite. Therefore, the team leader should be experienced with the dynamics of online communications and prepared to quickly identify and address misunderstandings, frustrations, and pending hostilities.

Since online volunteer teams do not last long, it is difficult to find and cite examples and even harder to find examples that have information online. But here are three:

- OpenOffice.org Community Council (http://council.openoffice.org/)

- The Wikimedia Task Force on Community Health (http://strategy.wikimedia.org/wiki/Task_force/Community_Health)

- The team of online volunteers that moderated the online discussion forum that took place during the onsite events for UN Open Day in Geneva, Switzerland, in October 2001 (http://unv.web.cern.ch/UNV/programme.htm). The forum was sponsored by the UN Volunteers program.

Unlike the late 1990s, when this *Guidebook* was first published, there is now a plethora of books, academic articles, white papers, and other information about virtual teams. Any keyword search on your favorite Internet search engine will give you a long list of suggested titles for further information about working with teams online.

Employee/Volunteer (Onsite and Online) Relationships

Tension between paid employees and any type of volunteer is a frequently discussed topic among VRMs and one of the most often requested training topics by people who work with volunteers. Despite removing onsite interaction, the cyberspace environment does not eliminate employee/volunteer tensions. All of the factors that lead to employee/volunteer misunderstandings onsite can also happen online, some with even more intensity:

- Volunteers and employees can misread text-based communications, interpreting a message or status update as hostile or insulting.

- Volunteers can read an employee's online messages and somehow feel that they have been left out of an activity.

- Employees can read volunteers' online messages and feel that a volunteer is stepping on their turf.

- Employees can feel that volunteers are getting more recognition than paid staff for their work online.

- An employee can define a prompt response as getting back to a volunteer's question in just 48 hours; the volunteer can feel slighted because the response came two days later rather than within minutes.

- Online volunteers, some of whom are using the latest devices and online tools, may feel superior to employees who are not as tech savvy, despite the staff's extensive expertise and merits in non-tech areas.

Tension most often arises from misunderstandings. In chapter 3, we emphasized the vital role of well-planned and clearly-written volunteer position descriptions, tools that are fundamental to successful working relationships among everyone. The person in charge of the work should help design and express what the volunteer will do; develop the implementation plan for accomplishing goals; and define such things as "frequency of ongoing contact needed." The position description then serves as a guide to recruit the most qualified and interested volunteer, who agrees to the activities required. With this as a basis for beginning a virtual assignment, confusion or misinterpretations can be prevented.

No matter how well planned, there is potential for error any time humans interact. However, there are several ways to limit or overcome common working relationship problems, most of which require the intervention and leadership of the VRM:

- Employees and leadership volunteers who supervise and support online volunteers must be regularly and easily accessible to these volunteers, answering questions and providing guidance as needs arise. As we've already mentioned, the speed of replies and support (on both sides) should be discussed and, if necessary, negotiated or online volunteers may become disgruntled, feeling they are not getting a timely response.

- Include at least a mention of online volunteering activities in every update provided to anyone about the state of volunteering at the organization. If you are asked to say a few words at the next staff meeting, for instance, make sure at least some of those words are about what is happening online. Similarly, always add an update about online volunteers in any written report about all volunteers. Keep a log of these updates—what you said and when—so that if someone claims, "You never told me online volunteers were doing such-and-such," you can quickly point out that you did. In addition, report on both successes and problems in staff meetings, showing you are aware that things do not always work perfectly.

- The VRM should provide staff the training and support they need regarding virtual volunteering. In addition to a lunchtime presentation or two, point staff to online resources that allow them to learn on their own, in their own time. Conversely, it's only fair to give online volunteers some sense of the demands on the paid staff. Remember that working remotely means the volunteers do not see for themselves how busy everyone is. Encourage a degree of patience.

- The VRM must stay in touch and in tune with those working with online volunteers. Stopping by someone's office and asking informally, "How are things going with your online volunteers?" can be a non-intimidating way to find out what is and is not working and doesn't require a formal survey.

- Credit employees when online volunteer successes are celebrated. When you laud an online volunteer for a task well done, include acknowledgement of the staff liaison who contributed to the success as well.

- Deal with complaints immediately. Ignoring hard feelings allows them to fester and grow. A text-based conflict can grow worse with more text, no matter how carefully you write. If needed, pick up the phone or walk down the hall and talk to the people involved to resolve misunderstandings and complaints quickly.

Troubleshooting Not-So-Virtual Problems

As with any traditional onsite volunteer or employee, it is inevitable that a problem will surface in a virtual volunteering assignment no matter how detailed and thorough your screening, preparation, and support systems are or how detailed your policies and procedures.

The more regularly you communicate with online volunteers, the quicker you will be able to identify potential problems and, ideally, prevent them in the future. Your goal is to recognize an issue, diagnose its probable cause, and create a course of action to address the problem and get the assignment completed.

When faced with a problem regarding an online volunteer, answer these troubleshooting questions:

- What is the problem, exactly? Even if you are not sure of the cause of the problem or who is at fault, what would you all agree is the challenge that you, the volunteer, and others involved now face? For instance:

  ○ The volunteer's assignment did not get done on time.

  ○ The volunteer's work did not satisfy the person who drafted the assignment.

  ○ The volunteer has not provided written updates as requested.

  ○ The point of contact for a team of online volunteers was not available for two weeks to answer questions from volunteers.

- Were all of the proper protocols followed in creating the assignment, recruiting volunteers, choosing the specific volunteer, orienting that volunteer, and preparing for the assignment? If not, where did the protocol break down? Does

everyone involved agree with your assessment of where the protocol was not followed?

- Has something happened in the volunteer's life that makes completing the task harder than originally anticipated?

- Has something happened in the employee's work or life that makes providing support to the volunteer harder than originally anticipated?

- Did the volunteer over-estimate personal skills or availability?

- Did the person who was supposed to be working with or supporting the volunteer over-estimate personal skills or availability?

- Could the problem be addressed with more training, better instructions, or additional tools for the volunteer or for the person working with or supporting this volunteer?

- Could the problem be addressed with a sincere apology and ownership of what went wrong by the volunteer or the person in charge of supporting this volunteer?

Your diagnosis will determine your course of action. As always, honesty is the best policy: Share concerns openly with both volunteers and employees. Use voice communication if that would lead to quicker answers and resolution; it is often better to have a short but uncomfortable verbal interaction with a volunteer to improve productivity or make a re-assignment than to jeopardize agency services.

No matter what you do, do *something*. Here are four important considerations:

1. If you do not act when a volunteer (online or off) is performing poorly, or when an employee is not providing proper support, you send the message that it does not matter or that you are in denial about the problem being real.

2. No one volunteers to do a bad job! If a volunteer is not doing something well, do not waste that person's time by letting the mistakes continue. Be respectful of a person's voluntary contribution and help that person to do the best possible job—or release the

volunteer to contribute to a different organization or to rethink volunteering altogether.

3. It is better to take a volunteer off the hands of a staff member who is not providing proper support than to create hostility or drive the volunteer away. If a staff member is not providing the support needed, say so, and ask how he or she would like to address the situation. Would it be best for the volunteer to be re-assigned to a different task and a different manager, to give the staff member time to reassess readiness to support online volunteers? The manager will probably appreciate your providing a graceful exit. However, to prevent similar problems from resurfacing, be honest about your concerns to the manager if the manager requests a new online volunteer in the future.

4. If a staff person is not providing the support needed by a volunteer but seems to be in denial about why this is a problem, it may be time to go to that person's supervisor to ask for help. Do not do so unless you have plenty of evidence to back up your case and you have communicated your concerns fully to the staff member first. But if you cannot change behavior that is interfering with volunteer success, you should be the in-house advocate and go to the next level of authority.

Online Volunteers Who Cross Behavior Boundaries

Some people share absolutely everything about themselves—and that may not be appropriate in the volunteer role they have accepted. While it may be flattering that they enjoy a trusting online relationship with you as their organization contact, confiding intimately-detailed information may make you uncomfortable. They also may have an expectation of confidentiality about their communications with you that would be unrealistic in any scenario. This can be especially awkward with a teenager.

For instance, what would you do if an underage person who is your friend on Facebook posted about engaging in an activity that is illegal for her or him at this time—leaving home, having sex, drinking

alcohol, etc.? Granted, experiences shared by teens through social media can be exaggerated and written to shock or impress. But what if a teen volunteer e-mailed you privately about committing an act of violence against themselves or another person?

A good way to approach how to handle such scenarios, particularly if the information came to you directly, is to first think about what you would do if an adult told you the same thing—after all, drugs and violence are equally illegal for all ages. Some responses should be obvious:

- If you have any knowledge of an imminent crime and can prevent it by reporting it, go to the police.

- If it involves anything like bodily harm to someone else, again, go to the police.

- If it is talk of suicide, contact the parents and, if it seems imminent, the police.

For talk of drug or sex experimentation, it may be time to call a school's guidance counselor for advice; you are not calling to turn in a student or to even share the student's name but, rather, to get advice on how to respond to any student's sharing of information with you. In the interim, while you are waiting to get this advice, take the Dear Abby approach and strongly encourage the teen volunteer to immediately talk to a parent or guardian.

If the problem surrounds the parents themselves, and the youth is in any danger of abuse, you are likely legally obligated to report your concerns to child protection authorities.

These issues often come up in working with teenagers in any context—as online volunteers, as onsite volunteers, or as clients. For example, at the volunteer program Susan ran for the Philadelphia Family Court in the 1970s, volunteers obviously had to be prepared for the possibility that the teen with whom they had been matched might talk about drug use or a crime—these were kids on probation, after all. The program differentiated between things that were outright illegal and things that skirted moral or values issues. Since these teens were under court jurisdiction anyway, a reporting system was available. But the program also wanted to preserve some sanctity of the volunteer/teen relationship, too. That is what friendship is all about.

Part of the responsibility of involving teens as volunteers, online or onsite, is creating a trusting, safe atmosphere where they not only provide service but also can learn and grow. Not every adult is good at working with young people, online or face-to-face. If your organization involves teens as volunteers, you may want to invite someone from a nonprofit, teen-oriented organization to join your staff for lunch one day to talk about how to handle different scenarios that come up—or could come up—in working with teen volunteers.

While we have just singled out teens for inappropriate behavior, it is important to note that such behavior also happens with adults. Use your established policies and procedures for onsite work among employees and volunteers to help you identify and address inappropriate online behavior, no matter the perpetrator.

Firing an Online Volunteer

Can you fire an online volunteer? Certainly! Your policies and procedures should define what activities merit dismissal of any volunteer, onsite or online. You should convey your expectation of quality performance during orientation for all new volunteers—including how the organization will handle unsatisfactory work or inappropriate behavior.

If a problem is a clear violation of stated policy, you must immediately make contact with the volunteer; confirm that he or she did, indeed, violate the rules; and decide if the violation merits suspension or outright dismissal. Often, if you both agree that the rule has been broken, you can give the volunteer the opportunity to make a graceful exit; it will be in your written records why the volunteer was let go, but it is not necessarily a reason that needs to be shared with others.

Of course, you hope to prevent the need to terminate service by properly screening and placing the right volunteer in the right assignment, but human behavior is not always predictable. Ideally, if a problem arises, you can troubleshoot and resolve the situation before it becomes serious. If it continues, you need to decide if re-assignment will neutralize the process and enable the volunteer to continue serving the organization more successfully or if the person is simply not able to do the work as needed.

Acknowledge performance that is below expectations as soon as it occurs, rather than waiting until what could have been a matter of training becomes an entrenched problem. That means you may write an e-mail that says:

Thank you again for completing the assignment. Per our conversation on the phone earlier today, the assignment was four days late. As we discussed in that conversation, completing online assignments on time is imperative. If you realize that you will not be able to complete an assignment on time, contact me ASAP so we can discuss either re-assigning the task or extending the deadline date.

Engage the volunteer in suggesting solutions or alternatives to set things right; this is often best done verbally rather than via a written e-mail. In those conversations, make it clear that being asked to stop volunteering is the consequence of noncompliance.

Document your interactions and assessment in writing so that you can justify your decision to let a volunteer go, if the need arises. You may want to consult with your human resources manager about the wording of such justification. If the volunteer disputes the reasons for dismissal in a public way, you may need to rely on your documentation to defend your decision to executives or the board.

If you need to let other volunteers know that a person is no longer with the organization as a volunteer, then say so simply: "Joe is no longer volunteering with us. His tasks are going to be taken over by . . . If you do not have his personal contact information and would like it, let me know and I will pass on your request to him." There is usually no need for further explanation to other volunteers.

If the volunteer disputes the reasons for dismissal in a public way, such as via Facebook or Google+, or a blog, you may need to provide further information to continuing volunteers about the dismissal. You may need to talk with your organization's public relations manager to address online criticism by a former volunteer; "dealing with online criticism" is discussed more fully in chapter 10.

After dismissing a volunteer, change the passwords of any online resource that the online volunteer could access; in fact, you might want to do this before you actually dismiss the volunteer. Remove the volunteer from your online forum for volunteers.

NOTES

1. Segments of this section were adapted from Jarene Frances Lee with Julia M. Catagnus, *What We Learned (the Hard Way) about Supervising Volunteers* (Philadelphia: Energize, Inc., 1999).
2. Excerpted from an e-mail interview of Hugh McGuire by Jayne Cravens, 2009.
3. LibriVox Online Forum <http://librivox.org/forum/>.
4. There is an ever-growing number of online tools that allow you to track projects and people. Some are even free! However, because of the vast number of these tools, we are not attempting to list them all here. Please see the TechSoup Community Forum (http://forums.techsoup.org/cs/community/f/) for recommendations and discussions regarding such online collaboration and project management tools.
5. Arizona Pioneers' Home Volunteers Association <http://www.aztecfreenet.org/azph/>.
6. YouthBeat, the youth marketing research service part of C&R Research in Chicago, conducted a survey in 2009 that said teens (14 to 18) and tweens (11 to 13) overwhelmingly prefer others to text versus e-mail them. Reported by Jennifer Kruger, "Teens Prefer Texting to Email," PMA Newsline Blog, January 21, 2011 <http://pmanewsline.com/2011/01/21/teens-prefer-texting-to-email/#.Ujc1fXnD8dU>.
7. "Oh My God!"
8. Section adapted from Jayne Cravens, "Using Real-Time Communications (VoIP, Chat, Instant Messaging, Etc.) with Volunteers," 2011 <http://www.coyotecommunications.com/culture/chat.shtml>.
9. Laura Hamilton, "SurveyMonkey Changed My Life: A Volunteer Manager's Perspective," *e-Volunteerism* (2010) XI, 1 <http://www.e-volunteerism.com/volume-xi-issue-1-october-2010/feature-articles/889>.
10. The authors apologize if there really is a Girl Scout Troop 1234567.
11. Cisco Systems, "The Psychology of Effective Business Communications in Geographically Dispersed Teams," 2006 <http://newsroom.cisco.com/dlls/2006/eKits/psychology_business_comm.pdf>.
12. *Ibid.*
13. Sirkka L. Jarvenpaa and Dorothy E. Leidner, "Communication and Trust in Global Virtual Teams," *Journal of Computer-Mediated Communication*, III, 4, published online June 2006 <http://onlinelibrary.wiley.com/doi/10.1111/j.1083-6101.1998.tb00080.x/full>.

Chapter 7
Advanced Techniques for Working Online with Volunteers
Making the Most of Evolving Technology Tools

New Internet and networking tools emerge *all the time*, and the borders between text, audio, and video, as well as between computers, cell phones, smartphones, radio, television, and other media, are disappearing. People watch TV on their smartphones, surf the Web via their televisions, and send video commentaries to their local newspapers. Because new tools are always just around the corner, and because the ways people use networking tools are in constant flux, it is hard to stay informed about communications developments and to separate the hype about a new tech tool from the reality of its practical value.

We wrote this book with an eye to principles that will always apply, no matter what networking tools come into being. This chapter is no exception: the names of various Internet tools for volunteers may change, and new tools may emerge to replace them, but we predict that the fundamentals will stay largely the same.

We have already acknowledged that it is impossible to use every tech tool available to you and that not every tech tool is appropriate for every organization or volunteer engagement scheme. Still, everyone who works with volunteers needs to stay on top of emerging trends; you do not have to try every new tool as it comes out, but you do need to know what tools your colleagues, volunteers, and even clients use and what is proving to be valuable to all these groups.

This chapter is part of the overall technology road map every volunteer resources manager (VRM) should follow—or adapt—in order to efficiently and successfully engage volunteers. Read this chapter even if you consider yourself a beginner or intermediate Internet tool user. It is a mistake to think you will never have to engage with volunteers in any of the more advanced online activities highlighted here. Eventually, you will likely need to use some of these tools or at least apply the principles of using these tools to whatever even newer tools emerge next.

As always, our first piece of advice is to connect with TechSoup to keep up with all the online tools and gadgets available to you for volunteer involvement. Besides keeping up with new technology and good deals on technology for nonprofits, the site has a learning center area[1] devoted to volunteerism.

Let's take a closer look at the ways you can use available technology to expand how you communicate and work with any volunteers, but especially those in virtual assignments.

Blogging by, for, and about Volunteers

The word *blog* is short for *Web log,* an ongoing record of observations (think the captain's log on *Star Trek,* but public instead of private). In addition to the writer or presenter sharing personal observations, others can post a response or make their own comments at the end of the blog as well, for everyone to see. Most blogs are in writing, but some people produce audio blogs (à la Captain Kirk) or even video blogs (vblogs). Blogging is not a new concept; people have been posting essays and observations online, and inviting feedback, long before the snazzy jargon.[2]

Most blogs are written in the first person, have lots of "I" statements, and read as if someone is speaking the words. They are an opportunity to relate facts but also to relate feelings and opinions. The appeal of blogs for an online audience is that they are more personal and less formal than other information on a Web site, in an e-mail newsletter, or in a traditional report. Readers or viewers who love blogs want to connect with an organization, cause, or a particular department or program on a more personal level; they are more intensely interested in an organization than the general public as a whole and will read or watch blogs religiously.

For a blog to appeal to readers or viewers, it must be frequently updated—at least bi-weekly, and some organizations publish a new text-based blog *every* day.

There are various ways people can be notified that a blog has been updated. They can chose to:

- Visit the Web site to see if something new has been posted.

- Subscribe to the blog via a special tool called RSS (Really Simple Syndication), which will automatically provide a link to the new information as soon as an update is made.

- Subscribe to receive blog update notifications via e-mail.

- Watch for notices about the blog via a status update from someone they connect to on Facebook, Twitter, LinkedIn, Google+, or another social network site.

How to Create Your Blog

You do *not* need special software to create a text-based blog; the most popular text-based blog platforms are free and very easy to use. (Refer to TechSoup or Wikipedia regarding your platform options and to view what colleagues at other organizations and current volunteers are using.) You can type your text directly into the Web interface provided by the blogging platform or cut and paste your text into it from whatever software you use for word processing or text editing. You can also configure your blog so that no comment on an entry becomes visible to the public until you have approved it.

The blog ideally should be part of or linked from your organization's Web site. If you produce a video blog, you can upload each edition to sites like YouTube or Vimeo and then link to it from your Web site and your various online social networking profiles. This saves bandwidth on your own Web site and helps your video reach a much bigger audience.

The nature of blogs makes them perfect tools for anyone who works with volunteers, as well as for volunteers themselves. Who might read or watch a blog you create? The potential audience includes

current volunteers, potential volunteers, employees, funders, potential funders, and even the media. Obviously, each of these audiences will be interested in different topics, so you should develop a communication strategy for what you most want your blog to accomplish. Among other things, your blog can:

- Inspire more people to volunteer.

- Recognize current volunteers and keep them motivated.

- Encourage both the public and employees to recognize volunteers' contributions and their importance to the organization.

- Help donors understand the time and effort needed to engage and support volunteers effectively.

What to Say in Your Blog

What was your first thought at the idea of producing a regular blog? Something like, "Where do you think I am going to find the time to do *that*?!"? Here's good news: *you* already *produce materials for a blog.* You can use excerpts from all sorts of things you and volunteers have already written—program reports, newsletter articles, or even interesting e-mails (with permission).

Consider this starter set of ideas for volunteer-related blog content, written from three different perspectives.

- A VRM can use the blog to:
  - Review challenges the organization is facing in recruiting volunteers
  - Talk about the introduction of virtual volunteering to the organization
  - Note some early successes with virtual volunteering
  - Highlight a particular experience with a volunteer (online or not)
  - Talk about a training session that was just held for volunteers
  - Describe a single "typical" work day coordinating volunteers

- ○ Reflect on the last year of volunteer involvement

- ○ Note how this *Guidebook* has, or has not, helped to engage online volunteers

- ○ Relate how he or she handled a particular challenge regarding volunteer engagement

- Other staff members who work with online volunteers at the organization can talk about:

  - ○ How online volunteers impact their work

  - ○ How volunteers, online or onsite, make a difference to the organization's work with clients

  - ○ What they have learned about working with others online through working with online volunteers

  - ○ One experience in particular regarding working with a volunteer

- A volunteer can talk about:

  - ○ What he or she does for the organization as a volunteer

  - ○ What happens during a single typical work day as an onsite or online volunteer

  - ○ Favorite online tools

  - ○ How and why to use social networking to talk about volunteering experiences

  - ○ One particular experience as a volunteer at the organization

  - ○ What the first six months or first year of volunteering has been like

A single blog can include any of these types of posts, or you can create several blogs for different purposes or audiences. Encourage volunteers to respond to blog posts and start a public discussion.

Coordinating blog entries is an excellent, high-profile task for a cyber deputy (see the end of chapter 2).

Micro-blogging

Micro-blogging refers to posting messages that have a very limited number of *characters* and are therefore limited to just a few words. If you micro-blog through the popular site Twitter, it is called *tweeting* and messages are limited to 140 characters. Some people consider status updates on Facebook a form of micro-blogging, since you are limited in the number of characters you can post in a message; users can configure their Facebook settings to send updates to their cell phones via text message, or they can use their smartphones to view the messages.

There are two ways to think about micro-blogs: those that are read on a Web site such as Twitter (viewed via computer or smartphone) and those that go to cell phones as text messages. The *reader* decides how to receive the messages, not you the sender. Why would a person want to receive micro-blogs via text message or to have their phone vibrate or make a noise when they receive a tweet? Because that person considers such messages to be urgent and wants to read them immediately.

The only way to know how people choose to receive your organization's micro-blogs is to ask. Most people will not want to receive your micro-blog messages as text messages, unless you are going to focus on infrequent, urgent, act-now style messages—and you make it clear to them that that is what the messages will be. Maybe things like:

- *The President of the U.S. just arrived at our offices! Come at once!*

- *Vote on state bill to prevent Dalmatian fur coats comes up this afternoon. Call your state rep now! More info on our Web site.*

- *Volunteers R gathering @ our offices to greet our executive director on her return from Afghanistan. Arrives in 1 hour. Come & cheer!*

- *A volunteer had to leave our booth at county fair; we need someone to come down ASAP & fill in! Please reply if U can!*

- *The annual meeting starts in one hour; we RLY hope you will be there.*

- *Online survey of volunteers closes in 4 hours. If you have not completed it, please do ASAP!*

- *Location of meeting has been changed; please be at our Main Street location tomorrow at 9 a.m.*

These are important, timely, and time-limited messages. By contrast, most people will *not* want to receive cell phone text messages from you such as: *the new annual report is out*, or *our executive director wrote a new blog about her trip to Afghanistan*, or *we have a new video on YouTube*! None of these last three messages are urgent. They might be good tweets for people to read via a smartphone or computer when they want to log in to a micro-blogging site, but they would not be good messages to send to all of your volunteers' cell phones via text message. This is why you have to find out how your volunteers like to receive micro-blogs and craft your message strategy accordingly.

Messages with a Purpose

As always, *develop a strategy* for why and when you use micro-blogging to communicate with volunteers, and explain your goals to everyone. You can have different micro-blogging activities for different purposes:

- You can create a Twitter account to promote new resources your organization publishes or produces or to make announcements about events or activities. These messages are probably going to be read by your target audience via a laptop or desktop computer or a smartphone rather than as a cell phone text message (though users can choose to receive messages however they wish). In addition to being a good way to reach current and potential volunteers, there are more than 100 million active Twitter accounts at the time of this book's publication, and many media outlets as well as corporations are particularly fond of it as a way to identify trends.[3]

- Use *hashtags* in your posts in smart ways (see sidebar, "Tagging Messages"). You can use popular, general tags such as #volunteer to help the public find your messages through an interest in the subject. But you can also create tags specifically for your organization's projects to allow volunteers involved in them to communicate together more easily. As one example, we encourage all readers of this *Guidebook* to tag anything they post to Twitter that relates to online volunteering with *#virtualvolunteering*, so we can all know

about the latest virtual volunteering news, resources, and activities!

- Create separate Twitter accounts specifically for special clusters of volunteers or your activist network, and post messages there that are only of interest to them. In order to get these messages, they will need to *follow* (subscribe) to your Twitter feed. For example, you might want to create a Twitter account specifically to report on legislation related to the mission of your organization

---

Tagging Messages

Tagging messages is essential when using a site like Twitter. You tag messages with keywords to reach those interested in various subjects but who do not subscribe to your Twitter feed or other micro-blog account. For instance, you may want to add #nonprofit, or #volunteer, or the name of your city with the # symbol in front of it (#Portland, #Austin) to the end of a message so that anyone searching for those terms will see your message.

The authors follow a number of different tags on Twitter to stay up to date on the latest developments regarding volunteering and other aspects of their work. We share these here so you can get a sense of the variety of tags you could use to give a message wider dissemination, as well as how you, too, can stay up to date on the very latest trending topics:

- #volunteer
- #volunteers
- #volunteermanagement
- #ttvolmgrs
- #virtualvolunteering
- #microvolunteering
- #nonprofits
- #nonprofit
- #ngos
- #nptech
- #humanitarian
- #ict4d

and focus messages on what followers can do to take action to support important bills.

- You can use micro-blogging as a form of *blast text messaging* at times when you want to make sure a pre-determined list of people receives the same information quickly and simultaneously. Require everyone involved to give you their cell phone numbers, so you can send the messages. Two examples are: send workshop registrants a reminder text message the morning of the event, and another an hour before it starts, to assure peak attendance; or send all volunteers engaged in disaster response a text message when a disaster strikes. In an emergency, you can either urgently call for their assistance or direct them to where they can find out immediately if they are needed. Just be aware that cell phone networks may not work in certain disasters or may be overwhelmed with messages when disaster strikes.

But micro-blogging is not all about one-way communication. Micro-blogging requires you to be interactive, responding to other people, not just sending messages to followers. If someone comments on your tweet, for instance, his or her comments will be seen by anyone following you on Twitter and you are expected to respond. In addition, you should be following the micro-blogs of volunteers who regularly talk about their experiences at your organization, as well as colleagues who provide information you might need in your work or that you might want to pass on to your volunteers.

No one wants to be overwhelmed with micro-blogging messages. Be strategic. Always have an answer to the question, "Why would our followers *want* to know this right away?" In addition, you should *repeat all micro-blogging messages*, in some form, in your more traditional or longer forms of communication with volunteers: your online discussion group, your e-newsletter, your Web site, during face-to-face meetings, etc. Remember that not everyone is reached by just one avenue of communication. Also, rare is the situation where micro-blogging will be the *only* way a VRM will interact with volunteers.

The Internet abounds in fantastic examples of organizations using micro-blogging to keep volunteers engaged, to support current volunteers, and to recruit new volunteers. Here are just a few that we like (but remember that you can go online and easily see *everyone* the authors follow on various social networks):

- @GWOBorg (on Twitter): Geeks Without Bounds, "an alliance of hackers, coders and geeks united by the common goal of assisting people and communities in distress."

- @NPSVIPNetwork (on Twitter): "Bringing together U.S. National Park Service VIPs, volunteer managers, and friends."

- @WTA_hikers (on Twitter): "Washington (state) Trails Association protects and maintains our hiking trails."

- @CrisisCamp (on Twitter): "Barcamp/hackathon-ish event (supported by CrisisCommons) to encourage tech ninjas & people of all skills to use tech to help crisis mgt and global development."

- Peace Corps (via Facebook): Profiles Peace Corps members in the field and provides important updates and tips for people who might be applying.

- Women of Uganda Network (via Facebook): Provides updates on their latest activities and contributions from collaborating organizations and volunteers.

- Humane Society of Henderson County, Kentucky (via Facebook): A good example of a small organization using status updates to keep volunteers engaged and recruit new supporters.

And, of course, you can view the authors' own Twitter feeds:

- @energizeinc: Updates from Energize, Inc. about resources especially for leaders of volunteers and those who specialize in community engagement.

- @jcravens42: Tweets by Jayne Cravens regarding volunteers and volunteering, as well as nonprofit/NGO matters, humanitarian/development/aid issues, communications, and her other areas of professional interest.

Micro-blogging Platforms

Which Web-based micro-blogging platform should you use? The one or ones that many of those you want to reach are already using. How will you find that out? You will ask and look. Survey staff, volunteers, donors, and other supporters. Ask them which platforms they use and on what device they like to read messages. Ask colleagues at other organizations as well. Follow organizations you admire, or that are similar to yours, and learn from them.

There are programs and Web sites that allow you to send one text message to several phone numbers via your computer, without using Twitter. One example is GeoChat,[4] a free tool from the nonprofit organization InSTEDD (Innovative Support to Emergencies, Diseases and Disasters). There are also others that will do this for a small, monthly subscription fee.

Some programs will cross-post your messages so that whatever you post on Twitter also gets posted as a status update on your other social networking accounts (Facebook, Google+, LinkedIn, etc.). One caution, however: each of these platforms allows for a different number of characters. For instance, if you type more than 140 characters on a Facebook status update and have your account linked to your Twitter feed, only the first 140 characters will be sent to your Twitter followers. We have seen some users forget this and their shortened messages have not been understandable! It is best to have a gateway where tweets also get posted to Facebook, but not the other way around.

Some organizations post the same message across all of their micro-blogging profiles. Others pick and choose, such as sending a notice about a training schedule change only on the organization's Twitter feed. You determine what message goes where.

Texting Your Location

One micro-blogging practice that people either love or hate is for individuals to send an automated text message to all their friends' cell phones or post a status message on the person's favorite social networking site simply saying *where* he or she is:

- *Jayne just entered the Starbuck's in Paducah.*

- *Susan has checked in at Heathrow International Airport.*

Some people even configure their smartphones with certain applications so that their location is sent out automatically as soon as they enter a restaurant, store, airport or other business that is also using the same apps.

Naturally this practice has evolved jargon names such as *mobile check-in services* and *location-based networking*. We call it *texting your location*. It is a type of messaging that can drive people nuts ("Why should I care where you are this second?") and is very popular with followers of celebrities. But as it happens, there are some interesting ways to use this micro-blogging convention to support your organization.

Mission-based organizations can leverage this practice to create more awareness about their organization by asking volunteers to text their location manually to their network (meaning they type it in themselves, rather than the location being sent out just by walking through the door). Here are ways it can work:

- At the start of your volunteer recognition event, display a message on an overhead projector and ask all attendees to take out their cell phones or smartphones and to text it or tweet it right at that moment to everyone in their contact list or to their followers or via their status update to their contacts. The message could be: *I am at the recognition event for volunteers of such-and-such organization. Great time!* And *then* ask everyone to turn their phones OFF!

- As volunteers start their first shift staffing an exhibit table at a public event, ask them to send out the message: *Come to such-and-such event @ number street address & look for me @ the such-and-such booth! Stop by & say hi!*

- Ask volunteer ushers at the opening performance of your theater season to send the message: *I'm @ opening night of such-and-such at name-of-theater. Call xxx-xxx-xxxx for tix. On with the show!* And then ask everyone to turn their phones OFF!

- Once volunteer firefighters finish putting away the equipment after a particularly intense or large emergency response, encourage them to send a message, as appropriate, to their network, such as: *Just finished response to factory fire in such-&-such-area. More than 30 volunteers responded. Photos soon @ Flickr.*

Remember that such messages need to be 140 characters or less, to meet the standards of most micro-blog platforms.

These posts send a personalized, informal message out to your volunteers' own networks—their friends, neighbors, and colleagues—showing how active your organization is and further building awareness about your activities and volunteer engagement. These messages can generate interest among new volunteers and new audiences, attract larger numbers of attendees to an event, and augment your other outreach efforts.

However, do not abuse this. Most volunteers, audience members, or clients do not want to send lots of messages on behalf of your organization to their networks, and their network members do not want to be overwhelmed with such messages. Of course, always make sending such a message entirely *voluntary*, never mandatory.

If you encourage volunteers, event attendees, and others to text their location at the start, during, or at the end of an event, track the results. Did you see an increase in the number of phone calls or e-mails to your organization regarding volunteering? An increase in phone calls requesting more information? More attendees at an event? Also ask your volunteers and other supporters what kind of responses they received personally to the message they sent out to their network on your behalf.

Live Tweet Chats/Live Micro-blogging

Live micro-blogging is an intense experience. A person or persons at an event begin sending messages regarding what they witness or participate in; people read and respond to those messages as they are posted, then people read and respond to each other's comments, and it continues as long as there is interest. It is real-time, instantaneous, synchronous communication, and the entire conversation is public—anyone can see it happening!

A live event on Twitter is called a *tweet chat*. A tweet chat that relates to volunteers could be:

- A Q & A session with your executive director or other high-profile, often-in-demand

staff person—someone people *really* want to talk to—answering questions from volunteers. This works best if you have a very large number of volunteers who are geographically dispersed.

- An event where volunteers talk about what they have liked most about being a volunteer, what they've learned, etc.

Such a live event needs to be focused on a single, limited topic; you cannot do anything that is too involved. This is not the forum to explore ways to reduce teen pregnancy or address misunderstandings between two religious groups. Keep your goals for the event *simple*. Also, pick a fixed date and set a definite start and end time (an hour is usually enough, though some organizations dedicate an entire day to such an event).

The fundamentals of a successful live tweet chat event are:

- Require that all participants use the same tag on *every* message they tweet as a part of the live event. This tag has to be communicated to all participants *before* the event. Participants follow the event by doing a search for that particular tag. For instance, if your organization's acronym is TEEKO, you could use the tag #TEEKOCHAT for your tweet chat session.

- Promote the event on as many other venues as possible: list it on the events sections of LinkedIn and Facebook and whatever other social networking sites you use; put the details on your Web site; blog about it; include it in any e-mail or print newsletters; post about it to your online discussion groups; and encourage staff and volunteers to talk about it in their own status updates on various platforms.

- Use status updates on your various online networking accounts and your Twitter feed to remind people of the event two hours before the event, again an hour before, and again as the event begins.

- Before the event, have your welcome message, opening question, some questions for midway through, and your ending message already written and ready to copy and paste into your Twitter feed at the appropriate time.

- Make sure something is posted regularly during the event; for an event that is just an hour, that means at least every 60 seconds! Arrange for a core group of volunteers to each have at least one question prepared and ready to copy and paste into their own Twitter feeds during the event. This core group should also prepare at least one resource or advice statement to post at some point. This core group can be designated employees or volunteers; talk with them beforehand so they know exactly what they are supposed to do.

- Have someone designated to thank every person who posts a question or an answer during the event. They can thank three or four people at once, as in: *Thanks to @ jcravens42, @ebarnhart + @LCMoy for great questions re: nonprofits + Twitter. #NPtwitter.* Now all of the followers of these people are going to see this tweet and have the tag to click on to jump in and see what is going on. You have just reached more people with your live micro-blogging event! And this is a great task for an online volunteer.

- Encourage participants to retweet questions and answers. Most will feel encouraged to do this if they see others doing it, so make sure your core group for this event knows they should retweet something at least once during the event.

- If you cannot answer every question that comes in, that is okay; save them and assure participants that all questions will be addressed on a follow-up Web page or blog.

- Capture every post and compile the information into a Web page or a blog so others can read the key information generated during the event, and respond to any questions that did not get answered during the event.

A live micro-blogging event is a great opportunity for online volunteers to help you prepare, run,

and follow up an event. Volunteers can serve in any or all of the roles we've just identified. However, a live tweet chat or live micro-blogging event is not for everyone. It is a focused experience that requires a lot of preparation before the start, a lot of concentration during the event by the organizer, and a lot of excited people who know how to participate (and want to!). But for the right participants, it can be fun and effective.

Volunteer management colleagues in England run a weekly tweet chat called *Thoughtful Thursday*. See page 99 for the details—and maybe you'll join in next Thursday!

Other Live Online Events

In addition to live micro-blogging, there are other ways to run live online events for and with volunteers. These can be just about anything that makes for an event in the physical world: conferences, training workshops, public forums, guest speakers, fundraisers, recognition celebrations, and more. The program content is presented in much the same way online as in front of a live audience, but volunteers see and hear the presentation in various ways on their computers. The techniques include: webcam streaming video capturing an actual live event while it is happening (but enabling people who cannot come to the site to participate as well); live audio (either by conference telephone call or by using an Internet phone service) combined with online slides; or a mixture of video and other asynchronous tools.

Live online events are not for the fainthearted. They are a lot like producing a television or radio program—it is a live performance! These events can look unprofessional when there is too much chatter or, worse, too much silence. Online events are a great tool if successful, annoying and frustrating if unsuccessful, and a public relations nightmare if a disaster.

Why might you want to create a live online event for volunteers? Only when it is worth the tremendous amount of effort involved! But there may be great benefits from generating real-time excitement by gathering participants together for a live presentation. For example, a live event is an excellent kickoff opportunity to start a project, campaign, or other activity that everyone will begin together as soon as the live program is over.

Thoughtful Thursdays

In 2011, a group of volunteer resources managers in England formed an advocacy project to champion the profession of volunteer management. As one of their tools, they launched a weekly live Twitter event called "Thoughtful Thursday," using the hashtag: *#ttvolmgrs*. Each Thursday, one of the group leaders opens the event with a single question, such as "Why do you think joining an association of volunteer managers is helpful?" or "What is your favorite volunteer recognition gift?" More recently, guest bloggers write a longer discussion-starting post on ivo.org (a social network especially for volunteers and leaders of volunteers), which is referenced throughout the day. Then the discussion takes off with all sorts of tweets.

Originally the tweets began around 9 o'clock in the morning, UK time, and dropped off by the afternoon. But now that the weekly discussion is gaining momentum in other countries, the posts keep coming well into the night in England, as the working day starts in the United States, moves across the continent, and gets to the Far East.

After the event closes, one of the group's organizers creates a PDF archive of the entire exchange and makes it available online.

See:

- "Thoughtful Thursdays from VMmovement" on ivo: http://ivo.org/vmm
- #ttvolmgrs tweets at https://twitter.com/search?q=%23ttvolmgrs&src=typdhttp://ivo.org/suevjones/events/thoughtful-thursday-tweetchat-ttvolmgrs-5

It can also inject new energy and maintain motivation at periodic intervals during the group effort or celebrate the successful conclusion. Live events can introduce new executive leadership or key volunteers to everyone else or share important information with volunteers when it is most pertinent. Because any online event can allow two-way communication, you can give online volunteers a live question-and-answer opportunity with decision makers (whether the questions are voiced by participants or sent by e-mail or text) or generate feedback on any issue.

A successful real-time online interaction with a group takes more than participants; you will also need people filling these roles during the event:

- *Facilitator:* to keep the group focused, to remind participants of the ground rules or topics for discussion, and sometimes to step in to calm nerves when arguments or comments get out of control.

- *Administrator:* to help with technical issues/problems, add/remove members, and archive the conversations (if possible). A technical problem can instantly kill a live online event; you need someone who can respond immediately to such problems.

- *Moderator:* to filter content (reading it before it is posted) and keep out improper posts (jokes, advertising, insults). Because this is a live event, this person will need to be vigilant and ready to respond instantly.

- *Expert* or special guest, representing a particular field or issue, who answers questions from participants.

Of course, online volunteers can fill each of these roles, based on their experience and interest. Just make sure the facilitator or moderator of the group, and whomever that person reports to, has extensive experience participating in these kind of online events and understands procedures (from both technological and group-dynamic perspectives) and the subtleties of live conversations (even just written chats).

Here are some additional recommendations for producing successful live events online:

- Tell all participants the purpose and rules for the event prior to participation.

- Make sure all participants understand the role of the facilitator or moderator. In the same vein, encourage participants *not* to dominate the conversation. This may mean sending out regular reminders to everyone or even communicating directly with an individual who is overactive.

- Encourage new participants to observe an online event for at least a few minutes before actually joining the interaction themselves.

- Send volunteers regular reminders about an upcoming online event, highlighting special features each time, such as noted guests or a particular topic of focus.

- Send an e-mail, instant message, or micro-blog to everyone 5 to 10 minutes before a real-time event, reminding them of the event and encouraging their participation.

- Emphasize that everyone must be on time; it is very distracting to others to have participants entering an online event after it has officially begun.

- Start the event on time. Let's repeat that, with greater emphasis: START THE EVENT ON TIME! No one likes waiting, even from the comfort of home or work. If your event starts and ends on time, volunteers will feel that their time has been valued, not wasted, and they will be more likely to participate in the future.

- Script the event as much as possible, to ensure that things run smoothly.

- Rehearse the event at least the day before, with even just one volunteer logging in to make sure everyone can hear or see what the organization wants to present.

- Encourage people not to multi-task during the event—trying to read e-mail instead of paying attention to the proceedings, for instance.

- If possible, make the archives of chats or conversations available via your Web site (probably in a private area), and remind participants that their posts will be archived and reviewed by others.

If you are going to make live events regular occurrences, then the information and interaction provided during these events must be seen as valuable by participants. Make the benefits or incentives obvious and valuable to increase and maintain participants' motivation. Some organizations include participation in online events as part of the commitment they ask volunteers to make. You may enjoy high attendance, but remember that not everyone can participate in such events, so be careful that you do not exclude some volunteers by making participation a requirement.

Podcasts and Videos

Podcasts are recorded audio segments that can be accessed via the Internet. The practice of producing podcasts was quite the rage 10 years ago, but excitement for them has tapered off as competition for people's attention has increased and as fewer people talk about actually listening to podcasts, as opposed to producing them. On the other hand, it's clear that someone is watching videos, even ones about volunteering. As of August 2013, a keyword search on "volunteer" on YouTube turned up 1,249,788 hits!

Before you start devoting lots of time and resources to producing either podcasts or videos, think about how much *you* listen to podcasts or watch online videos related to nonprofits, libraries, government agencies, or any organizations that involve volunteers. If you are not using such recordings, why do you think your volunteers will? People love to watch videos of kittens playing, but will they watch a video of your volunteers talking about what they do and why they volunteer? Will such a video get more people to volunteer or more financial support for your volunteer engagement activities?

This is not to say podcasts and videos cannot be worthwhile—and we've already talked in chapter 5 about using video for orienting and training volunteers—but think strategically about why you want to make them and how you will evaluate whether or not you have achieved your desired outcomes. Toward these goals, answer these questions:

- When do you expect volunteers (or prospective ones) to listen to the podcasts or videos? While cleaning the house? Mowing the grass? Driving? Riding mass transit?

- Why do you want volunteers to listen to a podcast or watch a video? Because it is part of their initial orientation as a volunteer? Because you want them to hear the voice of your executive director answering questions they have been asking in meetings and on your online discussion group? Because certain policies and procedures need to be reinforced, and you think hearing the volunteer resource manager re-asserting them will help in that regard? Because you want volunteers to hear a "thank you," not just read it?

- Would *you* listen to this podcast or video? How will you make the content and presentation compelling? Who will be speaking, and does that person have a pleasant, easy-to-understand voice?

- Will you make listening to the podcast or watching the video optional or mandatory?

- How will you accommodate volunteers who do not know how to listen to podcasts or watch online videos or do not have the equipment and access necessary to listen at home or at work?

- How will you know that volunteers actually listened to the podcast or video, as opposed to just downloading it or fast-forwarding through most of it?

- How will you evaluate the success of a podcast or video?

If you answer these questions and reach the conclusion that you do need to produce one podcast or regularly-produced podcasts, you can start exploring with your IT department the best way to produce and distribute your podcast. The good news is that volunteers can be recruited specifically to help produce podcasts and videos for or about volunteers.

Of course, even after all the cautions above, video recording an event, photogenic volunteer activity, or a presentation of some sort is probably always a worthwhile thing to do. If nothing else, you can use the video in-house for people who missed the original experience or include it as part of an in-person recruitment speech or exhibit. Once you have it (assuming it is interesting, even for someone who does not know your organization), it costs nothing to post it to YouTube or Vimeo, and you never know what viral connections it might make for you.

Online Activism

Susan often notes that "no one is paid to start a revolution," whether to fight government or to address a community need. Activism is a mix of volunteer activities that educate the public and pressure legislators and other decision makers to change their opinions and practices.

Online activism has been happening for well over 20 years, with virtual protests and public education aided or even led by concerned volunteers. Cell phones played a central role in activism online and in organizing offline activities from the beginning; grassroots advocates effectively used PDAs and cell phones to help organize and direct protesters during the 1999 Seattle demonstrations against the World Trade Organization, and protestors in the Philippines used cell phone text messaging to mobilize hundreds of thousands of demonstrators in January 2001 to help oust President Joseph Estrada.[5]

There are books, academic articles, Web sites, and even organizations devoted solely to helping others mobilize people to engage in online activism (see the Virtual Volunteering Wiki). This section is not a substitute for any of those excellent resources but rather a basic introduction to what activism by online volunteers might look like.

E-mail remains a key tool for organizations in their work with online volunteer activists, though micro-blogging (see above) is gaining popularity. Electronic messages to online activists are generally calls to action, meant to prompt the volunteers to text their friends about an upcoming vote in Congress, blog about a campaign being undertaken by your organization, or post to their status update on a social networking site about a demonstration they will attend in person.

Obviously, such calls to action must be used with caution because everyone is overwhelmed with messages. There is also the danger of crying wolf, urging people to "take action!" so often that the messages lose their potency. Activists should trust when they subscribe to your alert messages that you will communicate sparingly for only critical, time-sensitive issues.

If your organization already involves volunteers as activists in person, you are in a good position to involve online volunteers in virtual advocacy because you already have policies and procedures in place regarding activist activities. You also have a basic understanding of what is and is not legal and appropriate when it comes to public advocacy.

If your organization has not done formal activism before, or has not involved volunteers as activists, do some research to educate everyone about what activities you and volunteers can engage in legally regarding lobbying, advocacy, and other public policy activities. The rules will change from country to country and even state to state, and restrictions may be placed on some of your activities based on your type of organization: nonprofit, for-profit, or public. The resources in the Virtual Volunteering Wiki will be helpful.

We can give one piece of advice to nonprofit organizations in the U.S.: political campaigning by a charity in favor of or against a particular candidate in an election is strictly prohibited. Such a violation of IRS regulations may result in the organization losing its tax-exempt status. Advocating for nonpartisan issues, however, is generally allowed.

Having given the above caution, however, one of the unique strengths of volunteers is that they are both insiders and outsiders. Because they are not employees of your organization, they may not be as restricted as paid agents to contact legislators or the media about an issue needing attention. As private citizens, they are free to communicate with whomever they choose. This fact should *not* encourage you to circumvent the law by "strongly suggesting" or in any way instigating an advocacy campaign by volunteers that is really being coordinated by your organization! We raise the point simply to allow you to consider that volunteers have more freedom in some circumstances than paid staff. As one example, your funding may limit you from officially collaborating with any organization in another state or province. Volunteers, however, are free to drive across a border—or send an e-mail anywhere—and communicate with their counterparts to share strategies for tackling a cause that affects both geographical regions.

Spontaneous Volunteers Responding Virtually

When a big news story or disaster strikes, the result can be hundreds, even thousands of people contacting organizations to offer help, including potential online volunteers. It could be a natural disaster, an act of violence, or a particular issue suddenly becoming the hot item on the news. A nonprofit organization, NGO, school, or other organization could suddenly be swamped with e-mails and phone calls from people who want to help in some way online. These crisis-driven offers of help have come to be called *spontaneous volunteering*.

During a crisis or disaster, it is hard to deploy every person who wants to assist the response effort onsite because the immediate need is for certain key skills (search and rescue, medical, shelter setup, whatever) and there is rarely time, space or leadership to orient and train volunteers who are generalists. Providing there is someone designated specifically to respond to *online* offers of service, virtual volunteering is a way to get some important work done.

As soon as possible—or do this in advance so that you are ready when the time comes—put up a page on your Web site directed specifically at anyone responding spontaneously, *thanking* them for wanting to help in this time of crisis or intense attention. Then outline all of the ways they could help your organization both as financial donors and as volunteers, giving special attention to online volunteering opportunities (even those available all the time). Also refer them (with links) to other community organizations if there are ways to volunteer in response to the emergency through those groups. If you develop this page in advance, you can also ask these other organizations to cross-link to you, if you will be able to engage volunteers in useful ways during the crisis.

Provide an online response form for those who wish to serve virtually right away, and be sure to respond swiftly. Here are some ways spontaneous online volunteers could benefit your organization in a crisis situation:

- Invite the spontaneous online volunteers to subscribe to any communication vehicle that your organization uses to communicate the latest information on the emergency situation and actions to address it: your e-mail newsletter, blog, Twitter feed, or any social networking site. Once new volunteers are up to date, encourage them to *repost your messages* to their own blogs, status updates, and so on to educate their friends and colleagues about what is happening.

- Ask them to monitor media reports and bring certain articles or information to your immediate attention. Further, ask them to search for and let you know if they see misinformation online about your organization and its work in this crisis situation.

- If those caught in the emergency speak different languages, ask whether online volunteers are able to do any translation of some of your existing material or new information into those languages. Conversely, perhaps they can translate texts or blog comments coming in to your organization from another language into English, so you can read and respond quickly.

If the offers to do online volunteering come from people with technical skills, there are all sorts of amazing projects they can do individually and collectively during the crisis. They might gather research on what other organizations are doing, information that your organization might need to urgently know about. Or they could even create a special smartphone application for you. Here are two real-life examples from the response to the Haiti earthquake in 2010:

- OpenStreetMap created a crisis mapping project, mobilizing highly-skilled online volunteers to layer up-to-the-minute data, such as the location of new field hospitals and downed bridges, onto post-quake satellite imagery. This data was made freely available by for-profit companies including GeoEye and DigitalGlobe. The digital cartography—informed by everything from tweets to eyewitness reports—helped aid workers speed food, water and medicine to where it was needed most.

- CrisisCamp mobilized hundreds of online and onsite volunteers in Washington, DC;

London, England; Mountain View, California; and elsewhere to build and refine a variety of tech tools, including a basic Creole-English dictionary app for the iPhone to help aid workers.

These are not just nice things for online volunteers to do in a crisis; they are critical services. Depending on what the mission of your organization is, you might want to consider including how to deal with spontaneous online volunteering candidates in your crisis readiness plans.

Of course your organization should encourage all spontaneous volunteers, whether they want to serve onsite or online, to make a financial donation to the organization to help fund the crisis response effort. Be explicit about exactly what this money will be used for.

Virtual Board Meetings

Board members of a nonprofit organization are volunteers legally charged with governance authority and responsibility; their votes determine some of the most important actions and functions of an organization. The Internet can serve as a discussion forum and information review for board members, but whether or not the board may *vote* online depends on two factors: if online voting is legal in that region or country and if virtual governance is something that will serve the organization well.

In the United States, a nonprofit is governed by the laws of the state in which it is incorporated, and each state is different in terms of legal requirements for board meetings. The authors know that online board meetings are legal in California, Illinois, and Virginia but are not so sure about other states (and of course laws can change). Also, it can be a matter of interpretation: If a state law says that all people participating in a board meeting must be able to *hear* each other at the same time, does that mean they could use Skype or iVisit for a board meeting that includes voting? Your best bet for clear advice is to contact your city, county, or state attorney to ask about the legalities of online board meetings. Also, check your organization's bylaws to see what they require in terms of board votes; the policies may need to be amended to allow for online voting.

A few resources we have found regarding online voting and online board meetings in the U.S. can be found in the Virtual Volunteering Wiki. We shall leave it to other researchers to compile information on this subject for other countries, since laws and practices vary tremendously from country to country.

Even if it is not legal for your board of directors to vote online in your area, it is perfectly all right for the board to engage in informal virtual discussions that could lead to actions later at an official onsite board meeting. Just as a small group of board members may have lunch together and discuss organizational matters, all or some members can have productive discussions online.

The dream many organizations had with the increased use of Internet technologies was that board members would be easier to reach, board feedback would be easier to gather, and board decisions would be easier to make—and, therefore, board members would be easier to recruit! Sadly, this dream has not been realized.

It can be a struggle to get a board of directors to take electronic communications seriously. E-mails are easy to ignore or get lost in a sea of other e-mails. You can request, "Please read the attached when you have time over the next two weeks," but that time may never actually materialize. Online board meetings may be more possible to attend than onsite meetings, but they are also more easily interrupted by anyone around the board member's computer at the time. Also, you cannot prevent board members from attempting to multi-task during online board meetings, checking their e-mail, or reading other documents instead of listening to and engaging in the proceedings.

Ultimately, the only people who can compel board volunteers to use the Internet as part of their role as board members are the members themselves. But staff at an organization can entice the board in a number of ways:

- Get to know each board member's online habits. Which ones use instant messaging or do online phoning via Skype, iVisit, or Google Talk? Utilize each board member's favorite way of communicating, as appropriate, to get each volunteer used to communicating with you online, and vice versa.

- Refer to online interactions in *onsite* meetings. If other board members keep hearing about instant messaging, for instance, they may be more inclined to use it.

- Keep e-mails from your organization to the board at a minimum. (Follow the suggestions we presented in chapter 6.)

- Keep e-mail text short but descriptive. Find the happy medium between no information other than "please read the attached" and overkill such as repeating most of the text of an attachment in the e-mail.

- Invite the board to join your online community for all volunteers. Make sure they understand how to set their preferences so that they can read the messages via the Web or know how to filter messages so that they all go into a separate e-mail box. If they see other volunteers participating online, they may be inclined to try it themselves.

Even if all of the above motivates just one board member to start using online communication tools with greater frequency, you have at least cultivated one board champion to help encourage the rest of the board to work virtually.

Some board members will actually prefer discussing issues via e-mail or a private online discussion group because it allows them to read and respond to materials whenever they have time. Others will prefer discussing issues live via a private chat room or online audio or video discussion. Test both methods more than once for the entire board and for subcommittees, and get a commitment from the board president or committee chairs to engage in either way of online discussion. This will encourage the board to adopt whatever practice it likes best.

Avatar-Based Environments

An avatar-based Web site is a virtual world. It is a simulated environment with digital buildings, digital streets, digital trees, digital lakes, and digital people called *avatars*. Perhaps *people* is the wrong word, however, because an avatar—the online image that represents the site participant to others in the virtual world—could be a pink elephant, a park bench, a giant Queen of Hearts playing card or just about anything else you could imagine. Avatars interact with each other one-on-one or in a digital space that can look like a classroom, a board room, or a hot tub. Their speech appears either in a bubble near their avatar (like in a comic strip) or as an actual, audible voice. The most popular avatar-based meeting space is Second Life.

There are many uses for these virtual worlds, many of them for fun and play or for new types of shopping. But avatars can also do serious things, such as attend a seminar or participate in a professional discussion with other avatars. As one example, TechSoup (the site we repeatedly recommend in this book as an advisor to nonprofits on computer and Internet technical matters) regularly schedules presentations in Second Life.

A few organizations recruit volunteers and donors through these sites, and there are also charitable events that take place in virtual worlds. For instance, in 2008, the annual no-sitting, no-sleeping, two-day Penn State University IFC/Panhellenic Dance Marathon (THON) that raises money for various charities happened both on the campus and in Second Life, allowing for a greater number of participants and donors.[6] Organizations have created virtual marathons, in which the avatars "run" the race but the real-world people collect pledges as for any other such event. In 2005, the American Cancer Society expanded its signature fundraising activity, Relay For Life, with an annual "Relay For Life of Second Life"[7] that has raised more than a million dollars and counting.

Young people in particular enjoy interacting in virtual worlds, because it allows a user to appear to others however he or she wishes, via his or her avatar. Many people find it empowering to be in control of their appearance and, therefore, people's immediate perception of them. Many users describe virtual environments as more like playing a game than working and say that it feels more personal than e-mail or a text-based message board.

However, it also takes most people a great deal of time to learn to use an avatar-based environment, let alone to feel comfortable enough navigating in such a world to want to participate in a meeting there. New participants need time to become oriented to the world, create accounts, learn how to navigate the site, and create their avatar. Not everyone likes meetings to feel like a game, and can find participating in a virtual world as a time-waster with a tech toy rather than something that is integral to their online volunteering contribution to a nonprofit organization. Participation also requires the latest hardware and a very fast Internet connection, two things that many people do not have, even in this information age. Use of virtual worlds also puts a large demand on the organization's bandwidth, slowing down the Internet for everyone.

The key to success in using a virtual world site with online volunteers is careful planning, ensuring that the activities will match the goals and objectives of the organization and will truly augment a volunteer's contributions. Have concrete reasons why and how you want online volunteers to use a virtual world for some or all of their interactions with your organization, each other, or clients. Also, volunteers must be enthusiastic about using the tool.

The best place to find updates regarding virtual world use and volunteers is TechSoup. It is also worth noting that Second Life, a for-profit company, has a real VRM who coordinates Second Life's own volunteer program and welcomes people experienced in interacting in that virtual world to guide newcomers around.[8]

Distributed Computing and Crowdsourcing

Sometimes scientific projects produce more data than their computers can process and need to find additional computing power. *Distributed computing* allows anyone with a computer to donate its idle time to projects as diverse as working to cure diseases, study global warming, discover pulsars, and many other types of scientific research. Your selected project automatically begins using your computer when you are not using it yourself. Think of it as online volunteering by your computer!

One of the best-known distributed computing projects is SETI@home, where volunteers download software to their computers that then uses their idle computer power to analyze radio signals for signs of extraterrestrial intelligence.[9] The Berkeley Open Infrastructure for Network Computing (BOINC) lists some of these projects and has a good description of what it calls *volunteer computing*.[10]

We expect that most of our readers will not really have any need for this sort of computer work, unless engaged in scientific or academic research. But in chapter 3 we discussed the related practice of *crowdsourcing* as a form of micro-volunteering. If you need to gather many different opinions and recommendations or parcel out a huge project in small chunks, this form of public participation may be extremely useful.

Keeping Up with Changes and Trends

As we said at the beginning of this chapter, new Internet and networking tools emerge *all the time*, and the ways people use networking tools are in constant flux.

Do not wait for an annual conference to tell you what trends are on the horizon regarding new Internet tools and virtual volunteering; instead, set aside time every other week to learn a bit about what is going on. For just 30 minutes every other week, set your phone to voice mail or turn your cell phone on vibrate, close your door with a sign that says "in conference" on the outside, and use that time to see what other organizations are doing to engage and support volunteers with the tools we have talked about in this and other chapters. Watch others and think about how you might adapt some of their practices. This is what the authors do, and this is how we have kept up to date on this ever-changing landscape of tech tools. We share much of what we do and learn online, for free, for you to view at any time.

Here is a good place to remind you of the Virtual Volunteering Wiki where we list tools and resources related to virtual volunteering, as well as working online in general. These links tend to change frequently, but if a new, significant development that relates to virtual volunteering emerges, you can be sure we will put information about it on the Wiki (or *you* can share what new tool you have found!).

In addition, exploring advanced tools is a great way to involve volunteers—onsite and online. You could recruit volunteers to give you a briefing on a new tool you heard about, research how organizations are using a new tool with volunteers, or do a training just for you regarding a new platform or application. Tech changes and trends present a wonderful opportunity to further involve volunteers directly in your work.

NOTES

1. TechSoup, "Managing Staff and Volunteers," accessed September 2013 <http://www.techsoup.org/learningcenter/volunteers/index.cfm>.
2. Jayne Cravens, "A Brief Review of the Early History of Nonprofits and the Internet (before 1996)," 2009 <http://www.coyotecommunications.com/tech/npo_and_net_history.shtml>.
3. MSNBC, "Just How Many Active Twitter Users Are There?" April 1, 2011 <http://technolog.msnbc.msn.com/_news/2011/04/01/6388683-just-how-many-active-twitter-users-are-there>.
4. GeoChat <http://instedd.org/technologies/geochat/>.
5. UNITeS, Section on "Advocacy" from "Handheld Computer Technologies in Community Service/Volunteering/Advocacy," October 2001 <http://www.coyotecommunications.com/unites/handheld/handhelds04.shtml>.
6. See a video made of the Second Life version of the 2008 marathon at http://www.youtube.com/watch?v=zLwtxObrpvo.
7. Relay For Life of Second Life description, pictures, and more at http://wiki.secondlife.com/wiki/Relay_For_Life_of_Second_Life#Pictures.
8. Second Life Volunteer Corps <http://maps.secondlife.com/secondlife/Tenera/72/90/0?title=RHN—Resident Help Network at Volunteer HQ&msg=Headquarters of the Second Life Volunteer Corps—Tools, information meeting spaces and support for volunteers. Information abo.> Also see "About Volunteering in Second Life" on the Second Life Wiki <http://wiki.secondlife.com/wiki/Volunteer_Portal http://secondlife.com/community/volunteer.php>.
9. SETI@home <http://setiathome.ssl.berkeley.edu/>.
10. BOINC Project, University of California at Berkeley <http://boinc.berkeley.edu/>.

The Student Volunteer Army at work registering onsite volunteers for clean-up after the massive earth-quakes in Christchurch, New Zealand, 2011. All registration and organizing was conducted through Facebook by students at the University of Canterbury.

Chapter 8
Online Volunteers Working Directly with Clients

Direct service virtual volunteering, in which volunteers work directly with clients and/or the public, merits a chapter of its own. Although all of the recommendations we have made for working with any online volunteer also apply to this group, there are some issues that deserve special attention, for two reasons:

- By definition, the work of direct service online volunteers has a personal impact on clients and customers, and missteps or mistakes could have much more dire consequences than an online volunteer making a mistake away from the public eye or far from any client or customer.

- Engaging in direct online service that is key to the organization's mission reflects on how the organization is viewed by clients, customers, the general public, the press, donors, and any other stakeholders.

Online volunteers are already working closely with clients and the public on behalf of countless organizations all over the world. Using a variety of asynchronous and synchronous Internet tools, virtual direct-service assignments handled by volunteers include:

- Electronic visiting with someone who is homebound, in a hospital, or in an assisted living facility

- Online mentoring and instruction, such as helping young students with homework questions or supporting adults learning a skill or finding a job

- Teaching people to use a particular technology tool

- Staffing crisis support lines and facilitating online discussion groups for people with specific questions or needs, on topics as diverse as depression, child care, and organic gardening

- Offering legal, medical, business, or other expertise electronically

- Working on a project together with clients and other volunteers, such as writing about the news of their neighborhood, school, or special interest group

To repeat, many onsite volunteers have already added an online component to the volunteering they do with clients onsite. But a growing number of organizations are choosing to involve online volunteers specifically and intentionally to meet their mission. In other words, an organization focused on helping a particular group of people or addressing a defined issue chooses to involve online volunteers as a primary way to deliver the services that accomplish its goals. This is especially true of online mentoring programs.

The first reaction we often get when talking about volunteers working directly with clients online is alarmist: *Online volunteers working with children? Outrageous!* Yet, the idea of direct service virtual volunteering is no more radical than any existing field assignment, such as bringing adult volunteers together with children for weekly one-to-one visits, volunteers driving to people's homes to deliver food, or volunteers counseling those in distress or having suicidal thoughts. Such personal client contact by volunteers is common in the offline world, and we need to remember that these volunteers are not monitored or supervised by their organizations 100 percent of the time. Many organizations have long ago resolved their concerns about allowing certain volunteers the freedom to do their work, make judgment calls, and act responsibly without constant staff surveillance. We view online volunteers providing direct service to clients, customers, and the general public as normal as any offline program that does the same with traditional volunteers.

Expanding Onsite Activity with Online Service

As we have said, perhaps the most dramatic, worldwide change since the first edition of this *Guidebook* is how Internet-based communication has become totally integrated into every part of life. It is almost hard to remember that in 2000, we could not assume that organizations or individuals were online. By 2013, this situation had reversed and almost everyone is online. Of course there are hold-outs—individuals who refuse to go online or use anything other than e-mail, and many organizations barely have a Web site. But the key point to remember is that *most volunteers* are *using e-mail, smartphones, and the Internet* in almost every facet of their personal and professional lives and, to a large extent, *so are your clients* or consumers.

We have long been in virtual creep—the slow, even *un*remarkable addition of online contact in scenarios such as these:

- A long-standing telephone reassurance program, in which volunteers call older or homebound people to check that all is well, evolves to using Skype or other online calling platforms that include webcam video.

- A school tutoring or after-school homework program still puts the volunteer at the same table as the students being helped but also allows volunteers and students to exchange e-mails outside of formal tutoring sessions, to ask more questions, or to provide a good luck message before a big test.

- Many organizations invite speakers and performers to educate or entertain their members onsite, from professional associations to rehabilitation centers. By projecting a webcam-aided online call onto a big screen, groups can also see a speaker or performer remotely and live (and vice versa!).

Think about how volunteers currently interact with clients and customers: might there be a way to expand this onsite interaction to include some online activity? Would this, in fact, serve your clients even *better* than offering service only onsite during your daytime hours of operation? Would you be able to attract additional, highly-qualified volunteers if they had this option for helping?

Yes, expanding your onsite direct service activities by volunteers into the virtual world means there are policies and procedures you need to put into place to make sure the online activities are safe for all. But if you follow this recommended method of natural expansion with current volunteers, you will not be working with unknown people, as these are volunteers you have already welcomed into your organization and whose work you have already approved.

Extra Attention to Direct Service Online Volunteers

Online volunteers who engage with clients should receive all of the training and support we have been recommending for any other online volunteers. But in recognition of the special demands of direct service to clients, this group deserves some extra attention.

Deciding to Interview Online or Onsite

In chapter 4, "Interviewing and Screening Online Volunteers," we outlined the considerations of selecting online volunteers in much the same way as you select onsite volunteers. Just as you do when considering someone for face-to-face client service, you will probably need to do background checks on someone volunteering virtually (personal and/or professional references, criminal background checks, child abuse history clearance, or credit checks).

An interview, which can be done online, seems a basic requirement to test for desired skills and attitudes. If your organization resists the idea of assigning someone to work with a client without first meeting him or her in person, you can make this a stipulation for acceptance. Most people who live close enough or have adequate transportation will be happy to come for a personal interview. An onsite interview also tells a potential volunteer much more about the organization and its staff, more quickly, than can be gleaned over e-mail or a computer image. However, recognize that this sort of onsite requirement will limit your recruitment to potential volunteers who reside within easy travel distance. If you want many and varied online volunteers, this screening process may be an obstacle.

In addition, you will have to screen candidates for online abilities. Engage a candidate online with all of the tools you intend for the volunteer to use (e-mail, online conferencing, text messaging, etc.) to ensure the person writes well, responds to messages quickly, responds appropriately, really knows how to use the tools, or anything else that will be needed.

Training

Training is key to the success of volunteers engaging with clients and customers online. Consider that traditional volunteers for a sexual assault or domestic violence phone hotline typically go through around 30 hours of onsite training and then are heavily supervised during a probationary period of several weeks when they start answering calls. As just noted for interviewing, volunteering candidates who will work with clients online may need to come *onsite* for intensive training in person, not only for you to ensure they have actually completed the training (it is much harder to determine if an online volunteering candidate has watched a training video online, for instance), but also because the training may involve role-playing and various preparation exercises that cannot be translated online.

Your organization will need to define protocols for how online volunteers should interact with clients and customers, including: how to introduce themselves online; suggestions for building rapport; how to deal with common issues and problems; what to do when faced with hostile or inappropriate communications; how to transition a client to another online volunteer; and even how to end an online relationship. All of these topics should be covered in the training you give new volunteers.

You can assign experienced volunteers to mentor new ones, encouraging them to be in contact by e-mail or phone, especially in the first few months of the newbie's service. Also use your online volunteer community as a question-and-answer forum for peer support.

Supervision and Communication

In addition to the online discussion group you have for all volunteers, set up a private online discussion group or platform just for direct service volunteers and paid employees involved in these client services. This gives everyone a site where they can discuss client-related issues without violating confidentiality. You might form smaller online discussion groups for volunteers who were together in the same training class or who work with clients who have similar needs or some shared characteristic.

We have urged that staff supporting online volunteers commit to respond to questions and requests within 72 hours; for direct service volunteers, staff should respond even more quickly. You may even want to offer an off-hours phone number so direct service online volunteers can immediately reach appropriate staff if they face critical or emergency issues during times your office is closed.

In the same vein, clients and customers must know who to contact at your organization if there is any problem or issue with an online volunteer. Frequently reach out to those being served or supported by online volunteers to learn how things are going and to identify any concerns or complaints. It is important for them to know that issues will immediately reach the appropriate staff at the organization, that these concerns and complaints cannot be blocked by the volunteer, and that they will be dealt with promptly. More often, asking clients and customers whether they are satisfied will elicit positive responses, allowing you to give recognition and motivating feedback to volunteers doing their work well.

Silence is deadly to any online relationship. It can be absolutely destructive to the goals of an online mentoring program, for instance, that is focused on helping a teen have a positive, trusting relationship with an adult. You will have to explore ways to be notified quickly if an online volunteer working with clients or customers has gone silent and quickly develop ways to meet the clients' needs through a new volunteer or an employee. This can easily be automated if you create a private online platform where all volunteer and client interactions take place; for example, the system could notify you if a client does not receive a response to a message within a set number of days.

Performance Assessment

The measure of success for direct service online volunteers differs from other online volunteers who take on tasks with definite start and end dates, work only with employees or a few other volunteers at an organization, or have a product to show at the end of an assignment (a brochure, a database, a list of academic articles, a video, etc.). Direct service online volunteers take on a *role*, and how they perform in that role, rather than the end result weeks or months later, is going to be the primary measure of their work. This may require the supervisor to record and save all online interactions and regularly review a sample of these interactions to ensure quality.

There is an abundance of books, academic articles, and Web sites dealing with specific types of online interactions. If your organization is focused on any kind of educational or human service program and wants to explore ways to deliver part of this service online, keyword searches on your favorite Internet search engine will lead you to these resources and where to purchase them or find them online for free. Some suggested phrases to search for:

- online counseling

- human service delivery online

- building trust online

- online tutoring

Risk Management

When it comes to online volunteers who interact with clients or customers, no list of suggestions would be complete without a discussion of online safety, confidentiality and privacy.

Most people have a fun, safe trip on ye olde information superhighway, including young people. Relatively speaking, the Internet is no more or less safe than any other public space, such as a school, faith community, or sports stadium. Fears of exploitation, abuse, or exposure to sexually-explicit or violent material should not prevent an agency from engaging in virtual volunteering, any more than such fears should prevent the involvement of volunteers onsite. There is risk in *any* volunteering, online or face-to-face. The challenge is to minimize and manage such risk.

An organization can employ several measures to ensure the safety of all participants in a virtual volunteering program. The best safety measures include exercising common sense, adapting your existing offline prevention systems to cyberspace, following the law, establishing good tracking of volunteer activities, and at least some supervision of interactions.

Online safety measures for direct service volunteering have four goals:

1. To prevent opportunities for abuse or exploitation of any participants.

2. To protect youth and other vulnerable clients from inappropriate or harmful activities or information.

3. To screen out people who would abuse or exploit participants or the computer systems they use.

4. To protect participants' privacy and personal information (whether clients, volunteers, employees, parents, or anyone else).

If you bring volunteers together face-to-face with clients or members and you have practices in place to screen out people who might be inappropriate as volunteers, you have already established the procedures to screen out people who might be inappropriate as *online* volunteers. But, of course, no system is perfect, and supervision is vital to keep clients and volunteers safe. How do you currently ensure that face-to-face volunteer/client interaction, whether in your facility or elsewhere in the field, is appropriate, that everyone feels safe, that confidential information is not being shared with family and friends, and so on? Should your online volunteers and clients use a software platform that provides ways for parties to remain anonymous to each other while allowing you, the host organization, to know who all participants are? Should you use a platform that allows a moderator to read and even edit any message from a volunteer to a client (or vice versa), ensuring that no inappropriate information is ever shared?

Keep in mind that no technology tool can guarantee safety; policy and practice will protect the safety of participants as much, if not more, than the tech tools you choose. In addition, online safety measures have to balance with a program's service goals, and this can be easier said than done.

Real-Life Example

Here is a true story of an online mentoring program that illustrates the difficulty in achieving the balance between safety and goals.

Two classes at Sanchez Elementary School, in Austin, Texas, partnered with a project at the University of Texas at Austin for an online mentoring program in the late 1990s, bringing together adults from all over the U.S. with students online for one-on-one interactions. To ensure the safety of all participants, the program was designed to be moderated entirely; no message could get to a student from a mentor, or vice versa, without being read first by one of the three program directors. Only students' and mentors' first names were used in exchanges, which were done via a private (password protected), customized Web site, and any message that had identifying information in it, such as an e-mail address, a full name, a phone number, a company name, a Web address, an online handle or screen name (AustinTwangGal or HannaSolo or Buffy88), was rejected—the author had to revise a rejected message and resubmit it before it would be approved and sent on to the intended recipient via the special Web-based messaging system.

The system worked very well from a safety point of view. There was no way mentors and students could contact each other outside the system because of the absolute moderating of all messages. However, this moderation ended up getting the program directors into trouble with the students. Although students had been briefed before the program began and told that all messages would be read by the program directors, the students had not made the immediate connection that two of these message readers would, therefore, be their own teachers. When students realized this after a few months, they were mortified, as several had made comments about their teachers to their mentors. The students felt betrayed and angry. So while the program did a great job from a safety point of view, it almost defeated some of the goals of the mentoring program, particularly around trust!

While it may have been appropriate for the Sanchez program to moderate every message, it would have been better 1) if the moderators were not teachers and 2) if students had been briefed more than once that teachers *could* have access to their messages at some point. (The materials for teachers, mentors, and parents who participated in the Sanchez Elementary School online mentoring program remain online for reference.[1])

The point of this story is not that safety is unimportant, on or offline—it is crucial. But how far can safety monitoring go in programs that depend on developing trusting relationships? Consider, for instance, the fact that Big Brothers Big Sisters of America (BBBSA) does not send a staff member along on all real-world visits between volunteers and the young people they are mentoring. This would be intrusive and undermine one of the primary goals of the program: developing a trusting, positive relationship between a caring adult and an at-risk young person. Instead, BBBSA has strict, intensive screening and training for volunteers, training for families with a child in the program, and ongoing staff interactions with all volunteers *and* children/ families served. In short, BBBSA balances safety and program goals.

More Suggestions

If you bring together volunteers and clients online, you have two options. You can set up a private system through which *all* messages are sent, reviewed before they can be read by the intended recipient, stripped of all personal identifying information by the moderator, archived for the record, etc. But if you decide against such a cumbersome, moderated, and anonymous system, you need to employ *all* of the suggested practices and legal requirements associated with bringing volunteers and clients together *onsite*.

Other considerations and suggestions:

- Volunteers, clients, and parents/adult children of any participants should be fully aware of any supervision taking place regarding online exchanges, your organization's policy concerning what constitutes inappropriate online behavior, and what your organization will do if inappropriate online behavior is exhibited— by either party. Also, if online exchanges between adult volunteers and youth are archived, volunteers, youth, and their parents should be aware of who will (and will not) have access to these archives.

- The best way to ensure that clients and volunteers are having positive online experiences is for program staff to stay in frequent touch with both, to encourage an atmosphere of open communication. Also, it is fundamental that you establish and clearly (and frequently) communicate policies regarding online exchanges between volunteers and clients.

- Are volunteers and clients allowed to arrange face-to-face meetings, online or onsite? If no, to whom should they report such an invitation? If yes, should they report such a planned meeting to the organization to get permission first or simply so the organization knows such a meeting will happen?

- Advise clients to immediately notify the organization if an online volunteer ever suggests doing anything that is in violation of the organization's policies, and give examples of what this could look like. Also advise the clients to notify their contact person at the organization immediately if an online volunteer asks them to keep a secret about anything the online volunteer has said or done.

- Advise all participants on how to deal with messages that are suggestive, obscene, belligerent, or threatening, or make them feel uncomfortable. If a volunteer receives such a message from a client, what should the volunteer do? People, particularly youth and vulnerable populations, will relate information about themselves online that they would not otherwise. Your online volunteers and supervising staff should be fully trained in how to deal with various subjects that clients may bring up. Conversely, if a client receives an inappropriate message from another client or a volunteer, what should the client do? And what might an inappropriate message look like?

These points must be referenced frequently with all participants—not simply covered once at the start of a program bringing together online volunteers and clients.

There is a plethora of Web sites and books offering advice on how to stay safe online. Also, use the index at the end of this book to find all of the different places in this *Guidebook* where we discuss ensuring safety, confidentiality, and privacy.

Balancing Privacy and Safety

If you are going to monitor and archive volunteer-client online interactions, it is imperative that you communicate this to clients frequently and that you clearly state who will and will not have access to these interactions. Of course, your motivation is safety for all parties involved, but it often feels like a gross violation of privacy to know that a third party can read one's written communications, no matter what the motivation to do so. Having volunteers and clients help craft the policy together can help prevent negative feelings later.

As mentioned earlier, there are many software platforms that provide ways for parties to remain anonymous, and anonymous interactions between volunteers and clients may be best for your organization, depending on the focus of your work. But while it may be appropriate for volunteers to be anonymous from each other, it is never appropriate for volunteers to be anonymous from the organization itself. If volunteers are providing service on your organization's behalf, you need to know exactly who is doing what online. For instance, someone at the organization needs a record of what *screen names/user names* on an organization's forum go with which *real names* of volunteers.

Online Boundaries

In chapter 4, we reviewed using a person's online social activities as part of screening new volunteers, and in chapter 6, we cautioned about volunteers using social network sites to talk about their volunteering activities. In addition to the considerations raised in these two chapters, we need to add more that are specific to direct service online volunteers.

If you have volunteers who go offsite to interact with clients in the field (such as youth group leaders, baseball coaches, or hospice visitors), then you should already have written policies about what is and is not appropriate regarding where and how these volunteers and clients can interact, applicable both in the real world and virtually. However, you may still need some policy adjustments.

Let us start with an example of real-world, non-online volunteering, to get you thinking:

> *You are a volunteer teacher at a local community center, leading classes twice a month to help people learn to use computers. You rarely see the people you help outside of the community center activities—maybe while shopping for groceries, but not much more. But one day, while attending a* Star Trek *convention dressed as the blue dancing girl from episode 12 of the original series, you run into two of your students from the community center. You have not done anything wrong, and neither have they, but your personal life just crossed paths with your volunteering life and it may make you very uncomfortable (or very, very popular).*

The same thing can happen in cyberspace with online volunteers providing direct service to clients. They may cross paths on an online discussion group for a favorite TV show or sports team. A student protégé may find her online mentor's profile on Facebook or another social networking site and ask to be online friends. A client may find the personal blog of his online counselor and read about his weekend partying. Should your organization have policies regarding these out-of-program online encounters? Once again, we answer with a hearty *maybe*.

We cannot provide a one-size-fits-all policy statement. What you decide depends on the nature of your work as an organization, the nature of online volunteers' work with clients, and your existing policies regarding outside-of-agency activities by volunteers and employees. This is yet another circumstance that might be better handled through frequent discussions rather than a written policy, so as to create a culture where employees, volunteers, and clients are being thoughtful about all of their online activities.

Online Mentoring

One of the most popular examples of direct service virtual volunteering is online mentoring. By the end of the Virtual Volunteering Project in 2001,

there were more than 40 such programs in the U.S. alone.[2] As there is no organization researching online volunteering at the time of this writing, and as programs come and go year to year, we cannot say how many online mentoring programs there are in 2013, but we do know that new programs emerge regularly and we believe the number is easily in the triple digits. A successful online mentoring program identifies practices that are relevant to a wide range of online client services: tutoring adults and children, online visiting of homebound people, professional coaching, support through an illness or crisis—anything in which an online volunteer makes a connection with a client or customer that requires building a relationship of trust and productivity.

Online mentoring programs often involve collaboration among different organizations. For instance, the protégés—those to be mentored—may be students at a particular school, the volunteer mentors could be employees from one corporation,[3] and representatives from both of these entities organize the overall effort (an external nonprofit organization with experience in administering mentoring programs may organize the effort, too).

We have observed many online mentoring programs that gave a lot of thought to the software platforms they used, as well as to online safety issues; but they gave little thought to the many program activities and administrative tasks needed to create a viable, meaningful program. Assumptions were made about what program partners would do, how protégés would be prepared to participate, what interactions would look like, and how quickly relationships would be built. Sadly, as a result, many online mentoring programs do not last past one year.

The Electronic Emissary, launched by Dr. Judi Harris at the University of Texas at Austin and then moved to the School of Education at the College of William & Mary, was one of the first online tutoring/mentoring programs in the world for K–12 students and teachers and became a model for other programs. Its still-relevant papers and guides remain available online.[4] In a paper about lessons drawn from the experience, "Taboo Topic No Longer: Why Telecollaborative Projects Sometimes Fail," Harris concludes, "Telecollaborative projects may be curriculum-focused, but they are most definitely people-centered. Without effective collaboration, none would succeed."[5]

Mapping Collaboration

Whatever your program's focus, and no matter how many partners it does or does not have, every person who will be involved should come together to chart exactly what the program will look like. In these meetings, create visual representations such as flowcharts to envision how things will work—from the organization's point of view, the volunteer's point of view, *and* the client's/student's point of view. Map every step of the process, from the initial expression of interest by a volunteer, through the first meeting of the mentor and client, through the end of the relationship.

One tool for this mapping exercise is illustrated on the next page: it is an overview of the key administrative tasks involved in the launch and maintenance of a successful online mentoring program. You can adapt this list as needed for any program that brings together online volunteers and clients. While anyone involved may contribute to each of the following tasks, there should be only *one* person who is ultimately responsible for actually doing each task or making sure that it is done appropriately by assigning it to someone else and following up.

Every task shown on this grid must be assigned and communicated. If this list seems too much to do, or if only one person is in charge of all of these items, your organization is not yet ready to involve online mentors.

If the program is a partnership between two or more organizations, then the tasks should be fairly divided, not leaving just one organization responsible for every listed task. As well, a single individual should not be made responsible for *doing* most of the tasks!

Also, every person who is assigned some responsibility from this task list should be a part of the planning meetings; no one should be saddled with responsibilities s/he was not involved in designing(this happens all too often in school-based online mentoring programs, where the classroom teacher is told to participate—*after* others designed the program).

Decisions on Program

How will you select the specific sites that will identify the students to be mentored? Start by asking a simple question: "Why does your site want to participate in this program?" Ask for the answer to this question in writing. If a site cannot articulate its goals, the site is not ready to work with online mentors.

We have generated the long list of administrative tasks in creating and running an online mentoring program. What about program-related activities that must be defined and assigned? Participants will also need to discuss and make decisions about these sorts of questions:

- What will mentors and protégés actually do together online? What activities will they do together in the first week? The second week? The third week?

- What deliberate actions will mentors take to create a sense of trust online with their protégés?

- How will success for the first month of the program be measured? For the midway point? For the first year?

- What activities and results need to happen to demonstrate that this online mentoring program fits perfectly within the mission of our organization?

Site Managers

Many online mentoring programs are school based, with dispersed online volunteers interacting with students at or through the school. Most programs using this model have a *site manager,* usually a teacher, who is involved and supportive at all phases of development. Without full, enthusiastic buy-in from a site manager, the chances are small that the online mentoring program will last longer than just a few months and show tangible results.

Before launching an online mentoring program, clearly define what is expected of site managers, communicate these expectations, and make sure they are agreed to by all parties. You also need to define the consequences for site managers not meeting these expectations.

Key Administrative Tasks for an Online Mentoring Program

Task	Partner Organization Responsible	Key Person Responsible
Recruiting mentors		
Producing orientation materials for mentors		
Producing orientation materials for protégés		
Delivery of orientation to mentors		
Delivery of orientation to protégés		
Web site/online platform development, launch and updates		
Training of staff that will supervise participants		
Communicating regularly with all partners		
Reviewing mentor applications		
Communicating regularly with mentoring candidates re: the program (answering questions, etc.)		
Performing background checks on potential mentors		
Approving and rejecting mentors		
Notifying accepted mentors		
Communicating regularly with mentors (soliciting feedback, answering questions, troubleshooting, etc.)		
Approving each protégé's participation (reviewing grades, parental permission slips, etc.)		
Communicating regularly with protégés (soliciting and tracking feedback, troubleshooting, etc.)		
Communicating regularly with parents of youth involved (orienting them, soliciting and tracking feedback, answering questions, troubleshooting, etc.)		

Continued

Continued

Task	Partner Organization Responsible	Key Person Responsible
Designing system (e-mail, Web site, forum) where mentor and protégés will interact		
Reviewing (and perhaps approving/ forwarding) each electronic exchange between mentors and protégés		
Tracking and reporting on results of exchanges between mentors and protégés		
Tracking and reporting results of recruiting and orienting mentors, working with mentors, etc.		
Tracking and reporting on results of working with protégés		
Tracking and reporting results of parent relations and parents questions, concerns and interests		
Reviewing and evaluating all results of all tasks as reported and communicating this evaluation		

A site manager does much more than gather the names of protégés and provide them to the program coordinator or mentors. Site managers:

- Help define the goals of the program and the measurements of success.

- Provide their own vision for youth and mentor interactions so that this can be incorporated into the program design.

- Help identify the tools and resources needed to support the program and their work as managers.

- Review the tools and resources as they are developed, provide feedback about them, and learn to use them effectively.

- Provide guidance for or direct the matching of mentors to students.

- Participate in the training of youth who will be mentored, including program goals, everyone's expectations, safety guidelines, and so forth.

For at least three weeks before youth and volunteer mentors are matched and begin online exchanges, site managers should:

- Introduce themselves to the mentors.

- Talk about upcoming onsite program/class work activities or program/school events and how the mentors can help support these activities through their online interactions with youth.

- Provide or reinforce suggestions for online activities with youth in the coming weeks.

- Provide a list of days the program or class will not be in session.

- Invite and answer questions from the mentors.

- Provide any additional information they think will help mentors get off to a good start with their student.

- Be *upbeat* in messages to maintain everyone's excitement about this program.

After the program is launched, site managers should continue interacting regularly with mentors online and continue their firsthand involvement in the program. They should:

- Send at least bi-weekly reminders to mentors of upcoming activities and events and how the mentors can support these activities through their online interactions with youth.

- Provide or reinforce suggestions for online activities mentors can do with youth in the coming weeks.

- Promptly identify, investigate, and address problems, such as mentors not writing regularly, youth not writing mentors, misunderstandings, and so forth.

- Have access to mentor and student interactions (or a way to view the dates that e-mails are sent and from whom, without actually seeing e-mail contents) so that they can watch how the mentoring is progressing, who is writing regularly and who is not, etc.

- Address pertinent issues, either individually with a youth or mentor, with all of the mentors via the regular e-mail updates, or onsite with the youth.

- Provide a regular report to the overall project coordinator that reviews activities that are working well, obstacles and how they are being addressed, program and support needs, learning that could help in the further development or expansion of the program, success stories, and so forth. These regular reports will be critical to the overall evaluation of the program.

- Again, keep messages *upbeat* and encouraging! Volunteers need to see and hear site managers' enthusiasm in all messages about this program to further maintain and cultivate their own excitement about their work.

A Testimonial

In an earlier chapter, we introduced Infinite Family, the U.S.- and South Africa–based organization that connects orphans and vulnerable children in South Africa with online mentors. Dana Gold, program director at Infinite Family, notes that site managers have been fundamental to the success of the program because they have ensured participation by children and local partners:

What we have on the ground at each site is called Net Fundies, which is the Zulu word for expert. These are mostly young adults. They come to a center an hour ahead of time to make sure things are ready. They receive training on how to manage the computer site, how to defrag the computers, how to fight computer viruses, how to report problems and so forth. They receive a stipend based on the amount of children who come to the sessions. Fundies also get mentors to help them, and we connect them with speakers and trainers to help. Fundies suggest what they want help with. Recently, they asked for training in child management—they wanted to know, how do we get the kids to listen to us? Many of our Net Fundies work in education. We also have junior net fundies. These are usually kids that are always at the site and are identified as leaders among the kids. They get responsibilities for helping at the center. They discourage kids from visiting inappropriate sites.

Sometimes kids do drop out. Maybe they've been moved away by their families or they've gotten sick, they have to go to work, etc. There aren't too many kids who just stop showing up with no reason. When we are doing everything right on the management level, we don't have too many drop outs. When local partners can't meet their obligation, and when things change for our Fundies and it affects their work, that's when relationships falter.

Where the Students Are

All those to be mentored must have regular access to the Internet. If they are students and interactions will take place from a classroom, then each student site must have a minimum number of computers with fully-functional Internet access *before* the program begins. Define what number of computers would allow every student to be online every week, and make that number a requirement for site participation.

Each project site *must* identify protégés well before interactions are to begin, brief them fully on the goals of this program, and train them how to use the tools associated with this online mentoring experience. Consider these questions:

- How are these students currently using Internet access? What activities do they already engage in online through your organization or in their classroom? (If a site manager cannot answer this, the person is not ready to work with online mentors or help students participate fully in such a program.)

- Is there a person at each site who will help those to be mentored write their messages, if needed? This person could also make sure that all students are regularly writing to their tutors.

Everything Else Still Applies!

As we said at the start of this chapter, all the other program management recommendations in this *Guidebook* apply equally to involving volunteers in direct service activities. Whenever volunteers interact with clients individually, it becomes a highly personal activity and requires everyone to be comfortable and open. Whether onsite or online, these interactions are human, not technical—you are connecting people, not computers and smartphones. The most important things to remember when planning to bring volunteers together online with clients are not the technical aspects but the human aspects—building trust, cultivating interactions, encouraging buy-in, and enjoying the effort.

NOTES

1. The materials for teachers, mentors and parents who participated in the Sanchez Elementary School online mentoring program remain online for reference at http://www.coyotecommunications.com/sanchezov/index.html.

2. A list of direct service virtual volunteering and online mentoring projects compiled in 2001 by the Virtual Volunteering Project is still available online at http://www.coyotecommunications.com/vv/orgs/mentor.shtml.

3. This model was used by one of the first corporations to launch an online mentoring program for students—Hewlett Packard—beginning in 1995; the program later became its own independent nonprofit organization, the International Telementor Program (ITP): http://www.telementor.org/. It was also used in the 1990s by IBM in its own program, now called MentorPlace, an online mentoring program that brings together IBM employees with students to focus together on activities that help with the students' academic work and career goals: http://ibm.mentorplace.epals.org. Both of these Web sites have extensive training and support materials for mentors, students, and teachers.

4. To find the Electronic Emissary archive, go to http://www.wm.edu and type the word "emissary" into the search function. That will produce a long list of documents free to download. Another excellent source of information about virtual mentoring is ENDAPT, a very successful professional mentoring program pairing experienced teachers (volunteers) with novice teachers online, http://endapt.wm.edu/modules/telementoring/info.php?template=about.html&menu=.

5. Judith Harris, "Taboo Topic No Longer: Why Telecollaborative Projects Sometimes Fail," *Learning & Leading with Technology*, 27, no. 5 (2000). Accessed September 2013 <http://virtual-architecture.wm.edu/Foundation/Articles/Failures.pdf>.

German volunteer firefighter, Stefan Dietz, editing his fire company's Web site on the road during a vacation.

Chapter 9
Accessibility and Diversity

Online volunteering can be out of reach for some people for various reasons you cannot control, such as low literacy or lack of an Internet connection. And you cannot make every online volunteering opportunity accessible to *everyone*. For example, if you need someone to translate a document from English to Spanish, you will exclude any candidates who do not speak Spanish.

But there are many things you can do to make virtual volunteering opportunities accessible to a variety of people.

We have noted earlier that different volunteers will be attracted to different assignments, depending on their skills, interests, and availability. If all of your volunteering assignments are the same—all technology related, all requiring a great deal of reading, etc.—you will largely attract the same kinds of volunteers. By contrast, variety in assignments will produce diversity among volunteers.

Many people hear the word *accessibility* and immediately apply it only to people with disabilities. Similarly, the concept of *diversity* to many people may only imply having participants from different minority populations. But with both concepts, the issue is much broader. Accessibility and diversity are about accommodating *everyone*, not just people with disabilities or people from minority groups. You want to make virtual volunteering—as all other volunteering—welcoming to the widest number of people possible.

Benefits of Diversity

Why seek diversity among volunteers? What are the benefits of reaching out to potentially under-served communities even if it means accommodating online volunteers with different needs? By diversifying its volunteer corps, an organization will:

- Improve its service delivery by recruiting new talent, different from what already exists among staff and volunteers

- Ensure that the diversity of volunteers matches that of the organization's clients

- Reflect the various communities it serves

- Gain a fresh perspective, new ideas and additional talent

- Attract funding by demonstrating that it reaches out to under-represented groups

- Enable people to be themselves, enriching your organizational culture

- Make sure everyone has the opportunity to provide the best s/he has to give as a volunteer

- Avoid being boring[1]

Creating accommodations for one group often ends up making a program more accessible to many more people beyond that group. For instance, much of what is recommended to create accessibility for people with disabilities turns out to be helpful to everyone. Adding subtitles to your online videos not only makes it possible for people with hearing impairments to understand the material but also increases its usefulness for people learning English and for people who do not have headphones handy and want to watch the video with the sound turned down so as not to disturb people around them.

What is a *disability*, anyway? Both of the authors wear reading glasses—our *assistive technology devices*—and many Web sites that use tiny font sizes are inaccessible to us without our glasses. Both of us know people with physical limitations who have far more expertise in various professional and technical areas than we do and, therefore, have far greater online abilities than we do. The point is this: Do not divide volunteers into those-with-disabilities and those-without-disabilities—just as you should not divide volunteers into those who are *real* and those who are *just virtual*.

Accommodating Language Diversity

If your organization interacts with clients in multiple languages, you may wish to involve online volunteers who speak those languages, too. This may mean the volunteers are not native speakers of English (or whatever your local language is). The key decision you need to make is whether to require that all volunteers be *bilingual* so that they can interact with the clients but also with others in the organization.

Move with caution in converting some or all of your volunteering recruitment and training materials into other languages; by doing so, you are claiming to be ready to work with online volunteers who speak that language. Is that claim accurate? How many staff members could talk on the phone or exchange e-mails with a volunteer in this language? Do you have the resources to quickly, accurately translate e-mails and materials an online volunteer produces in his or her native language? (Note that translation Web sites that use a computer program, not a person, to translate from one language to another may be adequate for short, simple text but can produce incoherent and even misleading translations of longer or technical material.)

By all means, consider recruiting bilingual volunteers to translate some or all of your organization's public materials, including subtitles on online videos, into another language that is spoken by those communities you are trying to reach. However, to ensure accuracy, be sure that someone who is fluent in the other language edits and approves all of these translations. Either be prepared to deal with the phone calls and e-mails in that other language that will result from publishing the translated information or make it clear in both languages that a prospective volunteer should expect to speak your primary language with organizational contacts.

If you need many speakers of other languages, you also have the option of recruiting bilingual

volunteer team leaders. These team leaders can work with online or onsite volunteers who only speak the other language and so serve as your liaison with volunteers who speak a language you do not speak yourself.

Accommodating People with Physical Disabilities

One benefit of virtual volunteering is that it can allow for the greater participation of people who might find onsite volunteering difficult or impossible because of a physical or mental disability.[2]

According to the 2000 Census, there are 30.6 million people in the United States between the ages of 21 and 64 with a disability, and 57 percent of them are employed. Also in 2000, a Harris poll reported that 48 percent of people with disabilities who have access to the Internet believed that it had significantly improved their quality of life, compared to 27 percent of adults without disabilities.[3] An article in *The New York Times* in 2003 noted: "Many disabled workers say they consider telecommuting to be the single most important factor enabling them to work."[4]

People with disabilities who have Internet access and professional skills are already in a prime position to provide volunteering virtually. From 1997 through 1999, the Virtual Volunteering Project gathered testimonials from people with disabilities serving as online volunteers for various organizations. Their comments, received through e-mails, online surveys, and volunteer application forms, are excellent illustrations of the value of virtual volunteering to this population:

From an online volunteer in Iowa: *I live in a very rural area. Any significant area to seek volunteer opportunities is approximately 45 miles, one-way. Also, I became ill, and wanted something to do at my pace from home. I gave up my job and went on disability due to Fibromyalgia. My ability to predict my health status and schedule activities lessened dramatically. Volunteering on the Web gives me scheduling flexibility, assists me in maintaining contacts and cognitive functioning. I love the ease of getting to the "work site," the flexibility of hours, and being able to serve at my leisure 24/7. Now, my skills and background have become better utilized. I was awarded Volunteer of the Month. I was given more responsibility. My input is more readily sought. I was given more prominence on the organizational Web site.*

From an online volunteer in North Carolina: *We live in a very rural area that makes the disabled feel cut off from the world. Due to my disability, driving is out of the question. I also have children at home so that limits travel drastically. [Now] I can volunteer from home. I feel that I have learned as much from those I've helped as they have learned from me. I'm helping others as well as taking care of my children. Internet technology allows people to leave their disabilities behind. We are all the same on the Internet. No disabilities, race, or religion. We are united as one person. I recently found out that the fellow I worked with (online) had no light perception. He is a wonderful, caring person.*

From an online volunteer in Arizona: *I have extensive technical resources at home. I also have several health problems that preclude driving long distances and working set hours. [By volunteering virtually], I can stretch my skills, work on my own schedule and still "meet" very interesting people. My health sometimes affects my memory and with computer work, I can organize and document work to allow me to deal with many more complex details and more projects than I could handle manually. I can take breaks when needed and not be affecting anyone else.*

From an online volunteer in Colorado: *My work schedule must be done in 20–60 minute increments with long rest periods between. The Net gives me the opportunity to work the hours I can. Working from my home, I am able to work for 20 or 30 minutes and then lay down to rest or lounge in a chair with my neck and shoulders supported. Since the injury involves degenerative joint disease in my neck this is very important.*[5]

As you can learn from these comments, people with disabilities volunteer for the same reasons as anyone else. They want to contribute their time and energy to improving the quality of life around them. They want challenging, rewarding, educational service projects that address needs of a community and provide them with outlets for their enthusiasm and talents.

A volunteer resources manager (VRM), or anyone working with volunteers, does not have to become an expert in disabilities to involve people with disabilities as volunteers. Educating yourself about various disabilities in general, however, can help you learn to better accommodate a variety of volunteers in your program.

Also, note that many people applying to your organization to volunteer online may never mention that they have a disability. Your volunteer application should *not* ask about disabilities. Not only could this be a violation of laws in your country, but it gives the impression that you match volunteers to assignments based on what they cannot do, rather than on what they can.

Give volunteers—all volunteers, not just those online, and not just those with a disability—opportunities to tell you what accommodations they might need to be successful in an assignment. If you discover an online volunteer has a disability, you do not have to avoid the subject, but neither do you have to mention it. If you are uncertain about the wants or needs of a volunteer, with or without a disability, *ask!*

If a candidate writes and says, "I can do everything but such-and-such part of this assignment," consider working with the candidate to accommodate this preference. Perhaps the assignment can be broken up, with different volunteers taking on different pieces, depending on their interests and skills. Such a request does not necessarily mean the volunteer has a disability, however; he or she may lack the skills to do a particular part of an assignment or not have the time for that piece. If the assignment cannot be broken up to accommodate a candidate, explain why. Encourage the candidate to apply again for other assignments with your organization, because a "no" to one request does not mean all assignments will be closed.

Adapting Online Tools

Unfortunately, many Web sites and online tools exclude people with disabilities and prevent people using assistive technologies from accessing them. Fortunately, just as the way buildings are designed and constructed to allow people in wheelchairs to navigate doorways, there are ways to accommodate persons with disabilities to serve in virtual volunteering roles.

Volunteers with disabilities probably know more that you do about assistive technologies—software and hardware that allows them to surf the Internet, write documents, and more—so you do not have to become an expert. But it is a good idea to be aware of some of these tools, to help you understand just how much a person with a disability can offer to your organization via the Internet.

For instance, people with sight impairments sometimes use a special screen reader that converts whatever is on the screen to audible speech—meaning that the person hears the site rather than sees it. Text is presented in one voice, while hyperlinked text (text that leads to another Web page or another Web site) is presented in another. Just like everyone else, people with sight impairments sometimes just want to scan the links on a Web page in order to find something specific. If your links are presented only as *click here* or *read more*, that is all a person using a screen reader will hear, over and over again. Not very helpful! Instead, link from identifying text such as "donor information," "volunteer application," or "history of our organization."

Here's another example: your Web site may require someone to hold down several keys at once in order to make multiple choices on a pull-down menu. This can potentially leave out someone who has limited hand use. An alternative is to place check boxes on a Web page, allowing a user to click on multiple choices.

Your primary goal for your online tools is that they adhere to standards of universal design. At The Center for Universal Design at North Carolina State University's College of Design, a group of architects, product designers, engineers, and environmental design researchers established seven principles of universal design to provide guidance for planning products and environments.[6] These standards were for physical spaces but are easily adapted for online spaces—which we have done for each standard with regards to accommodations via the Internet:

1. *Equitable Use.* The design is useful and marketable to people with diverse abilities. For example, a Web site that is designed so that it is accessible to everyone, including people with: slow Internet connections; older hardware and software; a Web browser different than the one your Web designer used; and assistive technologies.

2. *Flexibility in Use.* The design accommodates a wide range of individual preferences and abilities. An example is a podcast offered as a text transcript, not only for people with hearing impairments but for people who prefer reading to listening.

3. *Simple and Intuitive.* Use of the design is easy to understand, regardless of the user's experience, knowledge, language skills, or current concentration level. This means, on a Web site, both graphically-represented links (photos, icons, and other graphics) and links via text.

4. *Perceptible Information.* The design effectively communicates necessary information to the user, regardless of ambient conditions or the user's sensory abilities. An example of this principle is when an online video includes captioning.

5. *Tolerance for Error.* The design minimizes hazards and the adverse consequences of accidental or unintended actions. An example of applying this principle is an online training module that provides guidance and background information when the new volunteer makes an inappropriate selection, explaining to him or her what the correct answer is and why.

6. *Low Physical Effort.* The design can be used efficiently and comfortably and with a minimum of fatigue. An illustration of this is the earlier example of a Web site menu that does not require the user to hold down more than one key.

7. *Size and Space for Approach and Use.* Appropriate size and space are provided for approach, reach, manipulation, and use regardless of the user's body size, posture, or mobility—and regardless of the user's hardware, including screen size.

Even if you are not the Web designer or webmaster, you should be an advocate for making universal design and online accessibility a priority for your organization. Talk with your Web staff to see what they do—and do not—understand about online accessibility. Ask if they are familiar with the Web Accessibility Initiative (WAI)[7] and how your organization's Web site measures up. If you encounter resistance, take your case higher up in your organization. If the webmaster is willing but unsure of how to proceed, suggest possible training on accessibility, and encourage the designer to read the WAI site, which includes free tools for evaluating a site's accessibility and how to address obstacles to users.

You might find available training on this subject through local programs that specialize in employees with disabilities, such as Goodwill Industries, Knowbility, or a public agency focused on people with disabilities. But, as always, we also recommend that you ask your volunteers. You may already have an online accessibility expert in your ranks who could help get your Web site in line with industry standards. Ask board members and volunteers who work for large for-profit corporations or large public sector agencies (government offices, universities) if they have a designer at their organization who is an accessibility expert and if this person is available to provide an accessibility workshop at your organization.

Accommodating Learning and Emotional Disabilities

A person managing any online service delivery needs to have a general understanding of various learning, working, and information-processing styles. Volunteer management is not one-size-fits-all, and simple adjustments in management style can effectively channel the talents and resources of the greatest number of people.

In acknowledging and accommodating the different ways people learn and communicate online, you are creating assignments that appeal to a greater variety of people with a range of working styles. You are also creating a virtual volunteering effort that accommodates seemingly hidden or non-apparent disabilities, such as learning disabilities (the most common form of disability) and emotional and anxiety disorders. Unlike other disabilities, such as paralysis, blindness, or even chronic illness, learning disabilities and emotional and anxiety disorders do not offer obvious visible signs to the casual observer; they may not be recognized by someone working with online volunteers.

A learning disability (LD) is a neurological disorder that affects a person's ability either to interpret what is seen or heard or to link information from different parts of the brain. These limitations can show up as specific difficulties with spoken and written language, coordination, self-control, or attention. They may impair multiple skills and abilities or they may impair only one. For example, difficulties with spelling may affect learners' writing skills, but not their reading skills. However, people with an LD have normal intelligence and are sometimes intellectually gifted. LDs are really a group of disorders, including dyslexia and attention deficit disorder (ADD).[8] The National Institutes of Health estimates that 15 to 20 percent of the total population has an LD.

Emotional and anxiety disorders are also disabilities. These can include suffering from depression, frequent anxiety, panic attacks, phobias, obsessive-compulsive disorder, and post-traumatic stress disorder.

Do not confuse these disabilities with lack of intelligence or lack of talent! In fact, many people considered very talented or having very high IQs also have, or had, learning disabilities or anxiety disorders: Albert Einstein, Agatha Christie, John F. Kennedy, Whoopi Goldberg, Nelson Rockefeller, Cher, George Patton, Leonardo da Vinci, Alexander Graham Bell, Abraham Lincoln, Barbara Streisand, and many, many others. Perhaps you did not know that any of these famous people had a learning disability or anxiety disorder. And the same will be true for volunteers, online and onsite: you may never know they have such a disability.

The more you break assignments down by task, the more accommodating you will be for 1) volunteers who have non-apparent disabilities, particularly learning disabilities, and 2) online volunteers who have only a very limited time available to provide service to your organization. The byte-sized assignments (or micro-volunteering as we discussed in chapter 3) that take just a few hours over a few days to complete may be particularly appealing to people who suffer from anxiety disorders as well as to people who are available only for a short period.

Generous deadlines may also be welcomed by volunteers with non-apparent disabilities, as well as to online volunteers with work schedules that frequently change. Not every assignment can have a flexible deadline; if a task must be done by a specific date, state this clearly in the recruitment message so that those volunteers who cannot meet the set deadline can screen themselves out.

Sometimes candidates will ask to take longer to read through the full assignment description and associated materials, or to go through the online orientation. They may need more time because of their work style or because of a disability that requires them to work at a slower pace. If you can accommodate more time, by all means do so. If the original time frame is non-negotiable, explain this and encourage the candidate to apply for another assignment with more flexibility. Refrain from asking why extra time is needed unless you feel that further explanation is warranted.

Sometimes you cannot accommodate a volunteer: an assignment may require a great deal of reading of background material that is only available via text; an assignment may involve producing an audio track, which means a volunteer would need to be able to hear, at least on some level; or the assignment deadline is tight because of the vital nature of the task to be done. The outcome of the work is paramount, so you may not be able to change the process for an individual volunteer. That is okay—no one should expect you to involve *every* person who wants to volunteer with your organization. Most people will not sign up for an online volunteering assignment if they are not qualified or if they do not have the abilities to perform the work. Should someone apply anyway, screening methods that an organization should already have in place will help identify the obstacles and steer the candidate elsewhere, either to another assignment or to another organization.

Language That Welcomes Everyone

The words you use can make your organization feel welcoming—or unwelcoming—to various groups. And when it comes to the Internet, your words can live practically forever. Your language choices can be

a barrier not only to people with disabilities but also to people of a particular ethnic group or who practice a particular religion (or no religion at all); people from a particular geographic area; people who are older, younger, gay, straight, thin, overweight, dye their hair, women, men—in short, language can hurt just about any category of human being.

Your goal regarding online language and accommodation is not to create a language police, stifle free speech, or play a never-ending game of "gotcha!" *Everyone* will make some written or verbal faux pas in the course of work or volunteering—or just simply living. Emphasize welcoming language and try to avoid hurtful, exclusive language. Create an atmosphere that is friendly to everyone so that when mistakes are made (and they will be), they are more easily corrected and forgiven.

Your organization probably has a non-discrimination policy stating that it prohibits discrimination or harassment based on a person's nationality, ethnicity, religion (or lack thereof), age, gender, or sexual orientation. If language use becomes a problem among volunteers in online communications, you can go back to such policy statements regarding inclusion and equal opportunity, as this is something all volunteers were supposed to have read and agreed to when signing on with your organization. Often, people say hurtful things out of ignorance or carelessness and would willingly stop and even apologize if they knew they were being offensive.[9]

Finally, in your advertisements for online volunteers, as well as on volunteer-related pages on your Web site, you should say something that affirms your commitment to be a welcoming organization for all applicants. Here are three samples of such statements:

- *Our organization appreciates the diversity of human beings and does not discriminate based on race, age, religion, ability, marital status, sexual orientation, gender, or gender identity.*

- *Our organization is committed to the principle of equal opportunity. We do not discriminate against individuals on the basis of race, color, sex, sexual orientation, gender identity, religion, disability, age, veteran status, ancestry, or national or ethnic origin.*

- *Our organization has a strong belief that all employees, volunteers, and clients of our organization should be treated with dignity and respect. In accordance with this, our organization does not discriminate in choices for employment, volunteer involvement, or providing service to clients because of race, creed, color, religion, gender, sexual orientation, gender identity/expression, national origin, disability, age, or covered veteran status.*

Some organizations add a sentence such as this as well:

- *Our organization also has a harassment-free workplace policy, which prohibits sexual harassment as well as any other form of harassment.*

Reaching Out and Tracking Progress

Tracking the progress of how well your organization reaches out to and accommodates diverse groups can be tricky; asking volunteers to identify personal information such as race or religion, or asking them to tell you whether they have a disability, can be seen as intrusive and interpreted as an attempt to discriminate unfairly in assigning volunteering placements. Yet, you need to document this sensitive information to assess whether your diversity outreach efforts are successful.

As we noted earlier, *under no circumstances should you ask these kinds of questions at the time of the application.* You want to avoid any implication that you are using such information to accept or reject a volunteer candidate. But once volunteers are on board, you may ask whatever questions you like in surveys, provided that you explain why you need this data and how it will, and will not, be used. Assure everyone that their replies will not affect future volunteer placements. This message will need to be repeated more than once; include it whenever you survey volunteers, online and onsite.

If you conduct a survey, consider making it anonymous to elicit the most honest responses and further ensure confidentiality. If the survey is done in face-to-face interviews or by telephone, the person conducting the survey should be someone who does *not* work with volunteers and who can assure the volunteer that responses will be kept anonymous and confidential. Volunteers can be identified by a unique number that only the surveyor knows; the VRM or others cannot otherwise match volunteers with their responses. For surveys completed online, use a system that allows each volunteer to respond only once; every computer has a unique address that properly configured surveys can use to prevent multiple responses from the same machine.

Final Thoughts

We noted in an earlier chapter that until recently, most online tools were text based, allowing physical disabilities, nationalities, ethnicities, physical appearance, dialects, and other personal characteristics to be hidden (naturally if not purposefully). That meant that online volunteers were judged primarily on the quality of their service and their written communications; it was harder for prejudices, even those we may not be aware of, to creep into our choice or evaluation of volunteers.

With the increasing use of live online audio and video, however, synchronous tools are bringing back face-to-face communications—and, possibly, prejudices. Therefore, think carefully before requiring the use of a certain tool for online volunteers, such as Skype or Google Talk. Could you accommodate someone who could not use that tool because of a disability? Think this through before mandating anything.

This is not a chapter about catering to just one group or about being politically correct. And this is not an add-on chapter, with a list of things to do as an afterthought. We believe a diverse, welcoming online volunteering program is a *better* online volunteering program, one that will more quickly reach an organization's goals and result in happier, more committed volunteers than a program that does not deliberately consider and plan for diversity or accessibility. This is a chapter with advice that really should be integrated throughout your virtual volunteering efforts.

NOTES

1. Adapted from The Consortium of Lesbian, Gay, Bisexual and Transgendered Voluntary and Community Organisations (London, UK), "InVolving LGBT Volunteers," 2008 <http://www.lgbtconsortium.org.uk/c1/downloads/2008/InVolving LGBT Volunteers.pdf>.

2. The Virtual Volunteering Project researched and documented ways to encourage the involvement of online volunteers with disabilities, supported by a special grant from and in collaboration with the Mitsubishi Electric America Foundation (MEAF). This chapter's information, while revised, is based on that original research.

3. Taylor, Humphrey. "How the Internet Is Improving the Lives of Americans with Disabilities." *The Harris Poll* #30, June 7, 2000 <http://www.harrisinteractive.com/vault/Harris-Interactive-Poll-Research-HOW-THE-INTERNET-IS-IMPROVING-THE-LIVES-OF-AMERICANS-WITH-DISABILITIES-2000-06.pdf.>

4. Eve Tahmincioglu, "By Telecommuting; the Disabled Get a Key to the Office, and a Job," *The New York Times*, July 20, 2003.

5. Virtual Volunteering Project, "First Person: Benefits of Virtual Volunteering for People with Disabilities," 2000 <http://www.coyotecommunications.com/vv/atech/comments.shtml>.

6. The Center for Universal Design at North Carolina State University, "Principles of Universal Design," 1997 <http://www.ncsu.edu/ncsu/design/cud/about_ud/udprinciples.htm>.

7. Web Accessibility Initiative <http://www.w3.org/WAI/>.

8. National Association of Special Education Teachers, "Introduction to Learning Disabilities," 2007 <http://www.naset.org/2522.0.html>.

9. The Consortium of Lesbian, Gay, Bisexual and Transgendered Voluntary and Community Organisations, *op. cit.*

Chapter 10
Evaluating and Recognizing Online Service

Like so many other volunteer management elements, virtual volunteering needs *evaluation* and *recognition* throughout the volunteer's experience. Waiting until the end of an assignment to do these activities for the first time with a volunteer is too late. *Ongoing* evaluation and recognition are essential to make sure everything works well at every stage of the online volunteering process and that volunteers feel acknowledged and appreciated along the way. Evaluation and recognition can be accomplished through small, informal actions as well as by big, formal efforts.

Evaluation has two aspects: program assessment and volunteer performance review. The latter is integrated with supervision and needs to be done individually with each online volunteer. As we have said earlier, the expectation of evaluation should be included in every volunteer task description, so both online volunteers and managers know that it is a required part of online volunteering involvement. When the manager submits a task description and starts the recruitment of an online volunteer, that manager agrees to conduct a volunteer evaluation during the volunteer's service. And when an online volunteer signs on, it is understood that the work will be evaluated.

The value of virtual volunteering obviously centers on effective and successful activities conducted by all volunteers, so individual performance review results *cumulatively* become a component of overall program assessment. In this chapter, we first examine program evaluation issues and then add some thoughts on individual reviews. We should also add that all the suggestions in this chapter can be applied equally to evaluating any and all volunteering at an organization, as the many online survey tools are accessible to everyone.

Why Evaluate?

Evaluating virtual volunteering serves many purposes:

- To assess what online volunteers contribute to the organization: what they are accomplishing and what their contributions allow the organization to accomplish

- To ensure volunteers have a positive experience and feel supported

- To ensure paid staff working with volunteers also have a positive experience and feel supported

- To identify issues that need to be addressed, such as what assignments have the most turnover and why, what assignments are the most popular and why, etc.

- To see what volunteer recruitment methods work

- To examine how diverse the virtual volunteering program is, in terms of what people are represented among online volunteers, and what recruitment methods might need to be adjusted to reach particular groups

- To track what tools staff and online volunteers use to interact

- To see if virtual volunteering develops new skills among employees and volunteers (supervisory, communications, tech-related, etc.)

- To send a message to volunteers that their service to the organization is important and valued by employees and clients/customers

Note that evaluation is never limited to *numbers,* as in how many volunteers, how many hours served, quantity of activities, and so on. As with all other volunteering, focusing on outcomes and assessing people's perceptions are most important in demonstrating the impact of virtual volunteering.

Creating a Welcoming Culture for Feedback

Evaluation happens informally whenever you ask volunteers and staff "How are things going?" at every opportunity—providing that you listen to the answers! If you hear a complaint or even a glowing report, is it a one-time, isolated event or are you getting the same feedback more than once? Keep asking. Over time, your sense of what is going on will be confirmed or challenged.

Also pay attention to behavioral indicators. Do volunteers and their staff partners contribute new ideas on their own? Meet deadlines for reports? Participate often in your online discussion group?

Silence is a warning sign that deserves investigation. For example, if volunteers do not participate in their online discussion group, is it simply because they are busy and do not have time or is there something wrong? Might they be keeping away out of frustration with their assignment, disgruntlement with someone on the staff, displeasure at a policy change, confusion about a recent announcement by the organization, or something else you need to address?

Do not rely on your memory to evaluate online volunteering activities. Keep track, in writing (on paper or electronically), of what you hear or read informally—this includes compliments, complaints, observations, whatever. No matter what the comment about virtual volunteering, write it down (with the date) to investigate later or to use in an internal report. This ensures that issues are really captured and will, hopefully, actually be addressed. Negative issues do not go away on their own and may wait silently until remembered at the least opportune moment—like when the online volunteer posts to a blog about frustrations with your organization.

The goal of both informal and formal evaluation is to create an atmosphere where feedback and observations from online volunteers and those working with them are welcomed at *any* time—and receive a response. That way, you address little problems before they multiply or grow into bigger problems. It is also a form of volunteer recognition: you are saying to volunteers that you value their feedback.

Formal Evaluation Techniques

Formal evaluation defines a period of time with a definite start and end date and then identifies a specific data set collected during that period to review and analyze. Note the two components: gathering data (the *right* data) and then analyzing it (*correctly*).

What Do You Want to Know?

Evaluation begins at the start, not the end, of program activities. First, you have to know what the goals and objectives are for:

- The overall involvement of volunteers in your organization, whether onsite or online

- The contributions of online volunteers in general

- The impact of online volunteers in a specific service project, role, or assignment

Do not just think about it: *write it down.* The more specific you are in articulating goals and objectives, the easier it will be to measure success.

Everyone who might need information about virtual volunteering needs to be involved in brainstorming the desired outcome of evaluation. In addition, all of these people need to come together to review and discuss the results of evaluation activities.

Collecting Data

Once you have defined measurable goals, next you need to decide what data will help you track, monitor, and eventually evaluate results over time. How will you gather that data? Where and how will you record it? What reporting do you need others to do to accumulate the right data? You should be tracking the information you need all along, not only at the end of a fiscal year or at the end of a volunteering assignment. For instance:

- If you want to know which recruitment method is most effective for online volunteers, you need to ask all interested people who call or e-mail how they heard about your organization—at the time of the contact, on the volunteer application form, or during the screening interview.

- If you want to know whether online volunteers are supported in their work with your organization, you might ask: How often is there contact between the volunteer and the person in charge of the assignment? How is this contact made? Do both people follow through on commitments?

- The volunteer resources manager (VRM) will want certain data for internal reporting requirements and to justify training ideas and resource requests.

- The marketing manager may want data about the accomplishments of online volunteers or the innovations they have inspired at your organization for story ideas for the media.

- The fundraising manager may want data about the involvement of online volunteers representing underserved demographics for funding proposals and the annual report.

- The executive director may want to report to the board about the staff time needed to effectively support online volunteers.

Data can be obtained in any number of ways. You can ask direct questions for the purpose of evaluation through surveys, focus groups, e-mail, and interviews conducted online, by phone, or in person onsite. But there are often other sources of information developed in the ongoing activity of a virtual volunteering project that can provide insightful data, too. For example:

- Volunteer application forms, time and activity reports, and any other data inputted into your volunteer management tracking system

- User numbers and the content itself on an online discussion group during the period under study

- The reports that online volunteers submit at the end of every assignment

- Answers to exit interview questions from volunteers who are leaving or taking an indefinite break from volunteering

Surveying Volunteers

There are different ways to conduct a survey, depending on the situation, tools available, and in what form you would like the data. Here are some options.

- Put the survey directly into the text of an e-mail. Ask everyone to respond in a reply back to you.

- Attach the survey as a document to an e-mail. This gives respondents the choice of replying electronically and re-attaching the completed form to a return e-mail or printing out the survey and responding to it on paper, faxing or even postal mailing the form back to you.

- Post the survey as an online Web form or use one of the Web sites especially created for collecting survey responses, such as Survey Monkey or Zoomerang. Web-based surveys gather data in such a way that you can either have the information directly keyed into your own survey system or download or cut and paste the results into reports, including automatically generated pie charts.

- Use the survey tools offered by the platform where you created your online discussion group for volunteers. Yahoo! Groups, for instance, comes with an online polling function.

- Use an event that brings a large number of volunteers together onsite, in person, and distribute the survey on paper; ask people to complete it before they leave.

- Conduct a telephone survey. Call all or a representative sample of volunteers and ask a series of consistent questions. For telephone surveys, consider involving interviewers who do not work with the volunteers being surveyed, to better guarantee the anonymity of responses. If your organization has a telemarketing staff, they could be trained to undertake this phone survey. You could also try contacting professors who teach business or advertising classes at local universities to see if their students might volunteer to conduct such surveys and receive class credit. Be sure you notify online volunteers well before phone calls take place, so they do not think the caller is a telemarketer (someone trying to sell them something).

Any survey effort needs a lot of reminders to those taking the survey to guarantee an adequate number of responses. Place notices on your online forum for volunteers, in an e-mail sent to all volunteers, in your volunteer newsletter, on a flier in the break room at your organization, in a notice on your social networking accounts, etc. Announce when the survey will take place and ask volunteers to participate. Include a message about why this survey is being done, such as, "to help us improve our interactions with and management of volunteers." Include an explanation of what you are going to do with the feedback obtained: Will it be available for all paid and volunteer staff members? Will it be published in any reports? Include a personal assurance of confidentiality, such as:

We would greatly appreciate your honest feedback and hope you will be candid. While I may pass on comments to others at our agency, I will not identify the volunteers who said them, if you request such anonymity.

We developed a list of possible survey questions and present the list on the next page. Use this list as a starting point to gather the feedback you need from volunteers who have been involved with your organization virtually. These questions are designed to uncover the strengths and weaknesses in the management of volunteers who work offsite via their home and work computers or smartphones.

Note that there are different ways to format the responses to these questions. Some might be useful with just a "yes" or "no" answer. For others you might want to offer a multiple choice checkoff (always, sometimes, occasionally, never) or ask volunteers to score their preference from 1 to 5. Yet other questions lend themselves to short answers or essay responses. It all depends on how much detail

you want to get from online volunteers. Just remember that a survey that is too long will not be answered carefully, and you want data that can easily be compiled and compared at the analysis phase.

Also, the way you ask a question often determines the response you will get. As just one example, if you give people an odd number of rankings from which to choose, a percentage will default to selecting the "middle" one most often; so if you really want to know if people are leaning one way or another, provide only an *even* number of options to force answers on one side of the issue or the other. Pilot test the survey to see: 1) if what you ask is correctly understood; 2) if your wording steers people to a certain reply; or 3) if you have given respondents the option of disagreeing with the question or feeling conflicted about the answer. There are nuances in constructing an effective survey and you may need to recruit an expert volunteer to help with this.

Be sure to thank respondents for their feedback and to report on results to all volunteers quickly so they know their input was of value. In fact, a few days before the survey is to end, you might want to post or send a reminder message to elicit more responses, with a quick indication of the results to date:

Thanks to everyone who has responded to the survey so far. We are getting praise about the usefulness of the last training session, as well as hearing you loud and clear about your frustrations with our online form for recording your hours! We are looking forward to hearing from more volunteers before the deadline of May 15.

Not all volunteers will respond to survey requests. But for those who do, study their feedback carefully. Does their description of what they did for your organization match your assumptions of their intended role? Do they have a positive image of your organization as a result of their volunteer experience? What are the common themes in their feedback?

Surveying Paid Staff

Surveying employees may be trickier than surveying online volunteers. It is much more difficult for staff to provide feedback anonymously (their responses can reveal in which unit they work or allow others

Possible Evaluation Questions You Might Ask Online Volunteers

- What type of volunteer services did you provide for our organization in [this period of time]? (*You might find that volunteers have done much more than you have a record of!*)
- Who was your primary contact at our organization during this/these assignment/s? Was s/he helpful? Accessible?
- What other volunteers or employees did you work with during this/these assignment/s? Was s/he helpful? Accessible?
- Did you work with other volunteers during this/these assignment/s? How? Was such collaboration successful?
- How much of your volunteer experience with us was virtual (working via your home or work computer or your smartphone) and how much of it was spent onsite at our organization?
- How many hours would you say you have spent as a volunteer for our organization to date?
- Do you feel you completed your assignment? If not, why?
- How long have you volunteered? Did you volunteer with our organization online only or also onsite?
- What type of support did you expect from our organization? Did the support you actually received meet your expectations? Please provide details.
- What tech tools have you used with paid staff members and other volunteers?
- What did you like about volunteering via the Internet, as opposed to volunteering onsite?
- What did you dislike about volunteering via the Internet?
- How did our organization recognize/reward you for your volunteer contributions? Did you like this recognition?
- What would make your virtual volunteering experiences with our organization more satisfying to you?
- What types of virtual volunteering opportunities do you wish were available that you have not yet encountered?
- What are your impressions of our organization and our programs?
- Would you volunteer with us again? Why or why not?
- Other comments/suggestions:

Possible Evaluation Questions You Might Ask Paid Staff

- What type of services/support did volunteers provide you virtually?
- How many volunteers did you work with during this/these virtual assignment/s?
- Were these volunteers appropriately matched to their assignments?
- How much of your work with these volunteers was virtual (working via home or work computers or via a smartphone) and how much of it was spent onsite at our organization or by phone?
- How many hours of service have volunteers assigned to work with you provided virtually?
- What skills/contributions did you find most valuable in volunteers who provided services virtually?
- Did such volunteers complete their assignments? If not, why?
- What did you expect out of these volunteers' virtual service to you and to our organization?
- Did the volunteers' online work meet your expectations? Please provide details.
- What did you like about working with volunteers virtually via the Internet, as opposed to onsite interactions?
- What did you dislike about working with volunteers virtually via the Internet?
- What tech tools do you use to work with volunteers?
- How did you recognize/reward online volunteers for their services?
- What would make virtual volunteering experiences more satisfying to you as a supervisor?
- What types of virtual volunteering opportunities would you like to assign in the future?
- Do you think these volunteers will work with our organization again? Why or why not?
- Other comments/suggestions:

to deduce who is speaking) and they may be reluctant to say something that, while honest, will hurt a person's feelings. Or they may see this as just another hassle regarding volunteer management.

You may want to use a Web-based method of delivery and reply, since it has the most anonymity and is the easiest for collating responses. Or, you may want to be more personal and sit down with each staff member one-on-one, face-to-face, and conduct the survey in a conversational tone. Staff may be more open to speaking candidly with someone who will not be at the organization long-term, such as a student volunteering onsite as an intern or recruited specifically to help with the evaluation through an academic class. Depending on your organizational culture, your method of choice may be to bring staff members together onsite for feedback through group discussion.

Once again, we start you off with a list of possible questions to ask employees about virtual volunteering, presented on page 136. Pick and adapt from this list the questions that will mean the most for you, applying the same considerations about designing the response format as we outlined for getting feedback from online volunteers.

Again, be sure to thank respondents for their feedback, and let them know how the feedback is used!

Carefully study the responses you receive. Are staff comfortable working with volunteers virtually? Are there gaps in communication with volunteers working remotely? How do the staff responses match the volunteer responses regarding what volunteers accomplished? What training might need to be done to build staff capacities to work more effectively with volunteers?

Analyzing the Data

A favorite saying of Susan's (original source unknown) is that "statistics are like bikinis; they reveal what is interesting but conceal what is essential!" Nothing is more important to the evaluation process than drawing the right conclusions from the data.

If you really want to know how people feel about a specific aspect of the program, ask more than one question about it on the survey. Then you have some validating data rather than responses from a single question that might be misinterpreted or unclear.

Statisticians warn that *correlation* is not necessarily *causation*. In other words, just because you find that a majority of volunteers surveyed have a master's degree, do not conclude that people with less education do not want to volunteer. You may have a highly-educated group of online volunteers because you recruited through graduate schools or your virtual volunteering task description was written with lots of big words. Check assumptions and do not assume that data is self-evident in meaning.

The best way to ensure valid analysis is to involve a team in reviewing everything. If any part of the evaluation evokes differences of opinion as to its meaning, you may need to ask some follow-up questions to learn more.

Reporting

Share the results of the evaluation with everyone who participated, not just with executives, funders, community partners, and others with a strong interest. If confidentiality rules make some data inappropriate to share with everyone, then at least share a summary of the findings and a brief on how the evaluation will affect online volunteer involvement at the organization. But remember that you have given training (we hope) about confidentiality and have affirmed this training frequently, and therefore, volunteers will not be any more prone to sharing the data outside the organization than a paid employee would be.

Do not be afraid to share negative information with online volunteers or staff. If the evaluation uncovered problems, it did its job. What is more important is what you plan to *do* to improve things once you have learned what matters to people. On the other hand, be sure to highlight the things that are going very well!

Dealing openly with evaluation results demonstrates transparency on the part of the organization, something volunteers really value highly. It may even lead to the volunteers coming up with terrific solutions to various challenges, small and large.

Encouraging Ongoing Input

As noted earlier, no volunteer or employee should have to wait until a formal survey to give feedback about a virtual volunteering experience or to make suggestions to the organization. Opportunities for volunteer feedback and involvement abound—or at least they should.

Use your online forum for volunteers often to solicit feedback. Even an informal message such as, "I have not heard much from you regarding how your volunteering is going, other than your standard replies in reports. Really—how are things going?!" will generate responses. Or post a "question of the month" for volunteers to answer, such as these examples: "My favorite online tool is _____ because _____." "My favorite thing about the organization is _____ and my least favorite thing is _____."

Find ways to engage volunteers in other work. For example, if your organization is redesigning its Web site, negotiate with the Web designer for a draft to be made available where online volunteers can access it. Then invite feedback: "So, everyone, what do you think?" Pass their suggestions back to the Web designer.

Take the pulse of volunteers and managers on a regular basis to troubleshoot and prevent small problems from becoming large ones. Identify and celebrate milestones and successes and capture volunteer ideas to help improve your activities and expand your organization's services. Don't forget: Asking volunteers what they think is a form of volunteer recognition. It demonstrates that you value their ideas and comments.

How to Handle Online Criticism

As positive as inviting volunteer feedback can be, eventually someone is going to say something negative. All social networking tools—from the online discussion forum to blogs to photo sharing—are interactive public forums. They allow people to comment on posted information, photos, or videos and for others to see those comments. This means you have to be prepared to see and deal with online criticism of your organization in general and of volunteering activities specifically. In fact, if you have followed our advice, you have actually invited such criticism.

Some negative comments might come from individuals taking their personal complaints public. For example, they may come from someone who did not receive a reply to an e-mail offering to volunteer;

who thinks it is inappropriate that you do a personal reference check on volunteering candidates; or who has been turned down from volunteering. Other criticism may be focused on disagreement or discomfort with a decision made by the organization or an observation of something that went wrong in the delivery of service.

To be successful with virtual volunteering, an organization must be able to honestly and openly deal with online criticism from volunteers. Otherwise, the organization puts itself in a position to lose the trust of supporters. Once lost, trust and credibility can be extremely difficult to win back.

Before your staff panics at the idea of supporters not being so supportive, or the organization nixes an online forum altogether, remember that *allowing such discussions among volunteers reflects very positively on an organization.* Here are some tips for dealing effectively with public criticism (whether from volunteers or not):[1]

- Address criticism directly and promptly. If you cannot respond fully immediately, then at least immediately acknowledge that the complaint has been read by the organization and a response is coming promptly. A week or more is not prompt in online community conversations.

- Contrary to a widely-held belief and frequently-made suggestion, you do not disarm criticism by thanking someone for their feedback in the opening statement of a response! This has been done so often that most people see it as the beginning of a canned statement. Save the compliment for somewhere else in your response—and say it only if you can demonstrate that you truly mean it. There are a number of ways that you can demonstrate that you are really hearing the complaints:

  - Ask the critic(s): "What do you think would make this situation better?" or "How do you feel this situation could be improved?"

  - Assure critics that their comments and suggestions will be shared with the leadership at your organization and that they will receive an update regarding the leadership's reaction.

- If the criticism is going to result in a change or action of any kind, or a staff meeting to discuss further action, say so. Offer as many details as possible.

- If it is appropriate, you could even ask a critic to take part in a staff meeting or create a dedicated, short-term online forum specifically to address the issue being raised.

- If the complaint is legitimate (such as someone pointing out that the organization's past annual reports are not on the organization's Web site), acknowledge it, correct the issue ASAP (get the annual reports on the Web site), and offer an apology. Do not try to defend or excuse a mistake. Take the lumps with grace and honesty.

- If some part of a criticism is accurate, acknowledge it. That does not necessarily mean agreeing with the person fully. For instance:

  You are correct: our organization does not address environmental problems. I understand that this is a very important, even critical issue, but our nonprofit has chosen to focus on preventing the abuse of children, and here's why . . .

- Even better, can you think about the criticism from the person's point of view and therefore agree with some of it? That is a powerful way to turn a critic into a supporter.

- Is the critic actually doing you a favor by offering you feedback that may not have been discovered otherwise, when damage was done to your organization's reputation and credibility? Again, acknowledging a real problem can win support.

- Some excuses can make a situation even worse—even if they are true—and should be avoided because they are perceived as red

flags for incompetence or mismanagement. Try not to say:

- "We didn't have enough money."

- "We don't have enough staff."

- "We didn't have enough time."

- "We are an all-volunteer organization."

- "Our computer system wasn't working properly"

- "So-and-so was on vacation at that time."

Instead, take responsibility.

- You may need to ask for clarification or more information before you respond to criticism, and that is fine. This will probably be perceived by those watching the online conversation as a very positive step on your part. But do not say, "I don't understand why you are asking these questions." Every question is legitimate and should be treated as such.

- If a complaint does not present the whole story, then do so yourself, as quickly and thoroughly as possible. If a complaint is off-base, counter it with indisputable, dispassionate facts. And offer to supply any other facts that will clarify the situation. Ask the original critic if he or she has any questions or comments about the facts as you have offered them.

- Be detailed about how a complaint is addressed. If a decision is made by the organization in response to the complaint, explain clearly how the decision was reached and exactly who was involved in making it (by job title rather than name is okay). If it was not a democratic process, then say so. Not all decisions can be made by a vote, but no matter how a decision is taken, an organization should be transparent, especially if the action has resulted from a complaint by volunteers or other supporters.

- Do not post one or two responses and then ask for the debate to stop. A better strategy is to let the debate play out. If you respond to a criticism and someone says, "That did not address my criticism," then review the original post and respond again and/or ask the person what would better address his or her concerns. If it takes answering each question or sentence individually, do so. Also, ask the entire community how they feel about the debate—are their own questions or concerns being addressed? As long as someone does not meet the definition of a troll (see below), let the debate rage on. In the best of worlds, the community itself will bring the debate to a halt—and be your greatest defenders.

- If the criticism is of an action that is not negotiable or changeable, then be prepared to sincerely acknowledge the criticism but also to stand your ground. If, after considering the criticisms of your choice of a conference site, your logo redesign, your new policy regarding volunteer candidate screening, the closing of a branch office, or whatever, your organization decides it is not going to change the decision, then say so, and say why. But also acknowledge any of the legitimate grievances the critics have: Should you have made the decision-making process more democratic? Should you have solicited feedback before the decision was made? Should you have better communicated the reason why you undertook an action? Acknowledging such missteps and committing to altering future decision making as a result of the criticism can take the sting out of the loss for critics who do not win the online battle, because you show that, indeed, the criticism *did* have an impact.

- Always consider whether a complaint is an indication of a greater problem. Could there be a credibility gap among some supporters that could spread to others if not addressed? Could online criticism be an indication of a problem or perception among supporters of which you were not previously aware? It might be worth brainstorming with staff and supporters onsite, in a special meeting, to find out if there is something more to criticisms that might meet the eye.

- No matter what you say, your organization's *actions* are going to speak much louder than its words. Therefore:
  - If you say a response is coming promptly, then it had better come promptly. Again, a week or more is not prompt in online community conversations.
  - Do not just say you welcome criticism; allow critical messages to be posted to your online forum for volunteers or the comments board on your blog, so long as such criticisms do not use inflammatory language, encourage criminal behavior, contain obvious inaccuracies, include confidential information, or are not verbatim posts from the same person over and over again.
  - Walk the talk: If you state that your organization engages in activities to recruit a diverse representation of employees and volunteers, it had better be engaging in actions that back up that statement, obviously and clearly. If you claim to be a green (environmentally-friendly) organization, make sure a television crew walking through or around your office would see activities that demonstrate this.
  - Do not just say your organization is transparent and consults with membership—show it in activities that make this quality obvious.
  - Allow people to voice their opinions. Halting a debate/discussion too soon will result in people perceiving your organization as not open to criticism and will result in even more of it.

In short, keep this in mind at all times: When volunteers care enough to criticize, they need to be taken seriously, and you need to show that you have taken them seriously.

If you have worked to create trust with volunteers, you are more likely to learn of issues early and privately. If volunteers already trust you, you are going to have a much better time dealing with online criticism that does occur, and most volunteers will be ready to give you the benefit of the doubt.

Complaints That Go Too Far

Can online complaints go too far? Certainly, and it is entirely permissible for your organization to prohibit or censor certain topics from discussion on its own online groups, such as information about clients, internal documents, and other confidential information. Establish rules and enforce them. For example, you would be within your rights to censor foul language and to remove a volunteer for posting with offensive language; if you do remove someone, the group needs to know who and why.

Beware of *trolls*. A troll is the label given to someone online who moves from being an angry person with legitimate criticism to a person who is arguing for the sole purpose of derailing conversations and creating mistrust. A troll consistently strays from facts, makes insulting personal comments, posts the same information over and over again, and posts messages obviously designed to annoy and antagonize other members and engage them in fruitless confrontation. But be careful: do not automatically dismiss someone who is disgruntled, suspicious, or questioning as a troll when there might be reasons for the online behavior. Avoid being seen as just trying to shut down legitimate, although uncomfortable, conversation.

It is fine to remind users of the forum rules and what topics are off-limits. It is also a good idea for a staff member to occasionally enter the conversation to let participants know that staff are aware of what is being discussed, appreciate the feedback, and are taking action as a result of it.

If anyone is violating the policies of your organization, step in immediately with appropriate action. But do not shut down a negative conversation on your online discussion group just because it is negative. If you feel that an ongoing debate is stifling discussion of other topics, then consider creating a forum specifically for that subject and asking users to move the debate there to allow regular business to be done on the original forum.

Complaints on a Third-Party Site

Criticisms of volunteering with your organization can also be posted on someone else's forum, Web site, blog, or page on a social networking site. You cannot control what other people post on their own or someone else's site, unless they violate the law (though you may certainly fire a volunteer who violates your organization's policies with personal postings anywhere online).

If a third party site allows online discussion or has a comments board, you should engage in any of the activities suggested above on this other site and invite the other forum participants to contact you directly for further information or clarification. If the site does not have a discussion forum or comments board, write directly to the author or moderator with your information or clarification. You may also consider posting information on your own online forum in response if you feel that the criticisms could cause concern among volunteers.

How can you find out if online criticism is happening outside of your own online forums? Let Google search for you by setting up one or more automatic "alerts" (see sidebar about "Automated Notices"). Ask volunteers to be on the lookout for postings about your organization on the online groups, blogs, and social networking sites they frequent. Encourage them to pass on such information so your organization can be more in tune with public opinion, *not* so you can shut down criticism. Also, go to any online search engine and search for your organization's name or the name of your organization's executive director, VRM, or other key staff. You may find criticism or praise from a volunteer, donor, or client about your organization that you will want to address.

Note that a variety of Web sites have been created to assist prospective donors in evaluating whether or not to give money to a particular nonprofit organization. Along with giving access to what an organization is required to report to the Internal Revenue Service (or its equivalent in other countries), sites such as InsideGood and GiveWell also solicit comments from anyone who knows something personally about how the group does its work. Financial donors, employees, clients, and, of course, volunteers can submit an opinion. Also, some online volunteer opportunity registries encourage people to report on their volunteer experience for the benefit of others considering applying to the same agency.

Automated Notices about Online Mentions

Both Jayne's and Susan's favorite tool for tracking what is being said online about an organization or topic (or where our own names appear!) is Google Alerts. This free service automatically notifies you if there is any new content in a public space—including traditional print media that publishes their stories online—that mentions whatever phrase or phrases you want to track. It will not tell you about e-mail conversations, as those are private, or about postings on private online spaces such as a member-only discussion group or someone's Facebook profile with all privacy settings on. You can use Google Alerts or similar tools to track:

- Your name

- Your organization's name

- Your executive director's name

- Another organization (your competition, a partner, an organization you aspire to be like, etc.)

- A particular subject matter

- Almost anything else under the sun

Start with two Google Alerts at first—one of just your name, and one of your organization's name. Putting a name in quotes is best, so that you will get only exact matches. As Jayne explains: *I don't want every newspaper story that mentions Jayne and also Cravens, but specifically, Jayne Cravens, and that won't happen unless I put my entire name in quotes, like this: "Jayne Cravens."*

You will receive an e-mail when something is published online with your alert name, with a link to the mention. You can set the alerts to come as soon as the mentions happen (for instance, when the blog is posted that mentions your name), in a daily summary, or in a weekly summary.

Be careful when you choose subjects to track; you do not want to track something generic like *dogs*, because you will be overwhelmed with alerts. You would want to track something specific instead in one alert, like *dog rescue Naples Italy*.

Individual Performance Assessment

Evaluation surveys of volunteers and paid staff give insight on virtual volunteering as a whole at your organization. Clearly such organizational assessments *imply* how successfully (or not) individual volunteers performed in their assignments, since all the links in the chain need to be working together to achieve goals. But at some point, you will need to evaluate individual volunteers in order to understand where you should make improvements or try to multiply what is going well.

Many organizations are reluctant to do performance evaluations of volunteers, feeling that they should be grateful for whatever contributions volunteers make (even sub-standard work) and that formal evaluations make volunteering too much like a paid job. But some kind of performance review is necessary, even if it is informal. Why? First, volunteers who are doing great work can be recognized for doing so and kept motivated by the positive feedback. Second, volunteers learn how they can improve their contributions in the future and not keep making the same mistakes. Third, it is a way to assure paid staff that volunteers are focused on quality performance. Finally, volunteers who consistently make more work for an organization through poorly-performed tasks can be let go in an honest manner.

If you tolerate service that does not accomplish useful results, you allow both the volunteer's and the organization's time to be wasted. As we said in an earlier chapter, no one volunteers with the purpose of doing poor work. Volunteers—online and onsite—want to know that they are really helping.

Performance assessment starts with the volunteer position description, since that was what both you and the volunteer agreed to do together when the volunteer signed on. So the first set of questions presented to the volunteer should revolve around:

- How much of this description accurately outlines what you actually did with us?

- Do you (or we) feel you were successful?

- What else did you do that is not reflected here?

- What problems did you encounter?

Encourage whoever worked most closely with each volunteer to share honest opinions of the work performed. Staff may need training in how to do this; role-playing is an excellent tool, as well as sharing actual examples from other staff (but protecting all volunteers' identity). Spend time discussing how they give feedback to volunteers about contributed work—good or critical—and ask volunteers if they have received such feedback and their response to it. Take action as necessary to make sure such ongoing evaluation and feedback are happening.

The goal of performance assessment is never to be punitive. It is a feedback cycle that, ideally, will motivate volunteers and those that manage volunteers to learn new skills, experiment with new ways of doing things, and be even more successful in the future. You might choose to call the process not an "evaluation" but rather an "action plan" or a "mutual progress report." And make sure the feedback is two-way; this should be as much of a chance for the volunteer to express an opinion about the organization as for you to assess the volunteer's work.

Look for other activities that reveal the contributions of a volunteer. For example, review the volunteer's participation in your online community for volunteers. Is there any? Does the volunteer connect with the community in helpful ways?

Of course, engage online volunteers in a self-assessment process. Ask them what they feel they accomplished and what they would improve if they did it again. At the end, review the original position description and see if it accurately reflects the work the volunteer did or if it needs to be updated.

Rejecting or Firing a Volunteer for Personal Online Activity

It is not a new practice to fire a volunteer because of activities outside of an organization that staff believe is not in agreement with the organization's culture or work environment. As one example, Peace Corps Online, an independent news forum, reported that the Peace Corps pulled an invitation for a candidate for an assignment after officials read an online article in which he stated an opinion regarding government policy. It was not the particular opinion that caused concern but rather that he offered an opinion *at all* about the government in an online public forum; that made him unacceptable, given the nature of the

work he would have been doing and the culture and laws in the specific country to which he was going to be sent.

The permeation of online activities of all sorts has created new dilemmas for VRMs. For instance, many people, particularly those under 40, share a tremendous amount of personal information online, from explicit stories about how they spent their weekends to explicit photos that illustrate the story. They have created the expectation that what they post online from their private life is somehow out of bounds to employers, even though it is published to public spaces. Then they are often stunned when their online activities have consequences at the workplace, let alone where they volunteer.

The blurring of public and personal information requires some careful thought by volunteer-involving organizations, and perhaps some clear policies. What if volunteers—whether online or onsite—have social network profiles with views or photos that might make you uncomfortable? Should this be used as a reason to not involve online volunteers? Would you use it as a reason to not have employees?

Start by accepting that a volunteer—or a paid employee, for that matter—may engage in or promote activities via online profiles on social networking platforms that your organization does not wish to be associated with but are not in violation of your policies. Perhaps there are informal pictures of the person and links to videos or political events that cause you some concern. Remember that volunteers may be engaging in *offline* activities your organization would not necessarily be comfortable with either. Think about the t-shirts many organizations hand out to volunteers. Do they come with instructions as to where they should and should not be worn?

Whether or not you fire a volunteer for online or offline activities, the decision should be based on clear, stated policies shared when you first orient new volunteers. The decision may not be black or white, as the volunteer's role might need to be taken into consideration. For instance, a volunteer who is helping with your Web site and is arrested for drunk driving probably will not be obviously associated with your organization in the minds of the public or the press (unless you are anti-alcohol advocates, of course). However, if your high-profile board president, who frequently serves as your organization's spokesperson, is arrested for such an offense, there may be pressure for that person to go. In neither case did the volunteers violate your policies; the difference is that one inappropriate incident probably will not affect one volunteer's performance at your organization, while it probably will affect the other.

Likewise, a volunteer who is designing software for your organization and has a publicly-available online photo featuring partial or complete nudity may not matter to anyone; but a racy photo on a public space showing your volunteer public relations manager in a similar situation might get everyone's attention, because that volunteer is in the public eye as your organization's representative. Similarly, it may be irrelevant that the volunteer webmaster at your animal rights organization publishes erotica elsewhere, but it may matter very much if yours is a child safety organization—not because of illegality or immorality, but because of its contradiction to the mission of your organization and the reaction parents might have if they found out.

Linking to Personal Volunteer Sites

You may also want to consider creating a policy regarding why your organization might refuse to link to a person's profile on a social networking site and share this policy with volunteers. You could even ask for their help in drafting the language; by involving them in the discussion, you create a sense of ownership among them regarding the policy.

If you are going to screen candidates for volunteering (or employment) based on their online activities (typing their name into Google or Microsoft Bing and seeing what comes up on the first two pages or seeing if their profiles on Facebook are public and, if so, what is on them), say so in your interviews and orientation. Have a stated justification for this kind of screening. Your goal will be to allow candidates to withdraw from the application process if this kind of screening would make them uncomfortable. If a volunteer's online activities are of concern to you, articulate why you have that concern, as it relates to the organization, its workplace culture, its public profile, its clients, or your written policies. It is not sufficient to use "I don't like it" as a justification for dismissing a volunteer because of his or her personal online activities.

In the chapter 12, written for volunteers themselves, we have recommendations for volunteers regarding how to separate their personal online activities from those that relate to their persona as a volunteer or employee. A good exercise might be reviewing these recommendations with your organization's employees and volunteers. Decide together if there really is a need for any of these recommendations to become actual written policies at your organization or if talking about these issues occasionally is enough.

Recognition

Recognition is another one of the major elements of effective volunteer management. We are discussing it in this chapter because in many ways recognition is tied to evaluation. First you need to know what was accomplished and how well it was done; then you can celebrate it.

Recognition is much more than saying "thank you," although it is always appropriate to express appreciation for any helpful action, no matter how small. In fact, informal recognition that occurs as contributions are made is usually more motivating to volunteers than formal, annual thank-you events. Perhaps the most powerful form of recognition is listening to and then using a volunteer's suggestions.

In traditional, offline settings, much of the inspiration and recognition for volunteers occurs informally: volunteers come in contact with staff members over coffee; talk with board members and other volunteers at special events; see firsthand how their contributions are used onsite at the organization; and so on. Traditional ways that organizations provide formal recognition to volunteers are banquets or parties, special gatherings or outings, small gifts, or discounts at local businesses. Since organizations need to fully recognize the efforts of online volunteers without differentiating between the value of online and onsite service, such recognition activities may no longer be sufficient if online volunteers are too far away to participate. Of course, you can demonstrate your inclusion of remote volunteers by setting up a webcam during a recognition event so that they can also be present virtually!

As always, the best practices principles of volunteer recognition fully apply to thanking online volunteers. Here are some general recommendations:

- *Be timely.* The most effective form of thanks follows the completion of a significant part of an assignment. Do not wait until the project is completely over or until National Volunteer Week to express appreciation well after the fact. Find ways to immediately acknowledge a job well done. This can be as simple as an e-mail that says "thanks" and outlines how the volunteer's contributions are going to be used by the agency or the impact this work may have on clients.

- *Be consistent.* Whatever you do to recognize onsite volunteers, do for online volunteers, too. If something cannot be translated online (such as giving free parking or a mass transit voucher), then find a way to give online volunteers something similar (see the list of ideas that follows). Do not get caught favoring one group over the other—many people will be both online volunteers and onsite volunteers, and they will notice the difference in particular. Plus, you want all volunteers and employees at your organization to think of all volunteers as valuable, not just those who are able to come onsite. Again, there are no virtual volunteers—only real ones.

- *Appreciate contributions large and small.* It takes many small contributions of service—not just the big ones—to keep a program moving forward and meeting its objectives. Be grateful for the work of everyone involved, not just the contributions of the superstars who contribute huge numbers of hours or lead a high-profile activity.

- *Recognition is everyone's job.* Educate paid staff about the importance of volunteer recognition and how to provide it on an ongoing basis to the volunteers with whom they work. Help them survey volunteers to make sure they are feeling involved and appreciated.

- *Inclusion is key.* Online volunteers like seeing and hearing about the differences their work really makes, being invited to participate in decision making, and being asked to take on a high-profile role. This makes them feel truly a part of an organization.

A Starter Set of Recognition Ideas

Once you understand that onsite forms of volunteer recognition may need to be adapted to include online volunteers, you will look for new ways to say thank you. Be creative. It may even happen that your attempt to express appreciation for virtual service will uncover a great, fresh way to say thanks to all volunteers.

Here are some specific ideas to recognize online volunteers:

- Honor online volunteers the same way you honor onsite volunteers in newsletters, program updates, press releases, and annual reports. Emphasize the impact made by online volunteer services or the difference they make; do not just report on the numbers of volunteers and hours they have provided.

  - Give online volunteers the opportunity to sign up to receive any newsletter or program updates that are sent out via postal mail or electronic mail to donors, clients, onsite volunteers, and others interested in or involved with your agency.

  - If you give onsite volunteers a lapel pin (or any small gift) to honor them for the hours they donate to your organization, why not give the same pin (or gift) to online volunteers? Unless you have hundreds of online volunteers, the cost should not be prohibitive, even with postage. If cost is a factor, you can send an electronic image of the pin to each volunteer, encouraging them to post the image on any personal site that will be seen by their family and friends.

- If you have a bulletin board with pictures of onsite volunteers in action, be sure you invite online volunteers to submit photos as well. This is especially important if you create such a photo montage for an annual meeting or public exhibit. You may want to specifically ask online volunteers to send you a photograph of themselves (ideally at their computer, since you want to show "volunteers in action") and post these photos on a special board at the onsite volunteer recognition event. Then photograph some people looking at the board and post *that* to the Web site or your online forum for volunteers!

- In keeping with your organization's confidentiality procedures, ask the client recipients of services provided by online volunteers to join in the organization's recognition by writing messages about the importance of this service, even just a simple "thank you." These can be signed with first names only, to protect privacy.

- Don't forget to include the paid staff who partner with volunteers in recognition activities. They are an important ingredient in any volunteer's success. So photographs of onsite volunteering should also show participating employees. For online volunteers it may be even more important to let them see the people with whom they interact. Consider encouraging an exchange of photos between the volunteer and the staff member who will be working together. A fun idea for the photo montage suggested above would be to pair the photo of an

Plan in Advance to Use Photographs

Mention volunteers and their contributions on your Web site. Include pictures of both onsite and online volunteers in action. Always have volunteers sign legal releases if you intend to publish their images online or in print (no release, no photo). If confidentiality and privacy are particular concerns, then identify volunteers by first name and city/country of residence only. Children should probably not be identified by more than their first names, and you should get a legal release signed from their parents before even taking photos.

online volunteer at his or her computer with a "mirror image" shot of the paid staff member also at his or her computer. Post them together on the display, take another digital photo of that, and send it to both of them!

- Copy *all* volunteers with e-mail addresses on internal staff memos (as appropriate) relating to programs and services.

- As described in the first part of this chapter, invite the comments of online volunteers about programs and services, and ask them how they feel regarding support and feedback from staff, etc. Be sure to report back about how you are incorporating their feedback in some way. This demonstrates that you value online volunteers as part of your team.

- Invite online volunteers to special events, staff trainings, and celebrations, if it is geographically possible for them to attend.

- Some remote online volunteers may be in your area while they are on a business trip, visiting family or friends, on their way to another destination, etc. So give online volunteers an open invitation to visit your agency if they visit your city (but to call or e-mail first, of course).

- Send online volunteers your "swag"— promotional items with your organization's logo, such as coffee cups, bumper stickers, t-shirts, etc. You can make this a special gift for those online volunteers who have contributed a certain amount of time to your organization or who have made a particularly outstanding contribution to your organization in terms of service. Why not spread your organization's name to other parts of the world?

- If online volunteers are outside of the city where your organization is located, send them a postcard of a landmark in your city, with a personal note from you. This will be more treasured than you might realize (Jayne notes: "It is my favorite 'thank you' from organizations I volunteer for online outside the U.S.").

- Contact a national or international chain store that is very well represented everywhere to see if they would be willing to donate coupons for a small amount off of a purchase at any of their stores for all your volunteers. This may mean distributing such coupons to online volunteers via postal mail, or perhaps you can get the store to permit using a coupon code for *online* shopping (something even local volunteers may prefer these days).

- If you are hosting an onsite recognition or other event that will exclude some or all online volunteers because of their remote locations, consider these options:

  - Set up a computer terminal with Internet access at the event and have a live chat so that onsite attendees can communicate with online volunteers. Find a corporation or university to donate its resources and volunteers—many are excited at the idea of showing off their tech tools and expertise.

  - Set up a digital camera or webcam so that volunteers who cannot attend in person can do so via cyberspace. Note that these suggestions may benefit *all* volunteers, as an onsite volunteer who has to miss the event for any reason can also participate virtually.

  - Encourage volunteers and employees who attend the event to use their smartphones to send photos from the event or text their comments about what is happening to a private online area that offsite volunteers can access—or post to Twitter with a predetermined hashtag or to a social networking area you designate for the day.

All of the ideas above have the added benefit of *recording* your event for posterity! They allow some people to participate online in real time, but then they can also be viewed later by people who were not available when the event took place. And you can use some of the photos, videos, and text in reports, recruitment materials, new volunteer orientation, and more—with permission of the posters, of course.

Online Recognition for All Volunteers

Just as you should think of ways to adapt traditional ways of saying thank you to online settings, consider using the Internet to honor all your volunteers, not just those who provide online service. With cyberspace, it has never been easier to show volunteers—and the world—that volunteer contributions play a key part in an organization's successes. For example:

- Create an online volunteer recognition area on your organization's Web site and/or on a photo-sharing site such as Flickr. Post photos there of onsite volunteers (add or refresh the photos often) and request online volunteers to submit photos of themselves, ideally working on their computers.

- Profile a volunteer of the week or month on your Web site, and make sure you do not favor onsite volunteers over online volunteers for this prize. Do not create separate profiles

---

Asking for Feedback and Suggestions as Volunteer Recognition

The nonprofit BlogHer, which hosts blogs written by women, invited its members to adapt its official logo—changing the colors, adding additional images, adding a word or phrase—on their own individual Web sites, blogs, and online social networking profiles to show their support of BlogHer's first-ever conference. BlogHer also engaged in a variety of online and onsite activities to allow members to offer their recommendations on the agenda for the conference workshops.

As a result, BlogHer got more than additional recognition for its conference and great ideas for its conference; through these activities, volunteers were also being recognized as valuable, even vital, partners in the organization.

for online and for onsite volunteers—this creates a two-tiered system and reinforces the differences in these groups, instead of reinforcing the idea that they are all volunteers with you.

- Prepare customized, downloadable, signed certificates of appreciation for each online volunteer—something they can print out and display as they like (the same template can also be used for certificates handed out to onsite volunteers at onsite events). It is very important that these be individualized with the volunteer's name (be sure everything is spelled correctly!) and include a line describing the specific service provided. This last touch truly proves you know what the volunteer did to earn the thank you. Generic "thanks for being a volunteer" inscriptions have little meaning to anyone.

- As we have repeatedly suggested throughout this *Guidebook*, provide an online forum for all volunteers, whether they provide service onsite or online, where they can all talk about their experiences and questions relating to their volunteering with your organization. This creates a sense of community among all of your volunteers and may even provide a more comfortable forum for those onsite volunteers who are too shy to speak up during onsite meetings.

- Invite volunteers to participate in online advisory groups regarding a program, upcoming event, design of a new Web site, etc.—many volunteers see these additional responsibilities or opportunities as a form of recognition.

- Have the head of your organization prepare a short video thanking volunteers for their service. Just 30 or 60 seconds would be enough. You can post this to your private forum for volunteers or post it to a site like YouTube for easy access (it might even turn into a recruitment tool, as people outside your organization see how you honor your volunteers).

- Develop an online "badge" that volunteers can place on their own Web sites, blogs, Facebook pages, or other social media to show that they support your organization (added benefit for you: it can link back to your organization's Web site). You can also create a special graphic to award to any volunteer who has successfully completed a task for your organization, or develop a whole series of badges for special commendation or when certain milestones are reached. For example, celebrate a year of volunteer service, recognize outstanding or reliable expertise provided (perhaps a "guru" badge), acknowledge overcoming a difficult challenge as a part of the volunteer's service (perhaps a "tenacious" badge), and more. TechSoup[2] offers badges to its most active online volunteers who provide consultation and advice when site visitors pose technical questions on their forum. VolunteerSpot also offered a digital badge to volunteers as recognition.

Courtesy of VolunteerSpot.com—free, easy online volunteer scheduling.

- Develop a special profile on the social networking site most popular among your volunteers and allow only those who are volunteers with your organization now or have volunteered in the past to link to this profile as a friend. This is a particular draw for teen and twenty-something volunteers, who spend a lot of time on such sites already. Note that this would be a different profile than the one you might create for *anyone* who is interested in volunteering with your organization to join. (More on this recruitment technique in the next chapter.)

- Invite volunteers who attend a live online event to blog in real time from the event, either on their own laptops or on computers your organization provides (you will have to make sure there is Internet access at the venue). Let onsite and online volunteers chat throughout the event, sharing text, photos, audio and video live.

Many publications and articles over the years have offered volunteer recognition ideas. You can find lists of such ideas, plus more advice on recognizing volunteers, in many of the resources listed in appendix B and in the Virtual Volunteering Wiki.

Promote Virtual Volunteering Activities In-House

Recognition activities are not just about generating awareness and appreciation for online volunteers and the employees who work with them; they are also about promoting virtual volunteering within the organization.

Neither traditional nor virtual volunteering happens magically at an organization, and everyone may need to be reminded of this. Involving volunteers is also not *free*; there are always some costs associated with involving volunteers, online or onsite. The costs include some expenditure of cash, but most certainly involve expenditure of valuable paid staff time. So frontline volunteers, employees, managers and executives, the organization's board of directors (themselves volunteers, of course), donors, and other supporters need to know that online volunteers are contributing to the organization, what these contributions look like, and what it takes in terms of time and effort, particularly by the VRM, to make this happen.

To keep everyone informed, reporting on virtual volunteering activities needs to happen regularly. This can be done formally by monthly or quarterly written reports. But look for other ways to increase awareness about virtual volunteering as part of normal internal communication opportunities:

- If any staff member is officially assigned to maintain a public blog, ask the staff member to blog periodically about the role of online volunteers.

- Be vigilant in reviewing all internal and external reports and publications regarding the organization's programs and services to be sure both onsite and online volunteers are mentioned. If missing, offer edits or additional text about how online volunteers contributed to the results being reported.

- Submit a short, pithy report or paragraph of interesting data about online volunteers for every staff or board meeting, just as the fundraising manager probably does about donations and grants.

- Involve marketing or public relations staff in your outreach/promotion needs. For instance, ask marketing staff to help develop a video of testimonials by different clients talking about the impact volunteers make and/or by volunteers talking about why they enjoy volunteering. If marketing staff say they are too busy, consider involving volunteers to undertake this for and with them.

- Send an e-mail update or talk at staff meetings about something you have read about online volunteer engagement, from either a news article or blog.

- Send an occasional short e-mail update to all employees and volunteers to share something online volunteers have done.

- Celebrate staff members who create virtual volunteering opportunities or work successfully with online volunteers by expressing public appreciation at a staff meeting or sending around an e-mail to all staff, highlighting their activities.

Building and sustaining support for virtual volunteering is an ongoing process, and the organization will pay attention if information is regularly provided. It could even win over employees who have been resistant to involving online volunteers!

Notes

1. Adapted from Jayne Cravens, "How to Handle Online Criticism," updated 2012 <http://www.coyote communications.com/outreach/critics.html>.

2. TechSoup has a full online recognition program, which it refers to as "TechSoup Royalty." See details at http://forums.techsoup.org/cs/p/star.aspx.

Chapter 11
Recruiting Online Volunteers (Finally!)

We are finally ready to talk about recruitment!

As we have said throughout this book, we placed advice on recruiting volunteers near the end of this *Guidebook* because so many organizations make the mistake of recruiting volunteers *before* they have developed task descriptions and have a fully thought-out system to manage and support volunteers. Inviting people to volunteer without a method to immediately place them into a volunteer role is like advertising a product you do not really have. It can, and does, cause hard feelings and bad public relations about your agency. By waiting until later in the book to discuss recruitment, we want to emphasize the vital importance of *not* recruiting online (or any other) volunteers before your organization is ready to involve them from the moment they express interest in helping you.

The good news is that recruiting volunteers for online assignments is relatively easy—which is another reason to put this subject near the end, as the other components of online volunteering, such as task development, are not simple at all.

This chapter provides tips on recruiting volunteers specifically to provide some or all of their service online. However, you can use the techniques in this chapter to recruit any volunteer, even for entirely onsite tasks. Susan's *The Volunteer Recruitment (and Membership Development) Book* is the field's go-to source for an in-depth discussion of all things recruitment and we recommend it if you want to learn more on the subject.[1]

General versus Specific Recruiting

There are two views on recruiting volunteers, whether onsite or online. One is to recruit a number of volunteers to put onto a roster and then pick volunteers from that roster as assignments arise. This means volunteers apply to help an organization in general, are screened and approved to be placed on the roster, and then wait to be called upon when an assignment becomes available. The other approach is to recruit volunteers for specific assignments. This means recruitment is targeted for each available assignment and applicants respond as interested. If the right applicants are found, screened, and approved, then they get started on the specific assignment right away. It also means that a volunteer must express interest in doing a particular task in order to become involved.

Some organizations initially think the roster method of recruitment is best for online volunteers. It seems, at first, to be the one that requires the least amount of work: as assignments come up, staff members simply review the list of approved people who want to help (using a simple keyword search to find the candidates with the skills to do the work needed), then e-mail those volunteers with the assignment details, and the volunteers get started on the assignments. But the reality is often much different: by the time these pending volunteers are contacted about an assignment that matches their skills, weeks or even months have passed since they first expressed interest; in that time, their priorities, their availability, and even their contact information may have changed. They are, in short, no longer available. In the end, the volunteer resources manager (VRM) ends up having to recruit new online volunteers for the new assignment anyway.

So the better option (which we recommend for any type of volunteer) is intentional recruitment for specific assignments. Volunteers get started right away on whatever it is they want to do when their interest and motivation are at their peak—provided your orientation and screening protocols for new online volunteers are rapid. You will, of course, enter these new volunteers into your database (or ask the volunteers to input the information themselves via an online system) to track their contact information and record of service and connect them with your organization's online community for volunteers. That way, your online volunteer community becomes not just a roster of potential volunteers but a community of proven volunteers who stay engaged with your organization through the online community's discussions and debates.

Over time, all of the growing numbers of volunteers added to this community become the first people to whom you offer new assignments, and your proven volunteers screen themselves in or out for a particular project based on their interests, availability, and skills. That means you do not spend any time poring over a roster of relatively unknown people to try to find a volunteer; instead, your organization's proven volunteers read through the latest assignments, and if they are interested and feel qualified, they let you know. If no active volunteers steps forward, you can focus on recruiting new people for your current needs.

Start with Onsite Volunteers

As always, until you ask, you may be overlooking potential online volunteers already under your nose, in your current onsite volunteer corps. Once you have identified online assignments, begin your recruitment by first announcing the opportunities in-house to current volunteers:

- In your paper or e-mail newsletter for volunteers and other supporters

- On a bulletin board in the break room or lobby at your organization or anywhere else volunteers frequent onsite

- Posted to the online discussion group you have set up for volunteers

- On a shared online work space you use with volunteers

- At onsite meetings with volunteers

- Via an e-mail about the new opportunity sent directly to volunteers

Remember, you are not asking volunteers to *give up* their onsite service; you are offering them *more* opportunities to be involved with the organization. It is possible that *some* traditional, onsite volunteers may choose to work primarily online, but it won't happen in *most* cases.

Encourage volunteers to let their friends, family, and colleagues know about these online opportunities, too, as there may be some terrific candidates for online volunteering among their trusted associates. For that matter, be sure to also ask the paid staff to spread the word to their circles.

In addition, do not overlook past volunteers—people who are no longer able to come to your facility to volunteer or those taking a break from volunteering for whatever reason. Virtual volunteering may be a great way to re-engage people who might remain interested in contributing and have the skill to give service online.

Reaching Out Online

When we wrote the first edition of this book, many organizations did not yet have their own Web sites. Today, it is generally agreed that a Web site is mandatory for any credible organization, regardless of the organization's size or budget. Unfortunately, an organization's own site can no longer provide all the information and outreach needed because the public today uses a wide variety of search tools and sites to learn about anything and everything. So a smart organization will identify where its prospective contacts go and will create at least a few and, possibly, several online profiles at those sites, too, in addition to providing detailed information on its own Web site. The good news is that you can link your information on these other online profiles back to your main site; this allows you to keep the bulk of your information in one place and shortens the amount of information you have to type into your status update or profiles elsewhere. Naturally, all of this applies to recruiting both online and onsite volunteers .

As you plan your recruitment efforts, remember that many people may not be looking specifically for *virtual volunteering* opportunities. They may be seeking a particular kind of project or task—to design a brochure, translate text, offer business development advice—or they may want to help a particular cause—empowering women, protecting the environment, fighting a disease. It is an added bonus to many potential volunteers when they read that a task they really want to do can be done in whole or in part offsite via their own computer or smartphone!

Your Web Site Comes First

If people surf the Web and land on your organization's home page right now, would it be immediately apparent that volunteers are involved in any aspect of your work? Would they find information on what volunteer positions are open and how to apply if they were interested? Is there an online application form? Would they at least find the name, e-mail address and telephone number of a person to contact about volunteering? If not—you have work to do!

Yes, it is necessary to create social networking profiles and to register your volunteer opportunities with the online registries proliferating around the Web, but ultimately even those sources should direct prospective volunteers to your organization's own Web site. Will a visit to your site continue the recruitment process or become a dead end with no information?

Attracting Interest in Volunteering

The fact that volunteer opportunities are available at your organization should be visible to any visitor to your Web site, starting with something on the home page, where there should be a short blurb or at least a link to a section about volunteering. If your organization has a *How you can help* or *Donate now* or *Support our work* link on the home page, make sure that link goes to a page that offers more than financial donation information; volunteering is also an important way that the public can make a contribution to your mission and should get equal notice at that link.

Apart from the home page and the pages specifically devoted to volunteer information, make sure that there are links to the volunteer section of the Web site on all *other* pages and sections as well. Aim to make *How to volunteer* information as easy to find on your Web site as how to donate money. If your volunteering information is not just one or two clicks away from the home page or any other non-volunteering page on the site, it is too hard to find.

The Web pages dedicated to volunteer involvement should be informative, in depth, inviting, and easy to navigate. Here, share details about volunteers at your organization, beyond what assignments are available, virtual and not; also give information about orientation and screening, what volunteers are doing right now, testimonials from volunteers, photos of volunteers in action, and so on. Unlike a printed brochure, you are not at all limited in how much information you can share on the Web. Some people will read just a few paragraphs and be ready to sign up to help. Others will want to read several pages with more details. By having in-depth and easy-to-navigate information, different people will find the different kinds of information that most appeal to them.

Note that some people will check out your page for five seconds and then leave it—which probably means they realize that volunteering with your organization is *not* for them. This is not a bad thing; as a result of the information you have shared, they will *not* complete your online application and go through your online orientation, or receive an assignment and *then* find out they really do not want to volunteer with your organization.

Getting Specific

Your Web section on volunteering should have a *current, specific* list of *available* volunteer positions or should link to where you maintain this information on another organization's volunteer recruitment Web site (discussed later in this chapter). If you list the assignments on your site, give some thought to how you present or categorize them. Here are some of your options:

- You might want to show open assignments clustered under these headings: onsite opportunities, partially onsite/partially online opportunities, and entirely online opportunities.

- You can list opportunities by type of assignment (staff support, client support, as part of a team, etc.), being sure to note clearly whether or not the assignment can be done entirely or partially online.

- Many people seek volunteering in order to contribute certain skills or to learn new skills, so it can be attractive to cluster opportunities by type of activity or by skills needed (writing, Web design, counseling, coaching). Pro bono service, in which volunteers donate the professional expertise for which they normally charge a fee, can be recruited by describing the kinds of consultation your organization needs.

- Perhaps it makes sense to cluster opportunities by schedule or timeline: one-time tasks; short-term/less than a month/micro-volunteering; up to six months; long-term/ongoing; working in a team; etc. For volunteer assignments that must be done on a regular, specific schedule (whether onsite or online), you can post current time slots needing to be filled.

- Think about who might visit your site and cluster opportunities for special types of service: student internships, families who want to volunteer together (intergenerational activities), corporate employee teams, and more.

- Use the power of the Internet's reach to create a *wish list* of hoped-for volunteer skills. This is often done for tangible items such as office furniture or computer equipment, but you can do it for skills as well. What additional activities do you feel would benefit the organization?

Throughout your Web site section dedicated to volunteers, scatter photos of volunteers at work, taking care that the pictures show diversity of age, race, gender, or other characteristics that will communicate to prospective new volunteers that they will fit in. If you followed our suggestions in the last chapter about using photographs in your recognition activities, you should already have many shots from which to choose. *Caption* the photos to explain what (and possibly who) is being shown so that visitors know these are not commercial clip art!

Give visitors as much to see as they might want to see—some will want to view just a couple of pages, but others will want to learn as much as they can about volunteering at your organization. Offer links to full position descriptions, data on volunteer achievements, personal testimonials from volunteers

in certain assignments, and more. An added bonus is that the more you feature current volunteers, the more the Web site does double duty as a recruitment tool and as another way to recognize and show appreciation of volunteers' efforts. The point is that potential volunteers can read as much information as they want, and such information can make the right person eager to become a volunteer with you.

Inviting Unexpected Offers

One last thought: Leave the door open for prospective volunteers to offer their own ideas for how they might be of service. For example, consider including a statement somewhere on the page with this message:

> *Are you interested in volunteering with us but don't see an assignment here that matches the interests or skills you were hoping to contribute? Do you have an idea for a project to help our work that you'd like to explore? We invite you to contact us to see if together we can create a new volunteer role for you.*

A trend in volunteerism is to engage *entrepreneurial volunteers*. These are people (especially Baby Boomers, Gen Xers and Millennials) who prefer to participate in designing the volunteer work they will

---

Avoid the Vague

Never post a general call with a vague statement such as "we need online volunteers." We have said why this is a bad idea frequently in this book. Be specific as to what volunteer positions and tasks are available right now, what skills are necessary, and what time commitment you are asking. Even if you use another organization's volunteer recruitment Web site to maintain your most current list of volunteering opportunities, you should include a summary or overview of what volunteers do at your organization and specific details for each opportunity you have listed.

If you do not give prospective volunteers the right information up front, you risk misleading them and possibly signing on someone with no interest or intention to do what you really need done.

do rather than just fill a predetermined slot in your organization. Therefore this sort of open invitation will resonate with them as well as possibly uncover some hidden treasure you never expected.

Keep Information Current!

It is of the utmost importance that information provided on your Web site be accurate and *current*. Never advertise a volunteering opportunity, virtual or otherwise, that is actually already filled and not available to new volunteers.

Date all postings so show that these are up to date. Even if volunteer positions do not change that often, freshen the date often to send the message that all this is happening *now*.

Negotiating with or around a Resistant Webmaster

We are sorry to report that we have frequently heard VRMs say, "I can't have any more than one page on our organization's Web site. Our webmaster said no." Some webmasters claim limited server space. The real reason for saying "no" is probably that the webmaster sees a request for more Web space as unnecessary and does not want to maintain the additional pages.

The first thing to do in dealing with recalcitrant webmasters is *assert your position*. Webmasters are knowledgeable about software and technology but should never be the final decision makers about site *content* or determine communication priorities. If your webmaster resists your requests to post more than one page, keep the pages about volunteering current, create an online application form, or anything else you feel is necessary, ask questions to discover the true reason for the resistance. For example, is it technically difficult or is it mainly a lack of time and many demands? If the issue is fitting the volunteer program into the sequence of priorities, you may need to find the appropriate executive who can insist that the webmaster devote time to search for ways to meet your needs. The key point is that what you have asked for is necessary for effective recruitment of the best volunteers. Saying "no" to your legitimate requests for current Web pages amounts to interfering with your ability to fulfill your obligations to the organization.

Most IT professionals have developed problem-solving skills needed for translating complex computer languages into successfully operating Web sites. Challenge them to use those problem-solving skills to serve your online communication needs. Also, offer to recruit a skilled volunteer who can create or maintain all the needed Web pages regarding volunteers (following official templates as provided by the webmaster) and give them to the webmaster for simple posting to the site. This keeps control of the Web site in one place but removes all the common barriers implied in the argument, "This sort of updating is just too time consuming."

Going Independent

If, despite your best efforts, you fail to get past the obstacle of your webmaster, we have a suggestion that has worked at many other organizations: With approval, create your *own* Web site to focus only on volunteering at your organization! A single page on your organization's site can then point to the other, more comprehensive Web site. You can make your new site look *exactly* like your organization's site, with the same layout and graphics, such that a user would never know he or she was on another site. (Or, of course, you could choose to design something quite different, but with elements such as your organization's logo to tie both sites together.) You will never give out the new site's address publicly. Only the organization's main URL will be promoted in any messages because that is where a prospective volunteer will start, getting to your new site only when clicking from the main site.

Lack the know-how to create Web pages? Recruit one or even a team of online volunteers to do it for you! You provide all of the content—written text for all of the pages you want (a page detailing the orientation and screening process, an online application, a page providing an overview of what volunteers do at your organization, perhaps even testimonials from volunteers, testimonials from clients who have been served by volunteers, etc.)—and the skilled volunteers develop the look and navigability of the site. You also need to recruit at least two volunteers who will always be ready to make any immediate text changes/updates you need. Web hosting is incredibly cheap, currently around five U.S. dollars a month, and the online volunteers you recruit could also help you identify the best host for your needs.

When your Web site is done, you and an online volunteer can create the one page regarding volunteering that will sit on your organization's official Web site. This page will welcome the visitor, say a bit about why volunteers are important to your organization, and then link to all of the various pages you have created on your dedicated Web site, as well as to any other Web resources you are using (your blog, photos on Flickr, whatever). You should then be ready to give this one page to your webmaster to simply upload to the organization's main Web site.

For those of you who are hyperventilating at the audacity of this plan, put it into perspective. In some cases, such as the military, there may be actual restrictions that limit your ability to *go rogue* online. But for most organizations, we are talking about non-confidential information totally within the purview of a VRM's responsibility in running a volunteer program. You have all the position descriptions in your possession and know all the vacancies. It is your job to recruit. The organization wants the best volunteers. Demonstrating that you have enough recruitment skill to craft a vital tool in your outreach campaign is *reasonable*, not maverick.

There's a saying: *It's better to ask for forgiveness than to ask permission.* Based on our experiences and our observations, we find that it is better to proceed with your Web site plan and then tell your webmaster after it is completed. If you can find an ally in your direct supervisor or another manager while you build the new site, that's fine, but not essential. And remember: you will still publicize only the organization's main Web address to potential volunteers!

Web Sites Specifically for Volunteer Recruitment

These days we search for everything online—shopping, finding movie times, checking out restaurant menus—so it is hardly surprising that people would also expect to learn about volunteer opportunities online. Web sites popped up on the Internet in the early 1990s that allowed nonprofit and public organizations to recruit volunteers by providing a searchable online database of volunteering opportunities, and their numbers have grown ever since. In addition, VolunteerMatch, one of the first online recruiting sites, gave organizations the ability to recruit online volunteers specifically as early as 1994!

Most of these Web registries of volunteer opportunities are run by nonprofit organizations, but some are run by for-profit companies. Most are free, though we have found some that charge either volunteers to access the information or organizations to post assignments. Most of the sites are country specific, and some are targeted to an even more specific region, like a state or a city. Some are focused on a particular type of volunteering assignment or a particular type of volunteer (singles, students, a specific profession). We have provided a partial list of such sites in the Virtual Volunteering Wiki, and Energize, Inc. attempts to maintain a current list at http://www.energizeinc.com/prof/volop.html.

Each site has its own criteria for which organizations can post volunteer opportunities. Some require the nonprofit to provide proof of its government registration, for instance, or bar assignments related to partisan politics or religious evangelizing. All ask for at least basic information about the organization: its official name, physical address, e-mail address, etc. Once an organization is approved as a user of a volunteer recruitment Web site, the organization's profile is made accessible to authorized paid or unpaid staff who have the ability to post, update, delete, or edit the organization's volunteering opportunities on the site.

Site visitors can search these online databases of volunteering opportunities by a variety of criteria, from location to skill needed to cause helped. Some of these sites provide a way to tag volunteering opportunities as virtual or online. At the time of this writing, however, most do not.

When someone sees an appealing opportunity and wants to express interest, he or she fills out an online form and that information goes directly to the organization posting the assignment. What happens next is up to each organization. We hope that *you* will follow the recommendations we have made in this book, particularly in chapter 4, for screening volunteers and getting them into assignments as soon as possible.

Online volunteer opportunity database sites make it very easy for would-be volunteers to sign up for assignments—so easy that many people often express interest before they have considered the real time and effort volunteering takes, no matter where it happens. Proper vetting of volunteers by your organization, as we have detailed earlier, will screen out those people who clicked to express interest before really thinking about the commitment needed.

Some organizations pick one of these volunteer recruitment Web sites as *the* place to post *all* of their currently-available volunteering opportunities. If this is the case, the organization's own Web page regarding volunteering will then say, "For a list of all volunteering opportunities at our organization, see _____," with a link to the information on the third-party Web site. Some organizations choose this approach because it is easy and quick to update information on the third-party site, while doing so is much harder on their own site.

Choosing the Best Site for You

There are too many of these volunteer recruitment Web sites for you to try to use them all—there are not enough hours in the day! So, which of the many online databases of volunteering opportunities should you use to recruit online volunteers? Applying any of the following criteria will help:

- Which have been most successful in recruiting onsite volunteers for you in the past?

- Which allow for the specific recruitment of online volunteers (they allow you to tag the opportunity somehow as being online or virtual)?

- Is the site focused on the particular type of volunteer or geographic region that you need to reach?

- Have any been endorsed by a colleague who tells you, "I have recruited a lot of very reliable online volunteers via this Web site"?

If you are in the United States, you should definitely try VolunteerMatch as a tool for recruiting online volunteers; it is one of the only sites that allows opportunities to be designated as *virtual* and is probably the most popular volunteer recruitment site, in terms of Web traffic and number of assignments posted. Otherwise, start by choosing just two Web sites available to you. Keep track of the number and quality of responses. Experiment with other sites if you are not getting enough candidates

from your first two choices or you are not satisfied with responses.

You may come upon "aggregator" sites that pull postings from several different online registries to provide a wider range of volunteer opportunity choices than a single database might contain. Such sites do not always clearly identify themselves as using data gathered by others (especially ones posted by government agencies). There is nothing wrong with aggregators, but try to find out whether using one site automatically makes your vacancies accessible on other sites and track results. Also, before you re-post new information into a new registry, check to make sure this is not unnecessary duplication.

Appealing Posts That Attract Volunteers

Of course, your degree of success is not solely due to which site you choose; a huge factor is the effectiveness of the posts you make to describe each available volunteer opportunity! Spend time stating your needs in an appealing and informative way.

Do *not* post a general "we need online volunteers" announcement, trying to put all your volunteer positions in one posting. Using a cattle call for "volunteers" instead of focusing on each individual volunteering opportunity available is poor recruitment technique, whether in the real world or online. For Web-based recruiting, it also shows a profound misunderstanding of how people want to use the Internet to look for volunteering opportunities and means potential volunteers cannot find the service opportunities they are looking for. People who use volunteer opportunity registries want to be able search for *specific* types of volunteer work, whether their interest is in a particular issue, client group, geographic region, time period, or skill set (which was why we recommended earlier that you categorize or cluster volunteer opportunities on your own Web site).

Instead, post as many volunteer position opportunities as you have, individually. You can even make separate postings for the same position but focus on a special need, such as a hard-to-fill weekend evening shift or wanting a few volunteers in that role to speak another language. There is no cost for being detailed like this, but it gives you added visibility in a search and a much better chance to locate the prospects who best match your needs.

Though it takes more time at the start to post 10 individual, detailed descriptions of different online volunteering opportunities rather than just one mega-posting, it will actually *save you time* in the long run when you need to update information. Most important, your individual, specific postings will attract many more online volunteering candidates.

As we discussed in chapter 3, titles matter. Do *not* use the word "volunteer" in the title line at all! Remember that these sites are entirely about presenting volunteer opportunities, so why waste space by repeating that word? More critically, what you call a position frequently determines who will keep reading the rest of the description. Take a look at the following list of possible titles and consider how each conveys a very different tone, although it could involve the same work activities:

- Clerical Volunteer
- Clerical Aide
- Secretarial Assistant
- Office Coordinator
- Recordkeeping Team Leader
- Records and Reports Czar
- Information Control Central Coordinator

Which one appeals to you? Which would appeal to a graduate student? A person out of work for a year? If the title of the role is off-putting, or makes the work seem elementary, who will contact you to express interest?

Any online registry of volunteer opportunities will only give you a small space in which to describe each volunteer position vacancy. But all allow you to link the posting to your own URL for more details—which is why it is so vital to first create a Web area of your own that provides all the information you want to offer.

It is very worthwhile to do a bit of online intelligence gathering. Go to your selected volunteer recruitment site and pretend to be a prospective volunteer. Type in your zip code or area of interest and see what emerges. These are your competition. They are the listings the public will see when doing the same search. How do you stack up? Compared to the others, is your volunteer opportunity listing interesting? Welcoming? Current? Does it sound like fun as well as offering the chance to do something meaningful? Now go back and rewrite you posts accordingly!

Revisit Your Postings

As we advised earlier for your own Web site, to is imperative to keep your listings current wherever they appear in cyberspace. Keep track of all the sites where you post information, what you post to each, and the date of posting. This will help you find your notices later for editing or removal when the position is filled.

You may well have some volunteer opportunities that are ongoing and rarely change, and therefore you always need more applicants for them. You may feel that you can post such assignments once and just leave them up forever. But almost all the online databases ask for the date of a posting and, if you never revisit a particular assignment, it will continue to carry the original date. Would *you* be eager to express interest in something that has been posted for a year or more? Hardly. So return to every posting at least twice a year and—if nothing else—refresh the *date* shown. This communicates to the potential volunteer that the opportunity is still current and worth pursuing.

Out-of-date information reflects poorly on your organization, whether on your own Web site or on a volunteer recruitment site. The humorous but ironic term for a site that never changes is a *cobWeb*. What is not humorous is what potential volunteers will think when they see your outdated information, or when they apply to an assignment you have posted online but then get a response from you that, in fact, the assignment is no longer available. They may even blog about their frustrating experience trying to volunteer with your organization.

Online volunteers can be an excellent resource to help you maintain your online information and ensure that it is always up to date.

Using Other Web Resources

Once you have a central area on the Web where current and appealing information is available to prospective volunteers and you are using the best volunteer opportunity registries for your needs, you are ready to make use of all the other remarkable sites and tools in cyberspace to drive people to those spots.

Social Media

Online networking sites, whether social or professional in nature, provide a terrific avenue for recruiting volunteers in general and online volunteers specifically. If you need an online volunteer who runs a cleaning company to offer advice to someone in Afghanistan who wants to start a similar business, you can send out a notice to your Twitter followers, for instance, and they—or *their* friends—may have the contact you need.[2] The word gets out because friends are telling friends, or colleagues are telling colleagues, through whatever online networking sites they use.

At the time of this *Guidebook*'s publication, the most popular online networking platform is Facebook. However, there are still several million users of MySpace, Twitter is quite popular, some organizations are using Google+ exclusively, and new platforms are being announced regularly—no one knows what the most popular platform will be even a year from now. In addition, there are those that prefer to keep their online *social* networking separate from their online *professional* networking or their work as a volunteer and, therefore, may prefer using a platform like LinkedIn or Plaxo to hear about potential volunteering opportunities from colleagues.

It is humanly impossible to use every online networking platform out there. Instead, find out which sites your current volunteers and staff use, and research what different people in your specific geographic area use. For instance, is there a platform that is particularly popular among one age group or ethnic group in your community that you would like to reach?

The simplest way to use online networking sites for volunteer recruitment is to put a specific volunteer need in your "status update" (the terms and location will vary depending on the platform). You are usually limited to only a small number of characters, but even a brief message can be useful. Some examples:

- *We're looking for native Spanish speakers to help us produce subtitles for a ten-minute video. See <Web page link> for more info, and let your friends know!*

- *Know any Drupal experts? We need a volunteer for three months to help us develop some new forms on our Web site. See <Web page link> for more, and please let your network know!*

- *Fabulous Web designers wanting to donate their time to an organization that helps place abandoned dogs and cats needed to help us with our Web site. See <Web page link> for more, and please repost this message to your own status update!*

- *We have just posted 10 new virtual volunteering opportunities to VolunteerMatch! Click <Web page link> for more info.*

Note how every message refers back to a Web page with information about the online volunteering opportunity, and most messages also encourage people to *repost the message* to their own network. How many people your message reaches depends on how many people you have in your network and how many people in your network forward the message to others.

Encourage all employees and volunteers to post online volunteering recruitment messages in their own status updates, as appropriate. The VRM should be aware of these kinds of recruitment activities for tracking purposes.

Online Discussion Groups

People with mutual interests, no matter how arcane, can find each other and communicate amazingly quickly and cheaply in cyberspace. Online discussion groups span a mind-boggling array of subjects and therefore are wonderful for finding the specific skills and interests that match your volunteer position openings. The point for a recruiter is that such groups gather like-minded individuals who might be candidates as online volunteers. It is target-marketing heaven!

If you need an online social media expert, for instance, look for online groups for marketing and public relations professionals. If you need native or fluent Spanish speakers to help translate documents or test the Spanish-language version of your Web site, look for a discussion group for Latino businesspeople. Want to recruit online volunteers only from a particular geographic area? Find discussion groups for specific cities, towns, villages and neighborhoods.

It is always a good idea to spend a few days just reading messages posted to a discussion group ("lurking") before joining in the conversation by posting your own message. That way you will learn about the culture of each group, as well as the type of messages that are or are not appropriate. Some lists reject postings that read like an advertisement. If you explain who (and where) you are in your message and why you are using this format to locate someone with these particular skills, you should not have a problem posting your message. If in doubt, take the trouble to first introduce yourself to the group hosts and ask how best to address their group.

To find online discussion groups:

- Ask your volunteers and paid staff (if they are willing) to share the names of online groups they have joined for professional or social reasons. Explain that your interest is in learning what online communities might have potential as places to recruit online volunteers.

- Use your favorite search engine and type in various keywords based on the skills you need, along with the phrase "online community" or "online forum."

- Search Yahoo! Groups, Google Groups, Ning, and Facebook for professional associations of people with the experience you seek (Web designers, graphic designers, etc.) or groups focused on a particular subject or geographic area.

- Check CataList, "the official catalog of LISTSERV® lists," e-mail discussion groups, and distribution groups.[3]

Intranets

Most large and national corporations and organizations, including colleges and universities, maintain *intranets*—online but private communication systems that deny access to anyone outside the company, organization, or school. Such internal systems often have a space for announcements of activities that are hosted by other organizations but might be of interest to their employees or members. If you feel that a particular source holds potential for locating new volunteers with the skills and interests you most want, contact the person in charge of that site's intranet and ask if you could share a message about volunteering at your organization via this internal communications system.

Intranets often allow members to post messages themselves. In that case, ask volunteers who work in companies or study at universities with this type of system to advertise volunteer opportunities for you on their intranets. This has the added bonus of serving as an endorsement of the organization from a work/study colleague already involved as a volunteer.

By definition, someone who is using an intranet has the potential to become an *online* volunteer!

Traditional Communication Channels

Online volunteers still live in the real world. That means that they can be reached offline, too. Many of the communication channels you might use for recruiting any volunteer can also be successful in filling virtual assignments.

Traditional Mass Media

Traditional mass media is not dead! Many communities still primarily get their community news from printed newspapers. Even in large cities where readership is falling, sizable populations still read newspapers. In addition, many newspapers post their content online, reaching even more people with their information. That means newspapers remain a viable avenue for volunteer recruitment, including recruiting for virtual volunteering assignments.

Similarly, local as well as cable radio and television stations always seek community stories. They may be attracted to the concept of virtual volunteering and give you an on-air interview. Increasingly, local print media and Web-based media outlets are in partnerships with local or cable radio and television stations and present news and feature stories in multi-media format packages. So pitching a story to a newspaper or a Web-based media outlet may translate into additional coverage on radio or television, too.

Just keep in mind that mass media recruitment is indiscriminate, meaning you will reach anyone who is listening. This can result in a flood of inquiries that you may not be able to handle—and from people not necessarily qualified. On the other hand, mass media is ideal for a "needle-in-the-haystack" search for a very specialized skill or unusual situation. In that case, casting a wide public net offers a shot at finding that possible volunteer who can sign for the deaf in Vietnamese or keep in touch with the homeless about the times and locations of night-time food vans.

Volunteer Centers and Other Clearinghouses

City, regional, and national volunteer centers also remain excellent avenues to recruit online volunteers. Today, most volunteer centers will post volunteering opportunities in all of their member agencies online, either in a national database or on a Web page of their own. The center in your community may use a different name, such as Hands On <city name>, or be part of a United Way or a mayor's office.

Some colleges and universities maintain a campus office for community service and internships and welcome requests from community organizations for student volunteers. Obviously, all students today are Internet savvy, so recruiting online volunteers through higher education networks makes a lot of sense.

Target Marketing

When you want to recruit volunteers with particular skills or certain demographic characteristics, you need to figure out *where* you can be certain to find the people you wish to attract.

Developing a target marketing strategy for online volunteer recruitment requires considering the various angles to use to approach a desired audience. Say you want to recruit teen volunteers to create an online community calendar of weekend events young people might like. Given the elements of this search, three recruitment angles suggest themselves: *between the ages of 16 and 21, active in the community,* and *comfortable online.*

We assume that you do not need much help figuring out where you can find young people, though we encourage you to brainstorm a long list that includes schools, shopping malls, arcades, vampire movies, sporting events, and more. Once you have identified the possible places to look, you can narrow the list by asking yourself what *type* of young person is most likely to be at each place and

how possible it might be to get a recruitment message noticed there.

Now consider *active in the community*, meaning a young person who is already engaged in weekend activities and would most likely feel comfortable sharing the information with others. This might lead to a list that includes officers of after-school clubs, leaders of youth activities at faith communities and secular centers, youth staff at recreation centers, local movie theaters on the weekend, and so on.

Luckily, the majority of young people are digital natives and therefore very *comfortable online.* That means it may be relatively easy to find the online groups they frequent (see earlier in this chapter on how to find these groups). However, many may not understand the importance of spell-checking something before they post it online—do not let the unique online syntax of teens make you think they would not be terrific online volunteers.

Having created your three lists, you can look for crossovers and evaluate what places have the most potential for your recruitment efforts. Only when you have identified the source you will approach can you then design the recruitment *technique* and *materials* you will need to match that source.

We cannot explain everything about target marketing here, but there are many books and Web sites on this topic. Again, you can get more information on how to apply target marketing to volunteer recruitment in Susan's *The Volunteer Recruitment (and Membership Development) Book.*

Recruiting Experts for Specialized Assignments

As we already noted, the Internet provides easy and effective ways to reach people with specific areas of expertise. But if a profession or association does not have a public online discussion group, you can still make contact in more traditional ways. For instance, if you are trying to recruit an accountant but cannot locate an appropriate online discussion group, you can send an e-mail, telephone, or even write a letter on paper to any number of sources with the membership you need—a national accounting society or its local chapter, a local accounting firm—and ask them to pass on the volunteer opportunity information to their membership. A local university's business school would also be a great place to send your recruitment message, targeting both students and faculty.

We have mentioned the organization Sidelines several times in this book as an organization that matches women experiencing high-risk pregnancies with volunteer advisors who have been through the same experience. If you were recruiting for them, your possible sources for targeting both clients and volunteers could include:

- obstetricians' offices
- fertility clinics
- home nursing services
- midwife programs
- childbirth education classes
- stores that sell home health care products such as special pillows, back support equipment, and the like

These are real-world places where both onsite and online volunteers might be recruited. So you could actually distribute on-paper literature at any of the locations above, or you might find out how they use online communication to reach their constituencies and ask if you can share your message that way.

The principle is to be creative and specific about where you have the best chance of finding volunteers who are most qualified for or interested in your opportunities. There are national and international associations for every profession imaginable: architects, programmers, human resources managers, mechanical engineers, civil engineers, immigration lawyers, health educators, school psychologists, and more. If you are looking for people who have lived and worked overseas, you could target the nearest chapters of the National Peace Corps Association (formerly the Returned Peace Corps Volunteers). Someone with experience as an educator? There are many active and retired teachers' associations. A Web designer who's female? In Austin, Texas, you could contact HerDomain; in San Francisco, Women on the Web; or any similar group in many other cities and countries. And so on.

And remember: finding organizations and groups in your area where you can target prospective volunteers with a specific skill set is an excellent task for an online volunteer!

Your Recruitment Message

In chapter 3, we present the fine points of how to write a detailed task description for a virtual volunteering opportunity. Each task description is the starting point for crafting the volunteer recruitment advertisement that you will post on various offline and online channels. Your own Web site, as well as most Web sites that provide a searchable online database of volunteering opportunities, can include most or even all of the information from your volunteer task descriptions. However, your Facebook status updates, ads in the newspapers, or a flyer posted on a university English department's bulletin board cannot include this much detail, so you need to write a brief summary of each role, pulling out the most important elements of the task description (possibly emphasizing different points to appeal to different target audiences). Your short description must be enticing. You want to provide enough information to attract a reader to explore further by going to a Web site where more complete details can be found.

For third-party Web site listings, always include a one-sentence description of your organization or its work so that potential candidates do not have to click on a link and go to another page to learn that your mission involves services to children, protecting wildlife, or promoting women's equality. Of course, be sure that your contact information is visible (which may or may not be done automatically, depending on the site), including your organization's postal address, phone number, Web site address, and an e-mail address to someone who can answer questions about the posting.

Vocabulary Matters

We have already talked about the importance of titles in attracting the best candidates to a volunteer role. Except in times of disaster or crisis, almost no one responds to the generic call for "volunteers." People want to *tutor children, plant a community garden, advise on a strategic plan*—not *give time away for free*. The volunteer nature of the opportunity is part of the description of the project, used as an *adjective* ("this volunteer position is. . . .").

If every volunteer assignment is tagged as an "assistant" or "aide," you will probably appeal more to inexperienced applicants than to veterans. Conversely, a role titled "coordinator" or "manager" of a project will catch the eye of more advanced potential volunteers.

It is also important to choose your words carefully when you extend an invitation to volunteer to highly-skilled people; unfortunately, the word *volunteer* wrongly implies unskilled labor. Consider that a for-profit business consultant may be looking for the chance to offer *pro bono services* to nonprofit organizations to balance his or her work with corporations. University students preparing for future careers are often looking for unpaid *internships* as a way to get practical experience in their field of study. Know the terms that will resonate with your target audiences and use vocabulary relevant to them.

Prepare Your Organization

Make sure that everyone at your organization who has regular contact with the public—the people who answer the phone, respond to the general e-mail address, and maintain your presence on online social networking sites—knows that you recruit online volunteers via the Internet. That ensures that they will be ready to respond when someone first makes contact with your organization and refers to your recruitment messages. It also will help staff know just how vibrant your organization's volunteer engagement is (if they do not already!).

Talk regularly with your marketing, public relations, and fundraising staffs so that you can all be aware of what you are each doing to involve and talk to the community and perhaps even coordinate your outreach efforts. If your online volunteers are providing especially innovative services, such as an online mentoring program, you may attract press attention; your marketing staff will want to be involved in any conversations with the media.

You might now go back to earlier chapters and review the importance of having procedures in place to quickly respond when someone offers to volunteer. You want to immediately interview or place candidates for online volunteering into your orientation process, with the goal of quickly identifying the appropriate candidate and getting him or her into an assignment immediately—within days, or even hours, of an expression of interest. "Cyber-immediacy" is vital.

NOTES

1. Susan is working on the fourth edition of *The Volunteer Recruitment (and Membership Development) Book* that will go into more detail about many of the online recruiting techniques mentioned briefly here. Meanwhile, the third edition is available at http://www.energizeinc.com/store/1-128-P-1.

2. Which is exactly what Jayne did in Portland, Oregon, to recruit a cleaning company owner in St. Louis, Missouri, to mentor a man in Kabul online, through the nonprofit organization Bpeace, talked about earlier in this book.

3. L-Soft, "CataList: The Official LISTSERV® Lists" <http://www.lsoft.com/catalist.html>. Kept continually updated.

Polish online volunteers were interviewed during the 2013 "Discover e-volunteering. Change the WWWorld!" conference organized by www.e-wolontariat.pl – the first Web site in Poland dedicated to volunteering done via the Internet.

Chapter 12
For Online Volunteers

This book was written for people who work or want to work with online volunteers—at nonprofit and non-governmental organizations, charities, public sector organizations, communities of faith, grassroots groups, and various other organizations and institutions. But we know that some of our readers might want to become online volunteers themselves. This new chapter is specifically for you.

We also hope this chapter will be helpful to anyone who wants to see virtual volunteering from the volunteer's point of view. VRMs, especially, can use the topics raised here to create orientation and training materials for their organizations' online volunteers as well.

We also want to acknowledge the role volunteers themselves have played in initiating virtual volunteering at many organizations. Unlike many agency staff, most volunteers are sold on the idea of virtual volunteering from the moment they hear the term—no need for a presentation or a book to convince them. Web sites that allow organizations to recruit online volunteers, like the UN's Online Volunteering service, always have far more people interested in volunteering online than they have tasks for them to do. Often it is volunteers who introduce virtual volunteering to an organization, not employees. We have no doubt that volunteers themselves will continue to play a primary role in continuing the growth and success of virtual volunteering. We hope this chapter honors and supports these volunteers' efforts.

Before You Volunteer Virtually

It is so easy to say "yes" to volunteering via the Internet that many people sign up before really considering what online volunteering means in terms of time and effort. Too often new online volunteers cannot find that spare time they originally envisioned and do not complete assignments they committed to doing,

leaving the organization scrambling to get the work done by others. Saying "yes" to virtual volunteering but then not completing an assignment also affects the organization's opinion of all online volunteers; staff may decide online volunteers are not trustworthy or reliable and challenge or even halt attempts to expand virtual volunteering in more ways.

Before you sign up to volunteer online, make sure you are ready to volunteer online. Virtual volunteering takes *real* time and effort, and assignments have *real* deadlines; this includes micro-volunteering, where the assignment takes just a few hours or even just a few minutes. A good place to start determining your readiness is to consider how volunteering from a home or work computer, or even a smartphone, is different from working onsite with an organization:

- There is usually more flexibility in *when* you can do the volunteer work. A task may still take two hours and be due in a week, but you could do it at three o'clock in the morning, if you so choose.

- There is a greater degree of independence regarding *how* you work virtually. If you are at home, for example, you may like your favorite music playing in the background or prefer being dressed in your pajamas.

- You may never interact in person, onsite with most other staff members or other volunteers.

- You do not see what other volunteers are working on when you volunteer, as you might if you went onsite to an organization to perform volunteer service side by side with others.

- You have to be a self-starter, not relying on inspiration to come from others face-to-face; the organization's executive director is probably not going to stop by your home office and tell you, "Good job!"

Setting your own schedule is one of the chief joys of virtual volunteering. However, there is still a schedule; *waiting for spare time to do a task often leads to a task never getting done.* In addition, there is nothing virtual about the deadlines you accept to complete the volunteer work. Virtual volunteering is convenient, but it still happens in real time and space, even if that space is in your own home at a computer or at a quiet coffee shop with your laptop or smartphone.

Self-Quiz

Ask yourself the following questions to determine if you are ready to volunteer virtually:

1. *Do you have regular, reliable access to the Internet?*

   If you have access only at a university and the semester is about to end; if you borrow wireless Internet access from a neighbor without his or her knowledge; if your Internet access and availability for the next several days will be only at airports, between flights; or if you are about to switch Internet providers or computers or smartphones—now is probably not a good time to volunteer to complete a project virtually! Make sure you will have reliable, ongoing access to the Internet for at least the next three months before you start searching for assignments, even if you are looking for something you can complete in less than a week, as it may take several weeks before you find that perfect volunteer opportunity.

2. *Do you communicate well via the written word?*

   More and more online communication is being done via audio and live video, but the reality is still that most online communication happens via the written word. Even if you want to provide a highly technical service, such as creating a database, you have to be able to communicate what you are doing

to your contact at the organization and to write documentation to help others after you have completed that assignment.

3. *Do you stick to deadlines? Do you see a project through to its finish?*

   Organizations are counting on you to complete the assignment for which you have volunteered; there is nothing virtual about their need for you to meet your commitment.

4. *Are you comfortable working on your own, without direct, immediate supervision?*

   Virtual assignments are best for those people who like working on their own. That does not mean you cannot not ask for guidance when you need it or that you will never be a part of an online volunteering team all working together on a project. But even in a team situation or with a lot of regular contact with an onsite staff person, most of your service will be performed by you alone.

5. *Are you self-motivated?*

   Some organizations involving remote volunteers are good at creating ways to inspire those individuals during their assignments— they may call or text you just to say, "We appreciate your work" or to check in. The executive director may send out a personal e-mail thanking you for your volunteer contribution, but maybe not. When you work remotely, the inspiration to work on a virtual assignment has to come from you.

6. *Do you pace yourself well? Do you avoid over-committing to projects?*

   Most volunteers who do not complete their online assignments say that they thought they could do the work when they signed up, but as the deadline for the assignment approached, they realized that other things took priority: school activities, home duties, paid work projects, etc. So those things got done, but the organization expecting volunteer effort was left with an unfinished assignment and an unmet need. Think about your work style and your other commitments before volunteering virtually. If you are feeling overwhelmed by other responsibilities, now is probably not a good time to volunteer, online or onsite. Organization staff who involve and support volunteers try to be understanding about your job and family commitments—but they are also counting on you to finish assignments to which you commit.

7. *Do you have a set time of day when you will work on assignments?*

   Do not just assume that you will get to that three-hour virtual assignment some time before the deadline two weeks from now, in your spare time. Create a schedule for yourself on specific days and times to complete the project you have committed to do, or it will not get done. Let's say it again: *Waiting for spare time to do a task often leads to a task never getting done.*

8. *Will your work area be free of distractions while you are working on a volunteer assignment?*

   Any virtual assignment is going to take a certain level of concentration and intensity. Make sure your environment is going to allow you to devote the proper energies to your assignment, without distractions that could affect the quality of your service. Some people can work at a coffee shop; others require a quiet setting devoid of all conversation and music.

9. *Do you answer your online messages quickly (no more than 48 hours or two business days after receipt)?*

   The organization may need to contact you with a critical issue before you complete the assignment. Responsiveness is crucial to the success of your online relationship.

If you answered "no" or had difficulty answering any of these questions, perhaps you are not ready for volunteering virtually.

But your self-evaluation is not done. You have more questions to ask yourself before you begin to look for any type of volunteer opportunity. You'll quickly see that these are important to online service, too.

- Why do you want to volunteer, in general?

- What do you hope to gain and to give by volunteering?

- What kind of organization(s) or programs do you want to help?

- What sort of services and assistance would you like to provide—build a Web site for an organization, do online research, mentor a young person via the Internet, visit virtually with someone who is homebound? (For more ideas, check out our examples of ways an organization can involve online volunteers in chapter 1.)

- With what organizations have you volunteered before, whether onsite or online?

- What skills and experience would you like to bring to a volunteer assignment?

You will be asked repeatedly on various volunteer applications and during interviews for answers to these and similar questions. It will be easier if you already have this information in a file, ready to cut and paste into forms as needed.

Where to Find Virtual Volunteering Opportunities

In chapter 11, we discuss the various places where all sorts of organizations can recruit online volunteers, particularly Web sites established for the express purpose of connecting interested people with service opportunities. Review that chapter to get ideas for where you might go to find their postings.

In addition to registries or databases of general volunteer listings, there are some organizations that involve online volunteers exclusively—or involve them in very large numbers. We refer you to the Virtual Volunteering Wiki for the most updated list. At some of these organizations, you move up the volunteering ranks, and receive greater responsibility and recognition, by contributing a larger number of hours than the average user while providing high-quality, consistent service.

Of course, if you are already involved as an onsite volunteer or active member with an organization, you can offer your involvement as an online volunteer to them as well. Because the organization already knows you, staff may be more comfortable allowing you to do some or all of your volunteering service online.

If you see volunteer opportunities at an organization that interests you but they seem to be recruiting for someone to do the work onsite, explore the organization's willingness to try virtual volunteering. Ask if some of the tasks could be done from your home or work computer. For instance, if an organization is recruiting volunteers to help with designing brochures, editing videos, writing newsletter articles, and other similar activities, explain why you believe you could do those tasks partially or entirely from a remote computer and see if they will pilot test the idea with you.

Designing Your Own Virtual Volunteering Opportunity

When you approach an organization—unsolicited—to offer your services as an online volunteer, be ready to be very specific about what it is you want to do. Think about the following:

- What type of service do you want to provide? What type of activities are you willing to do, exactly? What type of service do you *not* want to provide? What type of activities do you *not* want to do? Leave those things off your list! The more specific you can be about the type of work you do and do not want to donate, the more likely you are to find the right volunteering opportunity

- How many hours a day, a week, or a month will you be available? How many days, weeks, or months can you commit to the assignment you are proposing? What is your ideal start date? When do you want to finish the assignment?

- What e-mail address should the organization use to contact you? Would you be willing to be contacted by instant messaging or via a live audio or video session (such as via Skype, iVisit, Google Talk, etc.)?

- What staff members do you need to talk with in order to do the service you are suggesting? What materials and support will they need to provide in order for you to do this work? How will you solicit their feedback on an ongoing basis?

- What costs might be associated with whatever you are proposing to do for the organization? For instance, if you want to build a customized volunteer tracking system, what software and hardware would the organization have to purchase? (Be forewarned that proposing service that will cost money may be a deal breaker or may delay your service until money is raised.)

You might even consider writing up a proposal for how you could donate virtual service and shop this around to various organizations, whether or not they are currently soliciting this type of volunteering. Just be prepared for some resistance—perhaps even disbelief. Many organizations will be unfamiliar with virtual volunteering and be uncomfortable about allowing you to work offsite on your own. Therefore, start with local organizations rather than ones at a far distance so that you can offer to come *onsite* for a face-to-face interview, orientation, and training. They may even want you to volunteer onsite at the start before they allow you to continue your service online.

Tips for a Successful Virtual Volunteering Experience

Based on feedback from various volunteers who have contributed time virtually, organizations that have involved such volunteers, and various telecommuting resources, we offer the following additional tips to help make your virtual assignment rewarding for everyone:

- *Discuss the volunteer position description and your expectations with your contact at the agency at the time the assignment is made.*

  If the organization does not put this description in writing, you should do so in an e-mail confirmation following up your meeting.

- *Expect an acclimatization period.*

  It takes a while for even the most organized person to figure out how to manage time, space, communication systems, and projects while working remotely. Even with all of the advice provided in this chapter, expect to encounter unanticipated issues. Be flexible enough to recognize when something is not working for you, and adjust it accordingly.

- *Set up a communications routine with the organization.*

  Report in at least once a week via e-mail about your volunteer activities, even if it is to report no activity. Review what you have accomplished and what your immediate next activities will be. It does not have to be a large, involved report; just a short, friendly update will do.

- *Be kind to office support staff.*

  Remember that people who work at the agency you are supporting have many roles and are expected to do a lot with limited resources. While your key contact at the organization knows what you are doing, other staff may not be completely up to date on your project.

- *Follow the policies of the organization.*

  Every organization has policies on chain of approval, confidentiality of information, how you may represent yourself on behalf of the organization, etc. These policies are meant to be taken seriously! When in doubt, ask for guidance. If the organization does not give you the same orientation that it gives traditional volunteers, ask for it. Learn the organization's mission, get an overview of the organization's programs and current events, and get a list of the staff and the board members, in case you encounter these people in the course of your service.

- *Radiate quality.*

  Meet deadlines (in fact, beat them!), spell check everything (including e-mails before you send them), double check information, report problems as well as offer solutions, and show that you put substantial time and thought into your service. If you are inputting information into a database or Web site and misspell a name or enter the wrong phone number, the work you have done is not just subpar; it can be damaging to the organization.

- *Avoid burnout.*

  At the office, routines structure your time. There is a routine for arriving at the office and getting settled into volunteering activities. When volunteering virtually, you may not know when to stop. This will lead to fatigue and burnout for you and frustration for the organization if you have committed to a particularly large and important assignment. One way to get around overwork is to set firm starting and stopping times for yourself: develop a routine for volunteering virtually (see earlier in this chapter for further advice on the importance of setting aside time). Take breaks during a long stretch of work; severe headaches, eyestrain, and neck and back pain are the result of working too many hours at a computer keyboard without a break.

- *Motivation has to come from yourself.*

  If you find yourself having trouble completing an assignment because you just cannot seem to get started on it, try re-reading the assignment description and reviewing the organization's Web site. Think about how your contribution is going to add to the worthwhile work of the organization. If you do not know how it will, ask. If you are an active member of the organization's online volunteer community, check in to see whether others have advice for sustaining momentum.

- *Keep your workspace manageable and free of distractions.*

  Set up your workspace with all your equipment and materials within reach. Make sure others in your household understand and respect your commitment to volunteering virtually. What interruptions will you allow? Define a policy in advance so you do not have to make individual decisions at each distraction. Define your "I-Am-Volunteering-Now" rules to help family and friends avoid interrupting your volunteer time. Do not assume that you will be able to get volunteering work done between flights in an airport, while waiting for the start of a sporting event, or otherwise surrounded by a lot of distractions—while competing for limited electrical outlets and bandwidth.

- *Review and follow the "Do's and Don'ts for Volunteers Sharing Expertise Online" presented below in this chapter.*

  If you are volunteering a particular expertise to an organization, there are some things to keep in mind regarding your interactions with the organization and the way you present your information.

- *Help the organization evaluate its volunteer involvement.*

  If you get a survey from the organization about your volunteer experience or future interests, take the time to respond to it. Your feedback will help the organization improve its involvement of other volunteers. Also, agencies rely on such feedback to help them meet the evaluation requirements for certain grants. Speak up if you have constructive criticism or a great idea. You have earned the right to give input.

You play a huge role in building the capacities of an organization to expand virtual volunteering opportunities. Your performance will affect the attitudes of various staff members regarding volunteers in general and virtual volunteering specifically.

Staying on Top of E-mail

In this information age, we can all feel like we are drowning in electronic messages. It is easy for an important e-mail to be lost in a sea of dozens of other online messages each day. An important e-mail can be misdirected by a junk e-mail filter. And people send you messages through a variety of sources: traditional e-mail, instant messages, Facebook or other social networking site messages, tweets, text messaging, comments on your blog, and on and on.

To ensure e-mails get where they are supposed to go during your virtual volunteering experience, follow these tips:

- Make sure your junk e-mail filter allows messages into your in-box from the organization you support. Here's an even better idea: set up a filter that automatically puts all messages from the organization with which you volunteer into a folder you create specifically for that purpose so that they never go into your junk folder or get lost amid other messages.

- Always write something in an e-mail subject line that helps the recipient pay attention to it.

  o Do not make it vague. "Hello" and "information" are too ambiguous, but "questions needing your follow-up" or "feedback on your work so far" are good.

  o *Change* the subject line when the content changes. No one needs a stack of e-mails in their folder with the same subject repeated 30 times. At a minimum, add something like "response, 3 February" to show that you have *added* to the chain of messages, not repeated it.

  o Use "urgent" sparingly in the subject line; if you cry wolf with every e-mail message, recipients will not respond seriously when you really do mean "urgent."

- Make sure the organization knows your preferred way of receiving e-mail or text messages, and respect their preferred way as well.

Do's and Don'ts for Sharing Expertise Online

Some virtual volunteering assignments are reserved for people with a specific area of expertise. A particular role may require a formal certification or degree, a minimum number of years engaged in a certain activity, or an extensive professional portfolio. Volunteers who qualify as the experts are often people who donate the professional services for which they usually are paid. These expert volunteers—also called pro bono, highly-skilled, or particularly-skilled volunteers—could be from any field imaginable, including:

- Translator, editor, or proofreader
- Web, database, or software designer
- Marketing director, public relations specialist
- Lawyer or paralegal
- Doctor, nurse, dentist, psychiatrist, or veterinarian
- Human resources manager
- Accountant
- IT expert
- Water and sanitation engineer
- Videographer

All of the suggestions offered in the previous section for online volunteers in general also apply to pro bono online volunteers. But problems can arise when a volunteer expert is assisting an employee or other volunteer with work or technology that the expert understands quite well but the other person does not. In these cases you will be acting as a *consultant* or even a *trainer* (making the organization your *client*), which may or may not be something you are ready to do.

To keep your volunteer experience beneficial rather than frustrating for both you and the person or organization you are trying to help, follow these guidelines:

- *Listen, listen, listen to what the organization says it needs* as a result of your donated services. Do not assume you automatically know what the organization should do because of your expertise. Ask questions before giving advice.

- *Mutually set concrete goals or desired outcomes* for your activities. Make sure you discuss both the organization's expectations and

what you are prepared to do. Such preparation will help prevent misunderstandings later.

- *Be clear about what you can and cannot (or will not) do.* An organization may mistakenly assume that you are qualified to do some task, or interested in doing a particular task, because of their assumptions about your expertise.

- The people you are helping are themselves experts in areas different from yours. *Respect their knowledge,* as you would expect them to respect your own. Do not forget that you are talking to professionals; a lack of knowledge about a particular area, not stupidity, has led the staff to request your services. Remember that you were a beginner, too, once upon a time.

- *Think about the language you use* to explain something. Using technical terms or jargon that only a fellow expert would understand will frustrate the people you are trying to help. Use common language whenever possible, and fully explain technical terms you need to use a lot. Learn what you can about your clients' work and put things into a context they can understand.

- *Respect the time of the paid staff and other volunteers.* They have many responsibilities outside of what you see as a volunteer, particularly one who works remotely out of the loop of everyday onsite activities. Staff members may not be able to devote as much time to an issue as you think they should; help them do the most they can with the time they have available.

- Nonprofits, non-governmental organizations, charities, schools, and other mission-based organizations are not the same as businesses, corporations, and the rest of the for-profit sector; *just because something works in the business world does not mean it will automatically work—or is even appropriate—for mission-based organizations.* The nonprofit sector encompasses important, unique expertise and resources; pro bono service is an opportunity for for-profit folks to learn about the vital work that nonprofit organizations undertake and even to discover approaches that might work back in the for-profit world.

- Organizations become frustrated when businesses or consultants expect them to be satisfied with whatever service is provided, whenever it is provided, because, "after all, it is given for *free*." This is an unhealthy and potentially disastrous attitude. *Treat the organization you are assisting as an important customer, just like your paying customers.* Their deadlines and expectations are just as real as any other client's, and the work you have committed to do pro bono is important to support the organization's services to the community.

- Not-for-profit and public sector agencies operate in a world of very *limited resources* and ever-shrinking budgets. Do not be surprised if they do not have a staff member devoted solely to human resources, or solely to legal issues, or solely to online outreach, whatever. Also do not be dismayed if they do not have a budget to buy and maintain a large computer system or smartphones for staff. Respect those limitations by helping them to do as much as they can with available resources.

- If you encounter resistance to a suggestion, particularly in an area in which you consider yourself an expert, try to *diagnose the cause*: Differing priorities? Lack of information about you? Lack of information about them? Bad timing? Preconceived assumptions? Once you have identified the reason for the resistance, it will be much easier for you to deal with it constructively.

- *Build sustainability.* Do not just do it *for* them—involve them in the process. Explain each step, clarify the context, and recruit someone to write down procedures or troubleshooting steps, if applicable. The most important part of your mentoring is that what you leave behind works and the organization can sustain it.

- *Provide documentation* about your service to the organization. That way, if you must discontinue work on the project, the staff has the information needed to easily integrate a new volunteer.

If You Are Volunteering Computer and Software Expertise

Virtual volunteering frequently involves consulting on software or computer hardware or some other technical support. In addition to the guidelines above, there are two other things to keep in mind if you are providing services in these areas:

- Make sure that whatever system you recommend (whether a type of software, organizational model, or anything else) *meets the unique needs of the organization* you are helping. Is this a widely-used system? Is there sufficient documentation available on how the system works? Can the staff effectively use or even alter this system without always relying on your expertise? What kind of support is available for this system?

- If you are designing a Web site, a database program, a smartphone application, or other computer-related product, *what you may view as a great feature may be viewed as unnecessary or distracting* by the staff member or other volunteer who has to use it. If a flashy interface does not provide an easy-to-use tool, it is not helpful.[1]

Phil Agre of the University of California, Los Angeles, offers additional excellent advice for people helping others with computer and software use. This information is for traditional, onsite volunteer settings, but many of the tips carry over into online work:

- *A computer is a means to an end. The person you're helping probably cares mostly about the end. This is reasonable.*

- *Their knowledge of the computer is grounded in what they can do and see—"when I do this, it does that." They need to develop a deeper understanding, of course, but this can only happen slowly, and not through abstract theory but through the real, concrete situations they encounter in their work.*

- *By the time they ask you for help, they've probably tried several different things. As a result, their computer might be in a strange state. That's not their fault.*

- *The best way to learn is through apprenticeship—that is, by doing some real task together with someone who has skills that you don't have.*

- *Your primary goal is not to solve their problem. Your primary goal is to help them become one notch more capable of solving their problem on their own. So it's okay if they take notes.*

- *Knowledge lives in communities, not individuals. A computer user who's not part of a community of computer users is going to have a harder time of it than one who is.*

- *If something is true, show them how they can see it's true.*[2]

Share Your Experience!

So long as you adhere to an organization's confidentiality policies, you may want to share your online volunteering experience with others. You can:

- Talk about it on your blog.

- Mention what you are doing as an online volunteer on your status updates on Facebook, Google+, Twitter, MySpace, LinkedIn, etc.

- List your volunteering role on your résumé, both the one you hand to potential employers and the online version you maintain on your own Web site or on a professional networking site like LinkedIn or Plaxo.

- Add a photo of yourself to the Online Volunteering Group on Flickr: http://www.flickr.com/groups/onlinevolunteers/

Sharing your experience could help the organization reach more volunteers and promotes online volunteering in general. Your story may help an organization start engaging online volunteers and even make the case for expanding volunteer engagement

to financial donors. It may also catch the eye of a potential employer. Jayne knows three people who said the online volunteering activities listed on their résumés were discussed during their job interviews, and all three were offered those paid positions!

Online Boundaries

There are two of you. Maybe even three of you, or more.

No, you have not been cloned.

There is the professional, *public you*: the one who works at such-and-such company, went to such-and-such university, serves on such-and-such board of directors, lives in such-and-such city, and uses your first and last name in your e-mails, online profiles, etc. This is the you that is easy to find by co-workers, potential employers, and even the media. The *public you* is the one that comes up in the first pages of a Google search.

There is also the *personal you*: the one who engages in activities you would not necessarily want all of your co-workers or potential employers to know about readily, writes Harry Potter *fan fiction*, is overtly politically opinionated, and does not use your first and last name in your e-mails, online profiles, etc. The activities of *personal you* may be easy to find online but are not so easy to *associate* with you by co-workers, potential employers, or the media even if they find some information, because you do not use your full first and last name, do not list the city where you are, never identify your employer, and so on.

You have to decide where each of your activities, online or offline, falls among these two—or more—yous. And then you have to think about how your different online activities might, or might not, affect your online volunteering. What might this mean?

- You may end up with two Facebook profiles—one for your professional life, your volunteering, and your university activities and another for your personal life, where you talk about politics and personal interests and that crazy thing you did last Saturday night. Facebook discourages this, we know, and may delete one of the profiles if they realize it is the same person, so be sure to make the profiles different enough that they do not raise suspicions (for instance, use your middle initial in one but not the other, don't list your employer in the more personal profile, etc.).

- You may want your Facebook or Google+ profile to be only for close friends, while you use professional networking sites like LinkedIn or Plaxo to link to fellow volunteers, organizations you volunteer with, employers, co-workers, etc.

- Maybe you want to keep your volunteering activities and books you read in your *personal you* online activities. Or maybe you want to share even more in your *public you* profiles. The point is: *you have control of the information you share online and where you post it.*

Be deliberate, or at least thoughtful, in what information you share online and how you share it. Consider who might see certain information and whether you want—or do not want—them to know those things about you. Remember that the more robust your public online activities, the more buried your more personal online information becomes in

a search via Google or Microsoft Bing (in association with a search of your name).

You Are Needed and Wanted!

Online volunteers were the first promoters of virtual volunteering. Individual volunteers began pushing for virtual volunteering opportunities back in the 1990s, before nonprofit organizations even thought of the idea! You are needed and wanted as a volunteer, online or onsite, but either way, the Internet will play a big role in your experience. This *Guidebook* is packed with suggestions for finding virtual volunteering activities—get going!

Notes

1. Adapted from Jayne Cravens, "Pro Bono/In-Kind/Donated Services for Mission-Based Organizations When, Why & How?" 2009 <http://www.coyotecommunications.com/volunteer/probono.html>.

2. Phil Agre has posted his excellent publications about computing's impact on community and social practice at his Web site, http://polaris.gseis.ucla.edu/pagre/. His comments here are from "How to Help Someone Use a Computer," 1996 <http://polaris.gseis.ucla.edu/pagre/how-to-help.html>.

Conclusion
What's Next?

This is *The* Last *Virtual Volunteering Guidebook,* but it is not the last *discussion* of the concept or practice! We want to see exchanges, debates, testimonials, research, and workshops continue—online and onsite, face-to-face! We hope discussions and research about working with online volunteers become integrated into all volunteering—that these discussions are not always regulated to a separate Web site or a chapter at the end of a volunteer management book.

We are frequently asked: *What is next for virtual volunteering? What will be happening a year from now? Ten years from now?* Here are our predictions:

- There will be less and less talk of two groups of volunteers—*online* and *onsite.* The boundary will not last much longer—we will talk about *volunteers,* period, justifying the title of this book! More and more volunteer management education will fully integrate virtual volunteering practices into their recommendations, doing away with the need for separate virtual volunteering trainings, articles, books and the like.

- There will be less talk about the types of online volunteering within virtual volunteering—micro-volunteering, crowdsourcing, etc.—as boundaries for these labels are further blurred.

- Facebook will eventually be usurped as the most popular online social networking site, just as MySpace was usurped, and America Online (AOL) before that.

- Being able to engage in virtual volunteering—involving and supporting online volunteers—will become a standard expectation of volunteer resources managers

(VRMs) in countries with common Internet usage. Those VRMs and organizations that have avoided virtual volunteering will slowly be pushed aside by people and organizations that have long known virtual volunteering is no fad.

- Volunteer ranks will become more and more diverse at organizations, as the Internet allows for the involvement of a variety of different groups. We don't think this change will happen quickly, but eventually it will happen.

- There will be more and more virtual teams of volunteers—teams of online volunteers—working on assignments together, as organizations become more savvy about creating assignments for these volunteers.

- As networked technology permeates our lives and becomes available just about anywhere, people will seek longer-term, more substantial commitments in volunteering that are in contrast to "quickie" tech experiences. Certainly micro-volunteering will still be around, but we predict an increase in the popularity of volunteering experiences that provide a deeper commitment, not a decrease.

- Text-based communicating will not go away. Naturally, different people will have different preferences, but there will always be a need for text-based communications alongside audio- and video-based communication.

- Onsite, in-person volunteering will *still* not be replaced by virtual volunteering.

- More academic researchers and research institutions will include virtual volunteering in their studies regarding volunteer engagement practices. A report about the state of volunteering in a country, for example, will include detailed information about how volunteers use the Internet as a part of their service and how organizations use the Internet to support and involve volunteers.

- Virtual volunteering will become much more widespread outside of North America, with many more examples from Europe, Asia, Africa and the Middle East.

- There will be much more information available online and in print about virtual volunteering in languages other than English.

- Just as different cultures approach volunteering and people management in different ways, they will put their own unique spins on virtual volunteering. What works in Bangladesh will be different than what works in Ghana—although the underlying principles are more universal than often acknowledged.

- People will continue to come up with new jargon for old practices. For instance, the current talk of *micro-volunteering* is merely a re-branding of *virtual volunteering*. The *cloud* is just another word for *cyberspace*. The challenge will be to figure out when a new technology term is actually referring to something truly *new*.

- *The fundamentals of volunteer management— and, therefore, of virtual volunteering—will stand.* There will *always* be a need for clear volunteer task descriptions, for instance. There will *always* be a need to recognize the contributions of volunteers in some way.

There will *always* be a need to know what online volunteers are doing.

With *The* Last *Virtual Volunteering Guidebook*, we give you the tools and information you need to support and involve volunteers now and in the future. We believe that the fundamentals for success we offer in this book will survive for the next five years for sure, and maybe forever, unless:

- Alterations are made in the space-time continuum

- The entire power grid is wiped out for many years and generations to come

- An affordable jet-pack is invented

- *Star Trek*–style transporters or holodecks are invented

Tools, and how we use them, *will* change, but the fundamentals of volunteer engagement have stood the test of time. The savvy volunteer resources manager is going to know how to adapt these fundamentals as tools and practices change. We are even more energized about virtual volunteering now than we were when we first started researching and promoting it back in the 1990s. We hope this book has convinced the last of the non-believers, as well as helped people long engaged in supporting and involving volunteers using Internet tools.

We hope to see you on the Virtual Volunteering Wiki, on Facebook or Twitter or Google+ (or whatever the hot new online tool of the day is), and in person, onsite, at traditional workshops and conferences. We want to continue to hear your stories and challenges regarding virtual volunteering. Let's all keep learning together!

Appendix A
Virtual Volunteering Myths

Here is a list of 16 of the most common myths that surface as resistance to involving volunteers in online service. This entire *Guidebook* debunks these false assumptions, but we put them here for easy reference to help readers respond whenever they are raised.

Myth 1:

Virtual volunteering is a very new concept.

False. Online volunteering has been going on probably as long as there has been an Internet (which itself is more than 30 years old). This history is detailed in the first chapter of this *Guidebook*.

Myth 2:

Virtual volunteering is great for people who otherwise do not have time to volunteer.

False. This is probably the biggest myth out there about the practice. Volunteering online requires *real* time, not *virtual* time. If you don't have time to volunteer offline, you probably also do not have time to volunteer online. Online volunteering should never be promoted as an alternative approach for people who don't have time to volunteer face-to-face. Rather, the appeal of online volunteering for individuals is that:

- It is an additional way to volunteer to help the community or a cause.

- It often doesn't require having to travel somewhere just to volunteer.

- It is an additional way for volunteers to help an organization they are already helping onsite.

- It is a way for someone with time to volunteer, but who cannot physically leave home or work to do so.

- It allows volunteering by people who have physical disabilities, problems with mobility, or no easy transportation options.

- It permits people to help an organization, cause, or issue of great importance to them, but for which there are no onsite opportunities in their geographic area.

- It can allow a person to help a geographic area anywhere on the globe, even where physical travel would not be possible or advisable.

Myth 3:

People who volunteer online do not volunteer face-to-face.

False. According to research by the Virtual Volunteering Project in the late 1990s, as well as anecdotal evidence since then from thousands of volunteers and organizations, the overwhelming majority of online volunteers *also* volunteer in face-to-face settings, often for an organization in their same city or region and often for the same organizations they are helping online.

Myth 4:

There are online volunteers and there are onsite volunteers, but these are entirely separate groups.

False. As stated in the previous myth, rarely will you find an online volunteer who doesn't also volunteer onsite or an onsite volunteer who doesn't use the Internet in some way to interact with the same organization. They are all *volunteers* and do not self-identify into separate online and onsite groups.

This myth is one of the primary reasons we've called the second edition of our book *The* Last *Virtual Volunteering Guidebook.* Going forward, we hope that books, trainings, and discussions about volunteer management will now always include discussions of the Internet to support and involve volunteers rather than consider online volunteers as an entirely separate subject.

Myth 5:

Working with online volunteers is completely different than working with onsite volunteers.

False. The key to success in working with online volunteers is the application of basic volunteer management standards—the fundamentals that make any traditional volunteer involvement work. All volunteers, whether online or onsite, need support, feedback, guidance, and recognition.

Some virtual volunteering is short term or episodic, which also has its roots in onsite service. People who come out for a one-day beach cleanup do not undergo a criminal background check, receive a long pre-service orientation, or fill out a lengthy volunteer application form, and they may never volunteer with the organization again. Similarly, online volunteers who participate in a micro-volunteering task may get started on their assignment just a few minutes after expressing interest. But just as offline episodic volunteering like beach cleanups is more about building relationships, creating cause awareness, and cultivating loyal supporters, micro-volunteering needs to have the same goals, has to be worth doing, and works only when established, tried-and-true volunteer management standards are in place.

Myth 6:

People who volunteer online do so for organizations that are geographically far from them.

False. Indeed, there are thousands of people who look for virtual volunteering opportunities to engage with people far away (one great example is the United Nations Online Volunteering service).

But most online volunteers are people who *also* volunteer onsite for the same organization (for instance, a volunteer designing an annual report may go onsite to meet with staff but perform most of the donated service via his or her home or work computer). Also, most people who volunteer online look for opportunities that are in their own geographic area, just as people who want to volunteer onsite.

Myth 7:

Online volunteers engage primarily in technology-related tasks.

False. Online volunteers engage in many tasks completely unrelated to technology, such as advising on business plans, human resources development, fundraising, media relations, researching topics, and facilitating online discussions. A review of online volunteering assignments posted to the UN's Online Volunteering service usually shows 50% or more assignments that are non-tech-specific.

Myth 8:

People who volunteer online are mostly young, affluent, and living in the U.S.A.

False. Online volunteers come from all age groups (once someone can use the Internet independently, usually around age 13), from various educational and work backgrounds, and from various geographies and ethnicities. The breakdown of online volunteers from the UN's Online Volunteering service is telling: more than 40% are from developing countries. Of course, each organization that involves online volunteers will have its own diversity, but it is not possible to make sweeping generalizations about the demographics of online volunteers.

Myth 9:

Online volunteering is impersonal.

False. Online interactions are quite personal. In many circumstances, people are often more willing to share information and feelings online than they are face-to-face. Also, volunteers can more easily share photos of their families and narratives about their interests via the Internet than, say, at an onsite volunteer luncheon. As author Jayne Cravens notes, "Online volunteers with whom I have worked are real people to me, not virtual people. When they have gotten married or graduated from high school or college or had a baby or gotten a job, I have celebrated, and when they have died or lost a loved one, I have cried."

Myth 10:

Interviewing potential volunteers face-to-face is much more reliable than interviewing people online.

False. Both methods of interviewing potential volunteers have strengths and weaknesses; one may be more appropriate than another for a particular situation, but each is effective. This *Guidebook* talks at length about why it is never a good idea to base your screening on face-to-face, gut reactions to volunteers and how to use tried-and-true volunteer screening for virtual volunteering. Note that it is becoming easier and easier to interview people at a distance using Internet voice and webcam platforms—truly face-to-face, even if not in the same room.

Myth 11:

People who volunteer online are very shy and have trouble interacting with others.

False. According to already-cited research, the overwhelming majority of online volunteers *also* volunteer in face-to-face settings. In fact, online volunteers tend to be excellent at interacting with others—it's that very hunger for interaction that often drives their volunteering, on or offline.

Myth 12:

The Internet is dangerous and therefore online volunteering opens an organization and its clients up to many risks.

False. The Internet is no more or less dangerous than the offline world. When people, including children, have been harmed as a result of online activities, it has often been because they or their parents did not take appropriate safety measures—they share

information that they would never share with random strangers at a bus station, for instance. There is extensive information on how to ensure safety in virtual volunteering in this *Guidebook*.

Myth 13:

The biggest obstacle to online volunteering is lack of Internet access.

False. The "digital divide" still exists but is rapidly disappearing as more and more people, of all income levels and around the world, are able to obtain computers or mobile devices at decreasing cost. For organizations, the biggest obstacle to involving online volunteers successfully, or at all, is lack of experience in basic volunteer management practices. If an organization does not know how to involve onsite volunteers effectively, it won't be effective with online volunteers either.

Myth 14:

Online volunteering requires building a dedicated online platform or using a specific tech tool.

False. If an organization has e-mail, the organization can involve online volunteers. Organizations can effectively involve and support online volunteers with Internet tools already in place (e-mail, instant messaging, an iVisit or Skype account, etc.), and there are many free Internet tools to support all volunteers (not just online volunteers), such as Yahoo! Groups or Google Groups. And organizations recruit online volunteers via the same offline and online avenues as their onsite, face-to-face volunteers.

Myth 15:

Micro-volunteering *and* crowdsourcing *are completely different than* virtual *or* online volunteering.

False. A rose is a rose. There is no consensus on vocabulary in this arena and new technology also evokes new words to match. During the time of the 1990s Virtual Volunteering Project, the term was *byte-sized* volunteering: online volunteering tasks that take just a few hours or a few days to complete. Recently the hot new term for this is *micro-volunteering*, introduced when service via smartphone became an unexpected reality. *Crowdsourcing* is perhaps the oldest term of all. See the discussion of vocabulary in chapters 1 and 3.

Any form of volunteering *in which service is provided online* is virtual volunteering, whether a short "just show up once and help" gig or a longer-term commitment.

Myth 16:

Much more needs to be done to get people to volunteer online.

False. There are plenty of people who want to volunteer online—far, far more than there are opportunities for them. Instead, much more needs to be done to help build the capacity of organizations regarding volunteer management and to incorporate information about online volunteering into this capacity building.

Appendix B
Recommended Resources

Virtual Volunteering Wiki

It has long been true that every book is out of date the day it is published, and that is doubly true for a book about the Internet. Not only do new resources continuously appear, but URLs and links emerge or break daily. The wonderful thing about writing a book like this today, however, is that we do not have to be constrained by printed pages; we have the option of creating a *virtual* appendix and placing all sorts of additional information online right away. Then we can keep updating the information over time. Even better, we can engage *you*, the reader, in also posting new ideas and resources. Please visit—and bookmark!—the *Virtual Volunteering Wiki* at http://virtualvolunteering .wikispaces.com/. There you will find:

- The URLs of every organization and online resource mentioned in this book

- Volunteer recruitment Web sites

- Online communities related to volunteer management, including virtual volunteering

- Latest news regarding virtual volunteering (RSS feeds, updated automatically every time an article or blog mentions a certain key phrase, like *virtual volunteering* or *micro-volunteering*)

- Research and evaluations of virtual volunteering, as a practice in general or focused on specific projects

- Further advice on where to find organizations engaged in virtual volunteering

- A list of online mentoring programs

- Links to non-American resources, including resources in languages other than English

- Resources related to telecommuting, virtual teams, and remote management

- A long list of possible titles we brainstormed for this book (humor)

- Examples of videos used for training and orientation of volunteers

- Brief explanations of available tech tools, by function (screening volunteers, scheduling volunteers, etc.) and by name (Twitter, Facebook, Flickr, etc.)

- A list of tags to follow and use on Twitter related to virtual volunteering

- Latest news on virtual volunteering

- RSS feeds that automatically link to the latest Web pages, blogs, and other online materials that use terms related to virtual volunteering (This is automatically generated content; we do not control what shows up on these RSS feeds or what online materials get linked.)

- Online safety resources

- Where to find training regarding virtual volunteering

- Various online resources by Jayne and Susan

Visit the Wiki to contribute your own knowledge about online resources related to virtual volunteering!

Volunteer Management Resources (in Print)

These days the Web offers a huge array of resources in many countries offering basic information on how to work with volunteers, whether onsite or online. We have listed the various online resources we recommend regarding volunteer management on the

Virtual Volunteering Wiki. But there are also a lot of excellent in-print resources, many of which influenced the writing of this book. While the following list is by no means intended to be all-inclusive, or even comprehensive, it is a starting point for learning more about the principles and practices of volunteer management. To find purchasing information about any of these publications, visit the Energize, Inc. Online Bookstore (http://www.energizeinc.com/bookstore) or your favorite online bookseller, or type the title into a search engine.

Campbell, Katherine Noyes and Susan J. Ellis. *The (Help!) I-Don't-Have-Enough-Time Guide to Volunteer Management.* Philadelphia: Energize, Inc., 2004.

Ellis, Susan J. *The Volunteer (and Membership Development) Recruitment Book.* 3rd edition. Philadelphia: Energize, Inc., 2002.

Ellis, Susan J. *Volunteer Management Audit.* Philadelphia: Energize, Inc., 2003.

Graff, Linda L. *Better Safe . . . Risk Management in Volunteer Programs & Community Service.* Dundas, ON: Linda L. Graff & Associates, 2003.

Graff, Linda L. *Beyond Police Checks: The Definitive Volunteer & Employee Screening Guidebook.* Dundas, ON: Graff & Associates, 1999.

McCurley, Steve and Rick Lynch. *Volunteer Management: Mobilizing All the Resources of the Community.* 3rd edition. Ontario, Canada: INTERPUB Group, 2011. There is also a UK edition of this book, under the title *The Complete Volunteer Management Handbook* by Steve McCurley, Rick Lynch and Rob Jackson. London: Directory of Social Change, 2012.

Noble, Joy, Louise Rogers and Andy Fryar. *Volunteer Program Management: An Essential Guide.* 3rd edition. Adelaide, SA: Volunteering SA&NT, 2010.

Nonprofit Risk Management Center. *No Surprises: Harmonizing Risk and Reward in Volunteer Management.* 5th edition. Washington, DC: 2009.

Although it is only available in electronic form, we also recommend *e-Volunteerism: The Electronic Journal of the Volunteer Community,* the international online quarterly journal available since 2000, http://www.e-volunteerism.com.

Web Sites with Resources for Any Type of Volunteer Management

There are hundreds of Web sites around the world with information relevant to leaders of volunteers. Here is a starter set of volunteer management Web sites that provide a solid basis for learning the fundamentals of working with volunteers, as well as more advanced or specialized information beyond the basics. These sites, in turn, link to many, many more resources.

Coyote Communications Volunteerism Resources
www.coyotecommunications.com/volunteer/

Author Jayne Cravens' own frequently-updated Web site with information about supporting and engaging volunteers. It includes a comprehensive list of volunteer management software and tips for working with consultants in computer-related tasks. The rest of her site features resources related to her other areas of work, such as communications in aid and humanitarian initiatives and world travel. The site also links to her blog, Facebook page, Twitter feed, and whatever new online tool she thinks looks promising.

Energize, Inc.
www.energizeinc.com

Author Susan Ellis is president and founder of Energize, Inc., which offers the largest Web site in the world focused exclusively on information for leaders of volunteers in any setting. With more than 1,200 free site pages, it provides an extensive online library and annotated lists of links, directories of volunteer-related resources around the globe, visitor-contributed quotes and stories, and much more. There is also an Online Bookstore with dozens of titles, most available as e-books. Subscribe to the free monthly Update, check the "Volunteerism News Watch" blog, and follow the company on Facebook, Twitter, and LinkedIn.

National Service Resource Center
www.nationalserviceresources.org

Site created for American national service programs (Senior Corps, AmeriCorps, VISTA, etc.) but with resources helpful and available to any service/volunteering initiative. There is an extensive online library of sample forms and policies, articles, profiles of suggested practices, and lists of conferences, online discussion groups, print materials and other related Web sites.

Nonprofit Risk Management Center

www.nonprofitrisk.org

The Center is a resource for any risk issue confronting nonprofit organizations but has long included volunteer-related risk as one of its focus areas. The site offers free online tutorials, including a volunteer risk management self-assessment tool, books, an e-newsletter, and answers to risk and insurance questions.

ServiceLeader.org

www.serviceleader.org

A project of the RGK Center for Philanthropy and Community Service at the Lyndon B. Johnson School of Public Affairs of the University of Texas at Austin. ServiceLeader.org offers a range of practical and research information about volunteer management. It was the original home of the Virtual Volunteering Project.

Volunteer Canada

volunteer.ca

Produced for Canadians, but Susan and Jayne consider Volunteer Canada's Web site the most useful source of good volunteer management information of any of the world's national "peak body" sites—and it is available in French as well as English.

VolunteerMatch

www.volunteermatch.org

One of the most established and largest online registries of volunteer opportunities in the United States, VolunteerMatch also offers many free webinars and other training resources to agencies and individual volunteers alike in its Learning Center. Under its original name of Impact Online, the organization pioneered the Virtual Volunteering Project in the early 1990s and remains the only volunteer matching site to offer listings and searches for virtual volunteering positions alongside onsite opportunities.

About the Authors

Jayne Cravens is an internationally-recognized trainer, researcher, and consultant. Her work is focused on communications, volunteer involvement, community engagement, and management for nonprofits, NGOs, and government initiatives. She is a veteran manager of various local and international initiatives and is a pioneer regarding the research, promotion, and practice of virtual volunteering, including virtual teams, micro-volunteering, and crowdsourcing.

Jayne became active online in 1993, and she created one of the first Web sites focused on helping nonprofits to use online tools. She has been quoted in articles in *The New York Times*, *The Wall Street Journal*, and the Associated Press, as well as for reports by CNN, Deutsche Well, the BBC, and various local radio stations, TV stations, and blogs. Resources from her Web site, www.coyotecommunications.com, are frequently cited in reports and articles by a variety of organizations, online and in print. She is a popular speaker and trainer at conferences around the world and has been a guest lecturer at various universities.

Jayne received a VERA (Volunteer Excellence Recognition Award) from Business Council for Peace (Bpeace) and the Dewey Winburne Community Service Award, named after the co-founders of the SXSW Interactive Festival. She was named one of the "Top 25 Women of the Web" in 2001 by the San Francisco Women of the Web.

Jayne received her BA in journalism from Western Kentucky University and her MSc in development management from Open University in the UK. A native of Kentucky, she has worked for the United Nations, lived in Germany and Afghanistan, and visited more than 30 countries, many of them by motorcycle. She is currently based near Portland, Oregon, in the U.S.A.

Susan J. Ellis is president of Energize, Inc. (www.energizeinc.com), an international training, consulting, and publishing firm that specializes in volunteerism. She founded the Philadelphia-based company in 1977 and since that time has assisted clients throughout the world to create or strengthen their volunteer corps. She is internationally recognized as a leading advocate for the value and impact of strategic volunteer involvement.

She is the author or co-author of 13 books, including *The Volunteer Recruitment (and Membership Development) Book, By the People: A History of Americans as Volunteers,* and *From the Top Down: The Executive Role in Successful Volunteer Involvement.* As the documenting consultant to the Virtual Volunteering Project of Impact Online in the 1990s, Susan was the lead author on the original edition of *The Virtual Volunteering Guidebook.*

Susan has written more than 100 articles on volunteer management for dozens of publications and writes the national bimonthly column, "On Volunteers," for *The NonProfit Times* (since 1990). Since 2000, she has been co-founder and editor-in-chief of the field's first online journal, *e-Volunteerism: The Electronic Journal of the Volunteer Community* (www.e-volunteerism.com), for which she continues to serve as editor. Susan serves as the dean of faculty for Energize's *Everyone Ready*® online volunteer management training program for organizations and individuals (www.everyoneready.info).

INDEX

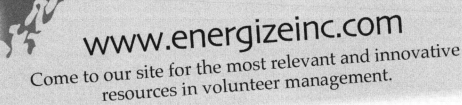

Printed in Great Britain
by Amazon